Letter to my 10-year-old self

AN ANTHOLOGY

Amanda Horswill
Anna Ball
Dr Catherine Jones
Charlie Giles
Chelsey Jean
Courtney Kynaston
Donna Gabriel
Ian Collins
Jess Weiss
Joanne Edge
Kati Britton
Kelly Ledger
Lisa Boorer

Luke Amery
Makaela Moore
Maria McDonald
Marta Madeira-Mulungo
Mary Wong
Michelle Beauchamp
Natasha Peake
Nyree Johnson
Rebecca Lang
Simon Bryant
Tara Nelson
Taryn Claire Le Nu

Compiled, edited, and published by CHANGE EMPIRE BOOKS

Published by Change Empire Books
www.changeempire.com

Edited & designed by Change Empire Books

LETTER FROM THE PUBLISHER

When my son came home, upset about events that had happened at school, I felt hopeless. As a parent, more than anything, we want our children to be happy and thriving. Even as a trained coach and self-development aficionado, I couldn't find the right words to say, the most helpful questions to ask, or the loving advice to give him that I felt would truly help him to learn and grow through the experiences he was having.

I had my own struggles when I was in school, and many of them were similar to those my son was going through. I was lucky to grow up in a loving home, but I still had issues with self-esteem, fitting in with the school system, and dealing with the fallout from toxic friendships.

I wondered, *What would have helped me when I was his age?* Beyond primary school, high school had all its own challenges, and of course, university and early adulthood were on an entirely different plane! I don't recall even talking to my parents about how I felt, so it's unlikely they were ever given the opportunity to help me.

If I knew then what I know now ...

Have you said that to yourself? I have, many times.

Would wisdom, advice, and support from a mentor or wiser, older voice have helped me?

I reflected on this idea for days ... If I could, what would I have prepared myself for?

What have I learned about life, love, and the world that would have helped me on my journey through adolescence and beyond?

What would have made me feel inspired about what was coming ... about the life I have today?

What would have helped me make better decisions?

What would have made my world an easier and kinder place?

What would have helped me get through?

In pondering these questions, I asked my community of authors and peers what they would tell themselves ... and through the flood of responses, the idea for this book was born.

With one successful anthology – *I Fly* – already published, I knew we could create something beautiful.

Twenty-five extraordinary everyday people joined me within a matter of days.

They all had wisdom to share with their childhood selves, and they were generous, open, and raw in sharing it. When the first draft letters were submitted, it was an emotional day. I cried from start to finish with many of the letters, touched by the love each author had for their childhood self. How they wished they could go back and hug that child close and tell them that they were loved, and how they wished they could protect their younger selves from some of the difficulties which lay ahead.

When writing their letters, the aim was not to try to change the future. It was about inspiring and guiding the child they were, and preparing them with tools to face and sometimes endure what was to come, knowing that the future lay in wait, and that it was going to be beautiful.

The result is a book which I believe will touch, move, and inspire readers of all ages, nationalities, backgrounds, and genders.

The letters you will read are true accounts, by real people. In some cases, names, places, and details have been changed to protect others. In some stories, events have been merged or changed for the sake of brevity.

Through coaching and multiple rounds of editing, we have sought to preserve the voice of each author. Some of the grammar and phrasing isn't perfect. We don't want it to be. We want it to be real. We have authors from different backgrounds and professions. They are all beautifully, uniquely different.

I hope that reading this book is a moving experience for you. These letters are sentimental but also inspiring. After I wiped away my tears, I immediately thought, *I want to read this with my son.* I want him to see the light at the end of the tunnel, even through his darkest days.

If reading this book triggers anything in you, I urge you to please seek professional help. Don't do this alone. Most of the authors have included their contact details at the end of the book so that you may reach out to them, but none of them are therapists or mental health professionals; please reach out to your support network if you are in need.

This book contains adult concepts addressed in a subtle way and therefore is, I believe, suitable for mature children nine+ and teens.

Every single one of these authors inspires me. I hope they inspire you, too. Please reach out to us using our contact details in the back of the book and tell us how you feel about this book. Please share it on your social networks and with your friends so that these letters can reach more of those who may need them. And please, leave reviews on your book retailer's website and buy official copies, as all these authors will directly benefit.

If your life has had its share of difficult moments and adverse events, I am so glad that you are still here, with us. I hope that you are thriving now and are able to look back upon your past as the collective experiences which made you who you are today. All of us want a better, more peaceful, and more loving world for ourselves and our children, and we believe that by sharing stories and wisdom, we are one step closer to achieving that.

I hope you love *Letter to my 10-year-old self.*

Cathryn Mora

Founder, Head Coach and Publishing Director
Change Empire Books

Instagram @change.empire.book.coaching
LinkedIn   linkedin.com/in/cathryn-mora/
Email   publisher@changeempire.com

CONTENTS

CHAPTER 1

You are Enough

Simon Bryant

Dear Simon,

You're about to have a pretty rough day ...

I know, because I was there. One of those mortifying days which has you wishing the earth would open up and swallow you whole. I was there, Simon, because I am you, the future version of you, travelling back across the bridge of time which separates us with a gift for us both. A gift of the opportunity to creatively influence the trajectory of your future, armed with insight into what is ahead of you – and, in doing so, to restore and redeem some of what's behind me. An amazing and mystifying gift, which I will not try to understand, but will rather embrace with open arms in the hope we can use it for our good.

Life is about framing the stories of your past in a way which gives meaning and power to your present, and about writing the story of your future to make the most of your life potential.

You can redeem your history and use it for your own good by reframing wounding former circumstances. You can significantly influence how the future chapters of your life story will turn out by taking control of defining the lore of your life, which informs the shape of every chapter of your story into the future. Your life-lore is the legendary, legacy-leaving essence of you. It captures the potential of your creation and life experience, articulates your

1

identity, and describes your unique brilliance, your future hopes, and what's important to you. It's the heart of every chapter of your life story. If you don't define your own life-lore and use it to shape your life story, someone or something else will.

Let me unwrap this for you.

Do you remember the first film you ever watched in Zambia – Born Free? And how you were entirely captivated by Joy Adamson (that's code for: You had a hopeless crush on her!) and the story of Elsa the lioness? Not to forget the lyrics and music of the theme song, 'Born Free' – which, truth be embarrassingly told, still brings a tear to your eye and goose bumps to your skin.

Actually, it gets worse – you turn out to be a 'chick flick' devotee. In case you're not familiar with that phrase … allow me to enlighten you! Do you remember the musty, mothball-scented trunk filled with Mum's Mills & Boon novels? Well, if you turn those into films, you have what is called a 'chick flick.' Crikey! You may not want to hear any more of your future after this revelation, but hang in there – you turn out okay.

But let's get back to the then-love of your life and her lion.

Elsa's story illuminates the allure and call of Africa, a call which is profoundly compelling for you. The endless extent of the savanna and the infinite expanse of the sky, in which everything that you see and experience precipitates a life of adventure, is the manifestation of true freedom and the revelation of the vitality and virility of a destiny fulfilled. An evocative call which informed Joy's perception of Elsa's life-lore and inspired her action. Action which aligned the trajectory of Elsa's life to the wondrous purpose of her creation. A trajectory which could have had a tragically different end had Joy not penned Elsa's story.

Elsa was one of three captured cubs, all tamed in Africa, two of which landed in the Rotterdam Zoo. But for Joy's intervention, Elsa's story would have been dictated by the deafening bluster of scientists and wildlife experts who believed a tamed Elsa was lost to Africa, her only destiny to join her siblings in a cage. Compelled by a vision of Elsa's identity and purpose, Joy wrote the chapters which ensured Elsa's future life was not a zoo cage under the grey and oppressive gloom of a European sky, but rather fulfilling the promise of her creation under the radiant sun and limitless blue yonder of Africa in Kenya's Nyambeni Range. She was home and free, embraced by a wild pride, and eventually birthed a family of her own.

For a time, you dreamed of finding Joy and working with her in Africa. But, inexplicably, the countless letters of an 8-year-old proposing to work as a wildlife conservationist went unanswered! If not with Joy in Kenya, where then will the future story of your life lead you?

Well, that's up to you.

Your history, of course, is written and cannot be changed. The first chapters of your life were authored by Mum and Dad and describe your moving country every two years of your life thus far. An exotic and somewhat colonial African adventure with your birth and first years in Sierra Leone, two years in England, two years of barefooted boy heaven in Zambia (you got to play with snakes, scorpions and slingshots under the mischievous spell of your Bemba friend Aaron) – and now South Africa.

Some would consider the enforced nomadic existence of your early years disruptive, but on the back side of reframing this part of your history, you will see how it helped you develop an explorative spirit, an expansive world view, and an understanding of different cultures. This sets you up to be inventive, flexible, adaptable and resilient, and gives you a life of discovery and adventure. These will be experiences which open doors to a wide and wonderful diversity of work roles in different places around the world – you're up to ten different countries on five different continents by the time you make half a century. The downside of your nomadic life in the early years is that, every two years, you need to adjust to new schools, make new friends, and leave friends behind.

And it is a new school experience, the stuff of childhood torment, which has me writing to you. It's your first week at your new school and the football teams need to be picked for the coming season. You settle yourself early (eager you are) on the spectator stands at the edge of the school football field with all the students in your year level. They are your competitors for a place in a team, all of whom have had three or four years of soccer seasons together, with their respective football abilities well known. You have heard how good the coach is and are inspired by how he likes to name the teams after the English Premier League teams, himself an ex-Premier League player.

The only football you have played to this point is with your idolised, football-mad older cousins in England, on the village green just down the road from their Nottingham home. Safe in being well-established football idols, they conspired to give you the glee of the 'nutmeg!' Surreptitiously letting your shots at goal

3

pass through their legs (how good does the 'nutmeg' moment feel?!) they then delighted you with their boisterous celebration of your goal-scoring greatness. Armed with these wonderful memories of cheering idols, nutmeg genius, and goal-bagging glory, you have hidden away in you a secret wish for fame as a Premier League footballer – and in taking this first step at your new school, you dare to dream a little.

The stand buzzes with excitement and anticipation as the coach picks out ten of his strongest players to be the Captains for the new season, and they begin to choose their teams, one pick per Captain in turn.

You'll have guessed by now that this story doesn't have a good ending for you. But what I hope we will discover together is that wounding events do not need to define the rest of your life story.

Horrid endings can be reframed into hopeful beginnings, if we so choose.

Lamentably, the earth does not swallow you whole! Instead, the shifting tectonic plates seem to have lifted you up on a precipice, with two hundred or more scornful eyes on you, or so it seems. You are the last one on the stands, unselected, humiliated, and holding a shattered dream in your hands. An awkward silence punctuated by the occasional snicker persists for what seems an eternity. All the teams are full and none of the Captains are willing to take you on, even as a reserve. You are shrouded in the fog of a confused mix of feelings that you will later understand to be shame, grief, and anger, in response to what seems to be a very public rejection. Your desolation is partially reprieved when the coach finally calls you down and deposits you as a reserve with the Rangers.

You will sit on the Rangers reserves' bench for the whole season, waiting to get a run on the ball. It will be a long, undignified season, and not once does the coach choose you to take the field. He is a man you admire, and you nurture a secret longing for his approval. You're forever hoping for him to call you out, recognising the seeds of football greatness in you. The call never comes, and the gates caging your potential start to close.

What happened that day, that season? Or rather, what do you think happened?

You were dismissed because all your peers and your coach thought you couldn't play football, thought you weren't good enough to make the team. Or so you believe.

The truth is – they just didn't know you. And, the Captains were under pressure to pick winning teams and didn't want to risk the season by picking an unknown player. Reframing the event with this new understanding, you would see it was not about you and your abilities at all, but was instead about their own fears of failure.

But, you made a choice. In choosing to believe what you did, you allowed your perception to change your life-lore. A change which will influence much of your life story, in sport and every other facet of life, a change in the form of a new belief – that you are not good enough, that you do not have what it takes. A life-lore change which, in the case of football, has you preferring to sit on the reserve bench rather than have everyone's belief of you immutably entrenched by making a fool of yourself on the field.

Sometime later in your life, you will come across a centre-spread newspaper advert which sparks an awakening in you. A full colour picture of a stallion running through a magnificent wilderness, entirely powerful, exuberant, and exhilarated in being free to be all he was intended to be. The advert had a bold caption: TRUE FREEDOM. (As an aside, the advert is for a personal loan from a bank, but take it from me – you cannot get 'true freedom' by taking out debt. The opposite is true, in fact!) Despite the dodgy morals of the marketing message, the picture will resonate with you because it calls you to the exuberance, vitality, and adventure of being entirely uninhibited in who you are created to be.

Simon, it is in your hands to decide upon the life-lore which shapes who you are in the future and how you enter into the wide open space that is the awesome legacy of your fulfilled life potential, and, in doing so, shining the light that is only yours to shine, making the world around you a better, brighter place.

If, on that day, during that season, you had reframed the circumstances to understand the restrictive fear of others rather than doubting yourself, your belief in yourself and your abilities would have radiated through in time, and you would have successfully contributed to the team fortunate to have you on their side. You would have taken your place on the field and run and played with gleeful abandon, knowing you are good enough, knowing you have what it takes. Your season would have been a very different one. Your life would be a different one, your potential completely uncaged.

Reserve bench-warming is a safe haven for much of your school life. In the absence of self-belief or words which call you out, you choose the safety of hiding your light, deciding that it's best to sit in the shadows rather than be picked for a position you think you will fail at.

The fourth team in hockey is the pinnacle of your sporting achievement in high school. In time, you hide not on the bench, but behind your strategy of making extraordinary effort to achieve acceptable prowess and gain the recognition and accolades of your peers and coaches. You run harder and farther than any of your teammates, chasing after every ball. But, the moment you have the ball on your stick, you are apprehended by fear of failure and you look for the first opportunity to pass it off rather than pushing through to discover what you're really made of. You are a brilliant defender though, chasing every ball back and recklessly throwing yourself into the path of the opponent or the ball. Defending is the one thing you find you can do, and you would rather be wounded in defence if it means avoiding the humiliation of overreaching yourself in an offensive move and being found wanting as a result.

Simon – you would rather cage your promise than fear being exposed as a failure.

The impact of the choice you make that day widens and becomes a series of decisions and choices which reinforce your belief that you're not good enough. A habitual thought pattern develops: I'm not good enough in myself to warrant being chosen or accepted or seen or appreciated ... but if I hide my feelings and work hard enough and avoid situations where I can't control the outcome, avoid circumstances where I'm not sure I can be successful, avoid situations which risk having two hundred eyes looking at me with scorn and pity – then I will make it through.

Paradoxically, it's a life strategy that creates a successful, though personally harmful career trajectory for you. Fear of failure drives you to perform and please. Working longer hours, overcommitting, and making unreasonable sacrifices elevates your standing in the eyes of your seniors, and they reward you with promotions and bonuses. Despite the material benefits, this is not the ideal way to live and work. You are habitually dissatisfied with yourself – restless to achieve, anxious to perform, itching to do more, to be more, to have more. This is a stressful and paltry state of existence which will ultimately harm your health and hurt those around you.

This may be hard to understand, but you can choose in the moment you are in to have a different future.

Do you remember the boat journey you took with Mum in emigrating from England to South Africa, the 12 magical days on the Edinburgh Castle? On the stormy days, you would go to one side of the ship and see a horizon filled with frighteningly dark clouds, and then, on the other side of the ship, there would be a magnificent sunset and a sky ablaze with warm, comforting, energising colours. You would choose to stand and watch the sunset. You were drawn to choosing to look at what made you more joyful deep down on the inside.

In the same way, you have an inner 'yes,' the true north of your created identity and purpose. By making good belief choices about yourself and what you can do in alignment with your true north, your gifts, your experience and your purpose, you will deeply affirm and reinforce who you are created to be. You become free to be true to yourself. You are at rest and naturally joyful. Your activity is charged with energy, your light is radiant, and you are inexorably drawn into everything you are meant to be.

The trajectory your chosen life-lore has placed you on is an often imprisoning and occasionally harmful one. But your life-lore can be reset and can be re-written, to release you into the glorious savanna of your life promise. It won't be long before life serendipitously presents an initial reset opportunity to you. Serendipitously ... that's a big word! It becomes one of your favourite words and describes how life brings you moments of amazing grace and wonderful providence in surprising and unanticipated ways.

To the delight and perhaps surprise of Mum and Dad, you end up going to university, where you are offered a student job as one of the managers of a local squash club. Why was this a moment of grace and providence? Well, the facility was owned by the South African No. 1 women's player at the time. And she will not only allow you free access to the courts to practice and play but also, seeing potential in you, choose to invest in your life by taking time to coach you. It turns out you have a natural talent for the game and spend hours practising on the court alone, enjoying the power, liberty, and confidence arising from mastering the skills you have learned. You become a very good player, which in time has you representing the Seychelles in an international competition during the two years you will reside there (that's a long story in itself!).

As you read this, Simon, know that you have seeds of promise and brilliance in you.

You are good enough. You have what it takes. As you discover later in life, you are actually a diversely talented sportsman, doing well not only at squash but also long-distance running and beach volleyball.

I wonder if this insight into your future serves to reinforce the belief you discovered in playing football on an English country green?

Clearly, this is not just about success in sport. You ended up believing a lie that day, when the earth should have swallowed you whole – a lie which says 'you are not enough,' not just in sport but also in every area of your life. You ended up believing that you are defined by how others see and think of you. You ended up investing so much of your energy in pleasing others and seeking the approval of others. You ended up not seeing or understanding how amazing you are, just as you are.

In order to sufficiently reset your off-beam life-lore, which will shape much of your life, you need to understand and accept the choice and power you have to choose your belief system, the foundation of your life-lore. You need to have insight into your life story as it's been written so far and be open to writing a new one. Fortunately, grace abounds in your future life, in giving you people and circumstances which take you on a journey of rediscovering your true north, entering into the infinite expanse that is the unlimited potential of you. It includes a wonderful family, a faith awakening, a life of self-discovery and rich learning, and the opportunity to make a difference to your world. As to the detail – well, I can't give it all away! I'll leave it to you to discover the wonderful adventure of your future that awaits.

In coming full circle, as life often does, future you has a masterstroke reset experience in the 55th year of your life. You reunite with your love of squash and start practising alone at the nearest squash club, a good 30 minutes' drive from your home in semi-rural Australia (yes, you do get around). A stranger walks into the centre unnoticed and is drawn to observe you. As you finish your solo practice session, the stranger comes on to the court and stretches out his hand, introducing himself as the captain of a state league team … and invites you to join his team.

Wait, what! What just happened here?!? A captain chooses you, Simon. You were seen and sought out. It turns out you are enough. More than enough.

And so, I write, presenting you an opportunity to begin with this end in mind, with the insights I have shared. For you to write the future chapters of our life, based on seeing yourself in a new light and holding on to the wonder of your promise and potential … not allowing your perception of others' thoughts and beliefs to take control of defining the life-lore which directs the writing of your life story.

You have what it takes, Simon. Those first captains just won't recognise it in you – and that will be their loss. Get off that reserve bench, leave it on all on the field, show them how good you are.

Marianne Williamson, in her book Return to Love, wrote this:

> *Our deepest fear is not that we are inadequate. Our deepest fear is that we are powerful beyond measure. It is our light, not our darkness that most frightens us. We ask ourselves, 'Who am I to be brilliant, gorgeous, talented, fabulous?' Actually, who are you not to be? You are a child of God. Your playing small does not serve the world. There is nothing enlightened about shrinking so that other people won't feel insecure around you. We are all meant to shine, as children do. We were born to make manifest the glory of God that is within us. It's not just in some of us; it's in everyone. And as we let our own light shine, we unconsciously give other people permission to do the same. As we are liberated from our own fear, our presence automatically liberates others.*

Be liberated from your fear and shine your light entirely, Simon. It will be wonderfully and redemptively contagious and it will bring us home to the wide open savannas of our life promise.

It has been wonderful to spend this time with you. I really love who you are. I can't wait to see who you become.

Simon (the future version)

CHAPTER 2

Fireworks

Amanda Horswill

Dearest Amanda,

People don't really call you that yet, though, do they? I remember now – you used to be 'Mandy' to everyone. It suited your ever-smiling face, with its freckled nose, brown eyes so dark they're almost black, and that sun-kissed blonde hair, cut into a fetching 1980s mullet; your skinny limbs always in constant motion (except when watching Doctor Who). Quick to laugh, and hug, and sing and jump and run and love without reservation. I miss you, oh so much.

That name – Mandy – was always said with a lilt of kindness. Except, of course, when you were in trouble.

You're ten now, and you've already heard your fair share of 'Amandas', haven't you? And you are yet to endure that one particular sunny central-Queensland Tuesday afternoon that will, in time, become the hallmark metaphor for your childhood.

On that otherwise unremarkable day, you will find yourself sitting at your kitchen table, slouching in one of the comfy, olive green velour dining chairs, in a sharp sliver of yellow light, staring in wonder at the floating, dancing galaxy of light thrown onto the living room wall by the glitter vinyl sticker on your candy pink T-shirt. There you'll sit, and stare, breathing in and out, in and out, watching the dancing rainbows of light, and then, as if possessed by that light, a million thoughts bounce involuntarily and uncontrollably into your mind, all at once: From that excellent scene in *Pollyanna*, of the prisms strung across the window to create 'the most beautiful room in the whole world'; to air-sketching the logistics of recreating that scene in your dining room, or wondering whether the west-facing lounge room would be a better stage; to wondering if humans could ever harness the speed of light to travel through time, even though they could only travel forward, surely, as travelling backward to meet yourself would mean creating a new set of parallel universes, or maybe not, because maybe time is flat and not dimensional so can be traversed backward ... When, suddenly, with absolutely no warning, the full three barrels of your name, the heralds of impending doom, are aimed at you, ready to fire – ready to bathe you in fire:

'AMANDA JAYNE BLAKE!'

Your mother's voice is lightning striking your ears, causing a sickening, piercing deceleration of thought that physically hurts your brain.

'STOP DAYDREAMING AND DO YOUR THREE TIMES TABLE!'

You will be frozen in fear, wondering from where this hurricane has sprung, and if it will obliterate you, atomise you – but you will feel anchored to the spot, rendered in wide-eyed stone.

'I'LL GET OUT THE FEATHER DUSTER ...'

All you will be able to see is the burning confetti of your shattered thoughts falling through the air. You will want to brush the embers from your shoulders, but your will won't comply.

'I AM GOING TO COUNT TO THREE! ONE ... TWO ...'

The magical powers of 'two' will break the spell, and, like the flicking of some internal switch buried in your sternum, you will dutifully resume the important task of learning your three times tables.

And, I can safely say that you, dear young Mandy, will never forget that 3 times 7 is, actually, 21.

Mum will never get to three. At least not until those dreaded teen years, but by then you'll have long despatched that atomic duster behind some paint tins in the scary cupboard under the stairs. And don't go filing pre-emptive child cruelty charges at your dear old ma, please. I firmly believe you were exceptionally lucky to have a mum – a teacher – that cared enough to wield such instructive power, and also lucky to have a dear old dad that loved you, too. Please be kind to your parents – you'll understand why when you have your own children. They were young and on their own. The 1980s is now considered the Wild West of parenting. Evidence? Just watch *The Goonies* in ten years' time.

And it may also help to remember that they don't know about your secret. The real you.

They couldn't tell, because you were a girl.

But more on that later.

First up, I want to reassure you that you'll be okay. The road is nearly soul-crushingly bumpy at times, but this 45-year-old version of Amanda is doing fine. I may have a few more dints and scratches than you probably hope for, but I have a wonderful family, a great job, a circle of understanding friends, and somewhere safe to call home. That's a lot more than can be said for millions of others in this crazy world right now.

So, dear ten-year-old me, even though I look back at pictures of you fondly and sometimes mourn for what could have been, I wouldn't change a thing, even if I could. Because if I did, I would not be me.

But that doesn't stop me from wondering.

The echoes of 'what if' and 'if only' haunt me still, and I do grieve for those lost years where knowing what I do now could have made all the difference. But I guess that's the purpose of that conundrum called hindsight, isn't it? To shine a spotlight on what we've learned, so that we can change our behaviour and stop history repeating itself. To break the cycle. That is my sincere hope. That what I've learned – what you are yet to learn – can help my children, or someone else's children, so they don't have to waste what are supposed to be the best years of their life feeling … less. Strange. Lazy. Incompetent. Stupid. Silly. Useless. Worthless. Worth less.

You are ten now, and I know you are already keenly aware of what I am talking about. How old were you when you realised that what was going on in your head was completely different to everyone else? That sometimes, you had thoughts so big that you thought they could crack the top of your head open and burst into life like some gory firework that could be seen from the moon? I remember how those thoughts zipped through your mind, multiplying into a cacophony of colour, weaving together and ricocheting, over and over and over. So much noise. And when you tried to transform that energy into muscle movements so your tongue could frame those thoughts into words and birth those ideas into the world, you just received blank stares or were told to 'be quiet,' 'do your work,' 'be a good girl.' Already, you have learned not to talk about those inner fireworks. But they still fizz and flutter against the spongy insides of your skull, trying to escape, don't they?

At the tender age of ten, the seeds of self-doubt and self-loathing are inside you and have been for a long time now. They've taken root, spawned that evil choir of voices in your head that sings your faults. Louder and louder they will sing, swelling in numbers, honing their craft, until, soon – oh too soon – they will be all you can hear.

Remember the song they wrote for you, after you read your Year 1 school report, your first official chance of taking your measure against the world?

'Amanda is capable of more at this time and it is only due to lack of concentration and "laziness" that her progression has been slow,' the faded blue biro marks state plainly. 'Thoughtlessness is the reason for this result.'

To others, it might not seem like much. Just one person's view of you. No biggie. But I know those barbs penetrated you deeply, anchoring something rotten at your core, in your identity, coalescing with the quiver full of identical arrows already buried there, irrevocably spoiling you.

That evil internal choir latched on to the word 'lazy' and sent you running blindly away from it, working harder, reading more, thinking more, wondering why your effort wasn't rewarded, which sent your pace upwards. Onwards. Perfection-seeking, the need for external approval, for everyone to like you, to think you were more special than anyone else, to prove the choir wrong. To shut them up. White-knuckling through long days of pretence and pretend.

Your coping mechanisms will gorge on your energy, devour your personality. You will have to let something slide, so your subconscious chooses just one thing. Then another, and another. One by one, they all fall. Another decade will dissolve like this, and you'll feel yourself dissolving, too.

It starts slowly, though. Already, you have started to sit inside your wardrobe, in the dark, on those big black plastic bags of other people's clothes, willing the warm, furry silence to hug you. In a few short years, your room will reflect the messiness of your mind, and your father, fed up, will throw everything out your window. You won't care. You will become addicted to television, devouring it as a balm against the world, deaf to all other sounds, even when your sister shouts straight in your ear. When friendships become too hard to understand, or you are afraid you can no longer keep up the false projection of yourself, you will abandon them. And you won't be able to care. It's mercenary, survival mode. Into adulthood, work will become an obsession above all else, years cloistered inside a room, in front of a screen, instead of really living, experiencing the world. And then the ultimate of all stressors – a child – will deliver you a blow that could so easily have provided a finale.

Instead, it will save you.

*

So, let me save you some pain, dearest Amanda, and tell you something now that will change your life. Maybe it will help silence that choir.

I have Attention Deficit Hyperactivity Disorder.

You have ADHD.

You are not lazy. You are not thoughtless. You are not doing anything deliberately to make your teachers angry, prompting them to put you in the 'stupid group' even though you can, eventually, do the work. Your parents don't know this about you, so they can't help. In time, you'll become so good at hiding, they won't see it. It's your secret. Your friends can't understand you sometimes because of it. You can't understand your friends sometimes, too, for the same reason. There is nothing wrong with who you are. It's just that your brain – your wonderful, intelligent, creative, loving brain – works slightly differently to everyone else's. Or most people's – because what is normal, really, but a set of statistics that cut out all the interesting things in life?

But you won't find out this pertinent fact about yourself – that you have ADHD – until you are in your fourth decade. By then, you will have been treated many times for bouts of anxiety and depression, been misdiagnosed with other psychiatric conditions, laid waste to your aspirations, and spent thousands upon thousands of dollars on professional help to try and patch up your flailing psyche. And, shockingly, you will come to understand that there are whole g+enerations of people who have had eerily similar experiences, whose lives could have been changed – could still be changed – if only they knew that they, too, were not broken but simply made a little more uniquely than expected.

I am so sorry I didn't know, didn't do anything sooner. But you don't know what you don't know, right? And I had bucket loads of misinformation drowning out any possible discovery. Like everyone else, I'd heard about the 'epidemic' of Attention Deficit Hyperactivity Disorder – the thing, as the prejudicial mantra goes, 'that makes little boys so crazy naughty their mothers have to drug them with speed.' And: 'Girls don't have it.' And then there's the media reports talking about over-diagnosis, risks of little kids hopped up on amphetamines becoming future druggies, of 'medicalising' normal childhood behaviour. 'Utter nonsense. Didn't happen in my day. Kids can be lazy, but all they need is a stiff kick up the arse.' And besides, don't those kids grow out of that silly 'childhood phase,' anyway?

So, while filling out a screening test for my child, it came as a huge surprise that I could also tick so many of the boxes.

I told a psychiatrist. She tested me, prescribed medication. And then the background noise subsided.

Quiet.

For the first time in my life, I could focus without extreme physical and mental effort. I could motivate myself to do something I didn't 100 percent want to do by just thinking that I needed to do it, rather than taking two days to mentally conjure an intricately detailed, Nobel-prize-worthy backstory to justify the energy expenditure needed to get it done.

The grey began to lift, and I could see a way forward. A future where I wasn't this exhausted ghost of a person trying to keep the zillion balls I had chucked into the air from crashing to the ground. I could work, and raise my kids, and breathe, all at the same time. It was going to be okay. I was okay. You will be okay. Eventually.

It's not a perfect peace, it's true. There are times when the medication makes me focus too much, and on the wrong things. Sometimes, it hampers my ability to change what I am paying attention to, which can make parenting naturally inquisitive children even tougher. I can't have (shouldn't have) coffee or drink alcohol. And, before we found the right magic pill for me, there was a very long period of trial and error. Some drugs made me cranky; one slowed my mind down to an unacceptable crawl; another made me wonderfully skinny but changed my personality so much that I was a stranger to those who loved me. To myself. It's a common theme among the medicated – what level of chemically induced 'normal' can you endure?

Now that the clouds have cleared dearest Amanda, I am left to ask: Why didn't I discover this secret sooner? How could I have missed this? I am a journalist. I've been writing about people for two decades, talking to thousands of men, women, children, from all walks of life, documenting everyday history. How have I never, ever heard of adult ADHD, or of someone being diagnosed with ADHD as an adult?

This huge thing that just happened to me, this life-changing diagnosis – how could there have been no warning, no red flags waving for all to see? All the times I presented to a medical professional with anxiety, panic attacks, with clear symptoms of being 'ADHD overwhelmed' – why did not one of those experts ask: 'How's your attention? Have you ever been tested for ADHD?' Why was it assumed that it was an inability to control my emotions that was making me so distressed? Why didn't someone see that it was, actually, everyday life that was hard for me? Normal, everyday things, trivial things like shutting kitchen cabinet doors after making a sandwich, which I could never do; important things like keeping up with the interrupting demands of a toddler, chipping away at my sanity like a crazed sculptor; workplace hiccups like reacting to competing priorities with unjustified angst, one day making me physically unable to leave my car; or that I only froze with anxiety when there was just too much to do? Too much input? Why didn't anyone see that my executive function was broken? Why, instead, did every single medical professional I consulted (and there were many) tell me that it was my inability to control my own emotions that was at the root of the issue?

And why did that somehow make it feel like it was all my fault?

You may detect, dear Mandy, a hint of anger here. If I am honest with myself – something I have had to relearn over the years – I admit that it's hard not to stumble into the black tarpit of bitterness and suffocate on my anger. But the enemies of bitterness are empathy and insight, the act of opening the mind to a possibility not yet understood. You have both those gifts in spades. They will come to define you more than any medical label can.

And so, I will ask you to call on those gifts now, and not give in to anger, when I tell you this: As a ten-year-old girl, growing up in 1980s Australia, there isn't even the remotest chance you will be diagnosed. Nothing will be done. You are on your own. The prevailing belief is that pleasant little girls who daydream the days away at the back of the classroom, not giving the teacher any specific sort of trouble, could never have something so debilitating as an attention disorder. The boys that climb the walls instead of learning their three times tables, who run and run and run and cause their teachers to despair – they will be the ones to face the doctor's diagnostic stare. The squeaky classroom wheel, after all, gets the most oil.

So, my advice to you, lovely Mandy, is to squeak. Squeak your loudest. Squeak at the top of your lungs! Squeak until the whole world can hear you say you are not okay. That you are not coping. That you need help to take control of the fireworks in your head, to harness their creative power.

And remember – there will be a time when being different is okay. The 1980s is not that time. But your children are living in it now. The work that you do on yourself in your first 40 years will be hard, but it will be worth it. Your children thank you every day for it, in their smiles, in their hugs. It's written on their delighted faces when they tell you that they just had a mind-blowing thought or an octogenarian-worthy insight about the nature of being, which you then ask them to tell you. And which you listen to. And understand. And congratulate them for. 'Wow,' you will say, 'I wish everyone could think like you.' And you will mean it, with every cell in your body, every strand of your unique DNA.

Because, Mandy, someday, you'll be glad you were made just that little bit differently. No, more than that – one day, you will be glad to be you.

Love,

Amanda

PS: Please buy Microsoft and Apple Macintosh shares. And in three years' time, just say no to your cousin, who offers you one of his crumpled menthol cigarettes in the chook shed at Nanna and Pap's Donnybrook place. Because, even as a 45-year-old who hasn't smoked for 20 years, you'll still crave a drag of those death sticks. They cost $60 a pack these days. Yep, that's right – for you, that's 300 bags of corner-store mixed lollies! xx

CHAPTER 3

One Day

Jess Weiss

Dear Jess,

I am writing this letter to you to let you know how much I love you. I am always with you, and I will never leave you. It must be difficult to believe because you haven't met me yet. You can't see me, hear me, or feel me. But one day you will.

For now, please trust me when I tell you that I am there for you. I am there for you when you feel alone and when you think that no one cares for you. I am there when you are afraid and you think that no one is there to protect you. Do you remember the nights when you talked to your stuffed animals in bed because you were so scared of the dark and you were alone at home because Mummy left you to go out all night? I was right there with you, wishing I could make you feel loved and safe.

I am there when you feel lost and don't know where to go or who to talk to. I am there when you are confused and don't know what to believe. I am there when you have good moments and when you have bad moments. I really wish you had more of those good moments when you were little, but one day you will.

I love seeing you smile; it makes me smile, too. I love seeing you happy. It's beautiful to watch your face light up when you see or touch a horse. You really love cuddling your face into a horse's mane. And horses love you just as much as you love them. They are so beautiful and magical; no wonder you feel so peaceful around them. One day, you will have your own horse –it will be your soulmate, and you will go on the most wonderful journey together. Keep believing in your dream, Jess. Your horse is somewhere out there, waiting for you.

I really hope this letter will help you to feel better. Remember, I'm writing this because I love you so much. Read it whenever you need to feel loved and understood and protected. Read it when you are upset or when you are happy. Read it when something special happened and you think you have no one to share it with. Read it to celebrate your victories, your small and big accomplishments. I promise I will celebrate with you and cheer you up when things go wrong.

I know you miss something that you don't even understand is missing. Being ten years old can be very confusing, but you are doing so well. I know you wonder why your dad is not with you and why your mum is away a lot. I know it hurts you so much that you think your parents don't love you. You wonder if you have done something wrong, or if there is anything you could do better for them to love you and to be with you.

One day, you will know that the world is a beautiful place to be and that you are so loved. But at the moment, everything is so confusing for you. The noise around you is too loud, and there are so many distractions. As you grow older, unfortunately, this will only increase. You may sometimes feel lost, but you are not. One day it will all make sense to you – big pinkie promise.

I know that many times you have been let down by the ones you trusted most. I know how deeply that hurts, and I wish I could take that pain away and give you a happy smile for your beautiful face.

Unfortunately, sometimes, the people that you need and trust most can't be there for you and give you what you need. That doesn't always mean that they don't love or care about you. Sometimes they just can't.

It's not your fault. It's not their fault. Please don't believe that it's about you doing something wrong or that you are not good enough or that you could do something to change them. They do what they can. They love you more than you can imagine, and one day they will tell you.

It's okay to be angry, sad, or disappointed about it. You are allowed to be, but don't hang on to those feelings – release them. Let them go to make space for some positive feelings. There is always something good in any bad situation; you just have to look for it. Smile to yourself in the mirror. It may sound silly, and you may find it awkward, but it helps. Give yourself a big smile – smile at others. A smile is like magic: Give it often and freely, and it will bring a little light into your darkness.

Please trust me that you are always loved, that you have everything that you need to be okay, and that everything that makes you feel desperate, alone, helpless, or scared will pass. It will pass and you will feel extraordinarily good about yourself. You are an incredibly strong and lovable girl and you have such a bright future ahead. Believe me, I know it, and I won't ever lie to you!

I know you have been lied to many times ... and it will happen again. Some people will lie because they never learned how to be honest. Some people will lie because they want to hurt you. Some people will lie to make you do things that they want you to do. Some people will lie because they think they love you and want to say something they think you want to hear. There are a thousand reasons for people to lie. It's very complicated and hard to understand, but you don't have to understand it all yet.

There are so many distractions out there, so many voices. They will tell you so many different things, and you will find it very hard to know which are the ones telling you what you need to know.

One day you will listen very closely to a very quiet voice, no more than a whisper, and you will know it's me.

You will find it easier when you surround yourself with stillness or the sound of nature. There is so much to find when you are outside. You can watch the clouds passing by and feel the warm sunlight on your skin, your bare feet touching the grass as you sit and soak up the beauty around you.

One of the most amazing things in life is to look at the night sky. There is some incredible magic in watching the stars, and every time you gaze at the sparkling little wonders above, I will be right there with you, and you will know it.

There are so many wonders around, Jess. Keep your eyes and your heart open for them. The smell and the look of some wild grown flowers, butterflies dancing in the sunny blue sky, a colourful rainbow after a summer storm. These are all miracles – and they are calling for you.

Go and climb some mountains and view the world from up above. Feel the soft breeze that refreshes you when you reach the top. Up there, you will experience peace and love. You will know that I am right there with you, and we will smile.

Cherish these moments and search them as often as you can.

Sometimes you will have to do it on your own, Jess. Sometimes nobody will join you and that's okay. There is a difference between being alone and being lonely.

You are never lonely. You will always have me, and you will meet a lot of wonderful people in your life. Some will become your best friends; some will only hang out with you for a little while; and some will show up when you least expect it and help you with something before they leave. Like the seasons, people come and go. Enjoy the time you have with them and keep the good memories when they have to move on. You are a wonderful friend; keep giving the gift of friendship to others and I promise feelings of loneliness will disappear like the fog on a sunny day.

I know you will reach that point, because I am there to guide you. You are here for a reason; you have a gift and you were sent to this world to have a positive impact. You may feel like you don't want to be special because being special feels so different. Being different can be scary. It can make you feel like you do not belong, and that can be really hurtful, I know that. But believe me, you will appreciate your gift when the time arrives. Until then, keep believing and keep trusting that everything will be alright.

You have to protect your gift and you have to protect yourself! This world needs you!

I know it will be challenging sometimes, and it will leave you feeling empty and tired. You are a deeply feeling soul, always wanting to give your all to others to make everyone feel better, to take away their pain.

This will become more intense when you get older and you start entering into romantic relationships. You will have a strong attraction to men in some kind of emotional pain; you want to be the one that makes them feel better. Just know that you can't save them all. You can't help everyone as much as you want to. Some people are not ready for you yet, and some never will be. You can still feel for them, care for them, and be there for them from a distance – but you can't let them take you with them. It is their journey; you have yours. Send them love, but let them go and move on. You are too precious to get caught up in their pain.

I know some of your classmates and older friends offer lots of temptations. I know you desperately want to be with them and have fun and feel part of something and just enjoy life. It will take some time until you find the right ones to stay with and know who to share your time and energy with. You will find the right ones, the ones who watch the stars with you, who listen to the wind with you, and who talk about exciting things with you. They will laugh with you, not about you. They will make you smile, not cry. They will touch your heart and your soul, not only your body.

In a few years' time, you will develop an interest in boys. It'll appear to you that you have to look and behave a certain way to be interesting for them, especially for boys or men who find you attractive at that given point in time.

Your mind will be occupied by the idea that you need to be 'sexy' as a girl. You'll compare yourself to other girls and women and want to look like them. You'll see them in magazines or on TV or even in your school, and you will think that compared to those other girls and women, you are not as pretty or beautiful or sexy.

Please never doubt your beauty. You are extremely beautiful, Jess.

The beauty that is most important is not the one you see from the outside. Don't focus too much on the outside. You want to be joyous and passionate and kind and curious and healthy and first and foremost – you want to be yourself. That is what makes you beautiful. That is what makes you sexy in the right eyes. But being sexy is not something to strive for, so don't waste all your precious energy on chasing it. It attracts too much of the wrong attention and it is not the one that I wish for you to get. You deserve so much more than attention.

Don't try to force something into a true loving and healthy relationship; it will happen when the time has arrived. Enjoy your life, build friendships, follow your dreams, and trust your journey.

You deserve unconditional, pure appreciation. Affection and passion with a wholehearted, genuine interest in you as a whole. One day you will meet someone able to give you all of this – and more. He will know how truly wonderful you are, and he will not abuse you but rather help you to grow. He will be witty and may sometimes annoy you, but he will never make you question your value.

You are enough, no matter what anyone is telling you. If someone keeps questioning your worth, just move on. You don't have to stay with somebody who does not appreciate you.

You can be so very proud of yourself. Don't be so hard on yourself, sweetie – nobody is perfect! The best you can do is keep a good balance. Life should be enjoyable and nourishing, never punishing or too restrictive. You have a wonderful soul, and my wish for you is that you learn how to keep yourself out of everything that is not good for you. I know you have the ability to stay away from harmful influences. Many people that you will meet as you grow up do a lot of harmful things, but you don't have to be part of those crowds.

You don't have to drink alcohol or take drugs and party all night long with strangers. These people are not your people. They may give you lots of attention, but they don't really care about you at all. Drugs and alcohol can make you feel extremely happy for a while; you may think it's the best feeling in the world, but that is only an illusion. Don't fall for it, Jess. Please don't let the illusion fool you. You are here to experience the real magic of life, not the artificial. You don't need to drink or take drugs to feel the way you desire. It's all in you. Pure and divine.

Now, let's move on to something inevitable for a growing young lady. You don't have to be intimate with someone when you do not absolutely feel good about it. You don't have to let someone kiss you or touch you when it doesn't feel right for you. Don't let them force you; you are strong and confident and you can say NO. Being intimate and having sex with someone should be a playful, exciting, and joyful experience for you. Make sure it gives you pleasure, not pain and confusion.

I know there have been times when someone you trusted did things to you that you didn't want and you couldn't make them stop. I am so sorry that this happened to you. You don't have to feel like that again, you have the power to stop it. It can't break you; you will only grow stronger. Remember, you are loved and you are safe. You've got this. Please don't ever doubt that. You did not do anything wrong. They did. It is not your fault. Keep loving yourself and cherish your beautiful body.

It's time for me to end this little keepsake memory for you, but I want to give you a few more little words of guidance that I believe will help you navigate through life.

Ready? Okay, here we go:

If you are talking to someone, look at them, and listen carefully to what they say. If you have a task to do, always give it your full attention and always give your best, even if it's boring and you don't really see why you should do it. Pay attention to detail.

I want you to have fun and to enjoy life to the fullest, but life isn't always about excitement and having fun. It's about doing what needs to be done first. Believe me, the joy and the feeling of accomplishment will be worth it.

There are very few things that are more important than honesty, so be honest, always. To both the people around you and yourself. Lying is never a good idea, so don't even think about it.

You have so many dreams. I can promise you each and every one of them will become true if you believe and put the right actions into them. It won't happen overnight, though. You'll have to work hard and be smart for it and sometimes it may feel like it's impossible and like you should give up – that is exactly when you have to push through. Never give up; never give in. If one way doesn't work, try another. Do something different. Be creative. Change directions if you must, but keep moving. Moving is progress. Don't mistake that for running away; it can be a bit tricky sometimes, but you will soon learn how to differentiate the two.

You are very intelligent, and you will always have that incredible open mind and the desire to learn and grow. That is one of your biggest assets; it's what makes you so very special and incredibly valuable, and it's what makes you successful in reaching your dreams. One day they all will come true.

Go for it, Jess! Don't be afraid if that means things feel unbearably hard at times, 'cause it is hard and I can't make everything easier for you. Sometimes hardship is just something that you have to experience. Acknowledge these struggles, overcome them, and build your empire with the rocks in your way.

One day you will be a mum. Your children will look up to you and love you with all their hearts, and they will see you for who you are. A beautiful, caring, strong, passionate, creative soul who always has the ability to smile at others and touches the hearts of many. A woman who shares her compassion with those around her and is trying to leave this world a little better than before.

One day you will be her. One day you will me.

Love and hugs,

me

CHAPTER 4

Oh, the Places You'll Go!

Ian Collins

Dear Ian,

Congratulations!
Today is your day.
You're off to great places!
You're off and away!

Can you imagine what it's like to be a grown-up? Me neither. I'm still working it out. And being a man, well, that's a whole other kettle of fish. What's a kettle of fish? And what's it got to do with being a man? No idea, mate.

So far, you might be thinking that when we grow up, we're not going to know very much. And you would be spot on. Because the weird thing is, we get taught all this stuff at school and from our parents, so we can go out there and stand on our own two feet, but then we realise that we've got a lot to unlearn. That's right. Unlearning. It's a thing.

So, don't take it all too much to heart. Don't worry about getting things 'wrong.' The other grown-ups? Most of them are just pretending they know what they're doing. Don't worry about having the answers. We're all just working it out, kiddo.

You'll have lots of friends, along the way, that will help you see where you're strong and soft. It's important to be both, you see. They don't tell us that when we're little boys, so I want you to know, straight off the bat, that real men do cry. That it takes true courage to feel those feelings. And don't be so afraid of the shadows. There's magic inside of them, and you, my friend, are an adventurer.

If I told you what was happening in your world many years from now, I don't think you'd believe me. Imagine far and distant lands, climbing mountains, crossing deserts, meeting goddesses (I know you're not into them right now, but trust me, that will change), and gathering riches untold. You'll weather storms on ships off the coast of Libya, jump out of planes and fly in hot air balloons in Australia, ride motorcycles across South Africa, bobsleigh down chutes in France, and ride sturdy horses on the plains of Mongolia. You'll encounter pirates in the Congo, find enlightening medicines in the jungle, and even send flowers to the real life equivalent of Darth Vader.

You'll be on your way up!
You'll be seeing great sights!
You'll join the high fliers
Who soar to high heights.

And then you'll look at all of that and wonder,

Who the heck am I?

(Big question for a young mind, but I wish we had started thinking about this sooner, so I'm throwing it out there.)

I think what you'll eventually discover is that no matter where you go, you will always be there. And it's not until you can be friends with you that you'll realise that all the high flying, motorbike riding, beauty queen dreaming, money making success kind of means nothing until you've got that. Sure, it's fun and we'll still do all that stuff. I wouldn't let us miss out on Congolese pirates or falling in love. We have to do that to let it go.

There will be times when you feel completely lost, scared, and even times when you didn't care if the plane landed safely. You will find yourself at the bottom of many bottles and dabbling in dodgy substances, all to try and find answers to the questions your soul yearns to know.

It will take something drastic to wake up, and it happens for us on the Italian coastline, after witnessing a friend's most extravagant and spectacular wedding – soon after the breakdown of your own marriage to an incredible woman. But you'll find your biggest answer after hiking up the steep face of a volcano. (More on this a bit later.)

We'll have a breakdown-heartbreak-dark-night-of-the-soul moment. That's something you can look forward to. But, really, every hero has to go through the part of the story where they might not make it. And we'll do that too, and it will be tough. But don't worry, we'll come out the other side, stronger.

You'll come to a place where the streets are not marked.

Some windows are lighted. But mostly they're darked.

A place you could sprain both your elbow and chin!

Do you dare to stay out? Do you dare to stay in?

How much can you lose? How much can you win?

You are surrounded by people who love you. Your big sister who always looks out for you, your parents who have always been there, doting aunties and uncles who adore you, an extended brotherhood, sisterhood, and global community – so remember that it's okay to ask for help when you need it. It's another one of those things that takes courage, so take a deep breath, reach out, and be willing to be vulnerable. You are not an island. I know that seems pretty obvious right now. You are clearly a boy. But you'll get what I mean at some point. Don't think you have to go it alone, my friend. One day, you will meet an amazing human and beautiful soul who will teach you how to receive. Until then, it's okay to keep on giving. I know you love that. Just remember, it's hard to keep giving from an empty cup, so make sure you always keep yours full too.

What is my greatest gift to the world?

Mate, let's get clear. The secret isn't about being whatever you want to be. The key you need to find is the one that unlocks the door to your greatest gift. We are each born into this world with a unique gift and a reason for being here. One of your good friends will call this 'becoming a genius hunter in your own life.'

(He's a poetic kind of guy. Which, btw, is very cool. You might think poetry is for girls, but you're wrong – which is fine, because, like I said before, you don't have to worry about getting things wrong.)

It was Aristotle who said that happiness is 'an activity of the soul in accord with perfect virtue.' Which basically means, find your inner genius and let him lead the way. You will be great at some things, average at others, and plain terrible at the rest, and that's okay!

All you need to do is to find your greatness, your genius and the thing that lights you up inside, and then share that with others. We each have something we are so special at that no one else has, a calling if you will. The question is whether you will answer it or not.

You'll eventually hunt your genius down while working on an oil rig in the shipyards of Singapore. You will see teammates get hurt until, one day, you'll witness a death on a neighbouring vessel and it will have a profound effect on you. From that moment forward, you will want to make the world a safer place for all, regardless of who they are or where they come from. Each day, you will get to work with some of the smartest people from some of the best companies on the planet to help them realise their potential and reduce the likelihood that they will make mistakes, particularly ones that can be catastrophic. Plus, some days, you even get to ride to work in a helicopter!

Am I living my life?

People will love to tell you what you should and shouldn't be doing. People love to 'should' each other. They mean well but you are the only one who knows what it is best for you.

You have brains in your head.
You have feet in your shoes.
You can steer yourself
Any direction you choose.
You're on your own. And you know what you know.
And YOU are the guy who'll decide where to go.

So how do you know if you are living your best life, and not the one someone else wants for you? You might not have learnt this yet, but you have an inner navigation system. Like the street directory in the back of Dad's car, but way better. And it's pretty simple. It's your emotions. Your intuition. That part of you that just knows if it's a big fat yes or a hell no way! Listen to how your body responds and follow that. Even if Mum and Dad say different, you really do know best. It might take you a while to really tune into this navigation system, like finding the right station on the radio, but once you learn how to, it will be your greatest asset.

Trust yourself, trust your intuition, and trust your inner guide. Remember that everyone is on their own timeline. You will have friends that get married, have kids, and buy a house when they do, while you're still gallivanting around the world. Don't worry about it. You are on your journey, my friend, an exploration of your inner and outer worlds. Ultimately, this is your life, your experience, and only you know what you really long for.

30

What do I value?

Right now, you probably value family, friendship, and the freedom to be outside playing. That's not going to change. Along the way, you'll develop a keen dislike for injustice and conflict, as you try to bring more safety, security, and peace to the world.

This journey that you are on is about becoming a more empowered, embodied, and whole man, and this means meeting all your different sides. You'll learn to harness your inner king, warrior, lover, and magician, and you'll meet their shadow sides, as you find a code you can live by. You'll get lost at times but stick to your values; follow that inner guidance, and you'll be just fine.

What do I want?

As you can probably tell by now, your life will take you on many amazing adventures. You'll want to experience the joy of jumping on a plane and discovering somewhere new. You'll want to experience the thrill of jumping out of planes and even hurtling down the ice chute of bobsleigh tracks. You'll want to experience the thrill of falling in love, staring blissfully into and getting lost in each other's eyes. And you'll want to remember the curiosity and exuberance that you have right now.

Most importantly, you will want to experience happiness, and this will come to you from a feeling of contribution. When you can know yourself as a contribution, someone who makes a difference in the world, in whatever form or capacity that may take, you will know true happiness.

Take care of your body and your money, do the housekeeping, and keep yourself in good working order so your soul can fly.

What would I do if I wasn't afraid of failure?

Mate, trust me on this – you are going to fail. You are going to fail in some spectacular ways! You will meet and fall in love with some of the most phenomenal women you could imagine, and you will stuff it up. You will get on stage in front of your colleagues and friends, and completely lose your voice. You will make an incredible amount of money, and then lose it all. These times will be tough, no doubt, but they are an important part of your path. And it's always worth remembering that, even in your darkest hours, you may still actually be the lighthouse in someone else's storm.

And when you're alone, there's a very good chance
You'll meet things that scare you right out of your pants.
There are some, down the road between hither and yon,
that can scare you so much you won't want to go on.

Failure will be one of your greatest teachers. Don't let it get you down. Keep going, mate, and know that all you need to do is pick yourself back up again. As someone great once said, the first 40 years of childhood are typically the hardest.

Do I have all the answers within me?

You have everything you need within you. On a deep level, you already know this, and I'm only here to remind you of that. What you will experience on that volcano was nothing short of an awakening and, while you have always felt its presence, it is the first time you really tuned into this universal life force we call source energy. You realise that you are in fact not a body with a soul inside, but the other way around. You chose to come into this body under the exact circumstances you arrived, to experience what this life has to offer. All the ups and down, the ins and outs, the wins and woes. As long as you keep remembering and knowing that you chose this, you will have everything you need.

But, enough of that for now. Go, jump on your bike, have fun and enjoy life, be kind to others, keep asking yourself these questions from time and time and always remember who you are.

So, like your buddy Dr Suess says...

Be your name Buxbaum or Bixby or Bray
Or Mordecai Ali Van Allen O'Shea
You're off to Great Places!
Today is your day!
Your mountain is waiting.
So ... get on your way!

Love you mate,

Ian

CHAPTER 5

Thoughts of Hope

Marta Madeira-Mulungo

Dear Marta, my little one.

I know it will seem strange that I am reaching out to you after 40 years of silence. Especially as I have not been good in keeping in touch with you, my little one, maybe because I didn't really know how I could, and partly because it has been so dark when I was there where you are. I just kept on moving forward, year after year, running away from the darkness.

Now, though ... this is a great way to reach out to you. There are things I want you to know – things that would give you more clarity than I had at your age. And maybe, if you know, you won't be trapped in so much darkness and silence. Maybe you'll be more free to be a child, more content with yourself – and perhaps more connected to the world and the people around you.

Right now, my little one, you look around and don't understand what is going on. You don't see where you start and where you end, how things are connected to each other, and that confuses you a lot. You have questions to ask, but you don't have words to interpret the questions. Your world is too closed, and there's a dark knot in your throat that you don't recognise; you want to speak, you want to participate in the conversation around you, but you're too self-conscious.

Should I say this, should I say that ... maybe I'll just listen.

You see, right now you are in a space where the adults are too occupied with everything else but you. Mom goes to work every day and comes back home really tired. Nana who sometimes comes in to stay is very quiet. Let me tell you some of the things that happened to you, that you choose not to remember. It's like you put a big mountain on top of those events. By choosing to pretend it's not there, my love, you remain in the dark, but it's your time to fly.

The War Left a Mark on You

When you were born, Mozambique's war of independence against the Portuguese regime had already begun. In 1973–1974, as the war progressed and spread across the country, danger crept closer and closer to home. Often at night, you and your family had to flee the house, running away from the soldiers scouring the neighbourhoods, looking for people to randomly kill.

You and your family lived in a small, two-bedroom house; there was no fencing and, needless to say, no electricity or running water. There were six of you kids – twin babies, a 2-year-old, and then two older than you – crammed into that little house, and the family's attention focused on the youngest.

Remember that drum, right outside the front door? The one Nana used as a punishment room when you children misbehaved? Remember how stubborn you were, and how often you were in there? Of all the times Nana punished you and put you in the drum, this is the time you'll always remember. You kept quiet, didn't cry or ask for forgiveness like your siblings. And then it got dark, and everyone went inside the house and forgot about you. You were so scared when you looked through the little holes the drum had and realised it was already dark – you couldn't see anything at all. But you didn't panic, just told yourself *it's alright, you're strong,* and hunkered down in the drum for a long stay. Strong, brave, angry, unapologetic – that's you!

It wasn't just a matter of sleeping in the drum overnight, though. You heard the gunshots and watched, through the little holes, as your whole family fled, running for shelter. You watched in silence as the soldiers went into the house, looking for people. And you watched, your heart in your mouth, as those soldiers came nearer to you, until one soldier kicked the drum, sending it and you spinning away, dizzy and scared. Another soldier fired two gunshots at the drum; the bullets zoomed right past you, adding another four holes to the battered drum. It felt like your heart was beating so loudly that they were sure to hear it, but you stayed as quiet as you could, and a few minutes later you heard one say to another that there was no one there. And then off they went, leaving you almost disbelieving that you'd escaped their notice.

You spent the whole night in that overturned drum, afraid to even touch yourself lest you find that you were bleeding. In the morning, your whole family returned, went right inside, and continued to chat with each other. At that moment, you felt like you did not exist, like they had not realised that you'd not been with them since yesterday. It was a couple of hours later that Nana finally asked where you were; only then did you have the courage to emerge from the drum and re-join the family. No one asked what had happened, so you kept your story to yourself. And it's stayed with you up to now, along with the darkness you'd felt throughout the night and the disconnect with the rest of the family. You felt empty and forgotten from that point forward.

Two years later, when the war was over, you and your big brother found yourselves in a boarding school very far from home. You just woke up one morning to find that your stuff had been packed, got into a bus, and travelled for many hours. Eventually you were delivered to the school, which was packed with other kids and felt like an orphanage built in an ex-military camp. No one ever explained why you were sent to that place – but if you had to guess, you'd say it's because your mother was living with the father of your three youngest siblings, and you and your other brother were not his children. So you were sent away. Your eldest sister was perhaps the luckiest; she was sent to live with a very nice aunt.

This was another episode that left you disconnected, closed off, and even deeper in darkness. You felt unwanted, unappreciated, as though you were somehow not good enough. You weren't even 10 yet, and being abandoned hurt so much. You and your brother stayed there for two years – you were forced to toughen up, to survive the hunger, to survive the cold, and to survive the overwhelming feelings of loneliness that came even though you were surrounded by people.

Back Home With Family

After two years, you woke up one day to discover Mom was there to collect you both. No warning, no explanation – it was just time to go home. And you obeyed, because that was who you were and that was what you did. You didn't ask any questions even though you had many; you just said 'okay, let's go.'

Back home was a totally different place than the home you left. When the Portuguese fled the country soon after independence, there were many houses for the Mozambicans to move into. The family moved to a really nice neighbourhood; the house was really beautiful, with three bedrooms, a nice garden and backyard, and water and electricity. The family had grown; there were two others, the children of Mom's husband, and you learned to call them brother and sister as well. You didn't really mind them; they were nice kids to play with, but Mom was worried. She'd constantly say that you shouldn't trust them, that you should keep your eyes open and watch what you eat – she feared they would poison you or something.

When you come to this part of your life, I want you to act differently and really connect with your new siblings. Feel free to play with them and develop a close relationship with them, just like brothers and sisters should. Fear is such a waste of time – such a waste of life! How can you be yourself when you are acting out of fear? Mom meant well when she asked you to not trust them, but she was acting from a place of fear, and I want you to act from a place of love. Your biggest power is love. Feel free to love them; as you do, you'll increase your ability to connect with people around you.

Lingering Darkness

You see, when life is unfolding, we can't always immediately find the goodness in it. Yet, despite the pain, the darkness, the emptiness that you experienced as a little one … Well. I'm here to tell you that it all works out well in the end.

You used to have many questions about life and its meaning, and why things unfolded as they did. Why was the sun yellow, why were the clouds blue, did God live alone or with somebody, who was GOD, etc. – but you would not ask anyone. You didn't know how to ask, perhaps because no one ever spoke to you about things that were interesting to you. And so, your world was quite closed; you felt darkness inside and out, and you walked with your head down, eyes stuck to the ground, like you were searching for something.

While the other kids were playing and seemed happy and laughing and silly, you would sometimes get very quiet and observe. Just observe. Sometimes you wanted to play and be loose and happy, but Mom had asked you to be careful not to trust. How could you play and be careful? How could you laugh and not trust?

You see, my love, while that part of your life had lots of unanswered questions, it was only the beginning of something really extraordinary. All those questions you had, some of which you still carry 40 years later, became your passion in life. They shaped your wonderful life today.

Thoughts of Hope

I am here today to lovingly tell you that, despite what it seems, you are doing just fine. The unanswered questions and the lingering darkness are the beginning of a path to self-discovery for you, and for the many that you'll shine your light on.

My dear, don't wish that things were different and that what happened to you shouldn't have happened. Nothing was supposed to be different; all is supposed to happen just as it's happening right now.

You see, being forgotten in the drum and spending all night in the open, alone, helped you to grow as a strong and brave person. As a result of that, you became independent and fearless; there are very few things that really scare you. You approach life with such tenacity, like nothing could go wrong; when you fall, you quickly bounce back. The voice that once said to you, it's all right, you are strong, is still with you, helping to coach you out of scary and challenging situations. You have come to name that voice GOD, and He is always there with you.

Because of the many questions you had, and how much you just watch people, you set out on a path to study psychology, and will later on develop a great interest in understanding the driving force behind people's actions and reactions. Today you have a great understanding of how people think, how they make such a big mess of their feelings, how to create results. You see, as you seek to answer your own questions, you learn to notice people's pain, and set out to help them dissolve the doubts and fears holding them back.

Marta, let's use some of the wisdom gained throughout the years to shine light into that darkness you're currently living. Let's explore those events and see what different results were possible, had you thought about things in a different manner – you see, thoughts create feelings, and it's your feelings that get you to act in a certain way.

Right now, my precious, I want you to mentally go back to the drum. When it got dark on that day, you chose not to remind your family that you were still in there. You loved to be by yourself; it gave you the power to listen quietly and not worry about joining in the conversations. You made a choice then. Can you see that?

Yes, I do see that. It was kind of a choice, though I never thought of it that way.

So own it. There is great power in owning your decisions and actions. You did well in keeping quiet, especially when the guns were shot, but I've always been puzzled by how you acted when you saw the family returning. So tell me, little one, how did you feel when you saw them arriving that morning?

I felt happy that they were safe, but I also felt jealous that they were together and that I'd spent the whole night alone.

I see. What meaning did you give that?

It meant that maybe I was not an important piece of the family.

Interesting. What else?

That they together were the family; I was not part of them.

Why did you choose those exact thoughts?

I don't know ... I guess I wanted to justify how I was feeling.

When you think 'I am not part of the family,' how do you feel?

I feel empty, lonely.

Interesting, isn't it? Can you see now that it was what you thought that gave you the feelings, not what actually happened? When you look back at that moment today, how would you have liked to feel and act, as you see them arriving together?

I would have loved to jump out of the drum and run towards them and tell them what happened.

That is so great to hear, my little one. How would you have felt if you had done just that?

Free to love them, to be loved, to be part of them.

Bravo. You see, with the thoughts 'I am not part of the family,' you suffer; without the thought, there is freedom, joy, love.

I see. It's very interesting that I created this horrible thought in my head and then spent more than 40 years believing it was real.

Don't worry. Now that you know, you can choose differently. Let's look at the drum again. You were in there; the soldiers had gone, but you stayed the whole night. Why did you not go back to the house where it was warm and comfortable?

Well, I was afraid.

Afraid of what?

I don't know. Just afraid, paralysed, I didn't want to move. I didn't want to think.

So, what you're telling me is that fear stopped you from finding the comfort of your bed?

Yes, that's right.

Isn't that interesting to know? That it was your fear that stopped you from moving towards the comfort of your bed or enjoying a good night's sleep.

Yes, I see that now, but I didn't then.

Please remember that always, and never let fear stop you. Always ask yourself, 'what are the thoughts that I am thinking?'

It's always the thought, isn't it?

Yes, you've got it. It's always the thoughts you choose, never the events.

You see, this is what we do now – we help people to see that. Humans often create a story of drama and suffering in their minds, when they could have been happier and created better results for themselves.

I want you to understand that it's never what happens that creates suffering. It's the way you think about what happens. Hang on to thoughts that give you hope rather than creating thoughts of suffering, even if they feel real to you. Each time you remember a story with drama and judgement, you feel the pain again, just as you felt when it happened. This doesn't mean you should hide from the truth; it means being open to finding out what the truth really is. The beautiful truth about you is that you are worthy. You are enough. You are complete as you are, and you are an important part of this wonderful universe and of your family. Your mission is to live life to the fullest – and that answers one of your questions, doesn't it?

Do not worry too much about the many questions you have. As life unfolds, one by one you'll find the answers. It's your questions that will stir curiosity and get you fired up to create a successful life. Being curious about life turns out to be one of your gifts. Because of it, you'll go forward and create a wonderful life of achievements. Your desire to know more and understand the principles of the universe will lead you on a path of self-development where you study with some of the greatest teachers and go on to create a fantastic life.

You'll travel the world, seeking more wisdom and knowledge – not just to improve your own life, but also to impact the life of others, as you have come to genuinely care for other human beings. Your work will lead you to meet and shake hands with Queen Elizabeth and Princesses Anne of Great Britain, statesmen, and leaders of this wonderful world. You will visit palaces and castles and get to see this beautiful world's many wonders.

You will inspire others to live their dream and unleash their potential. The world will open to you as you open to it; it will love you as you love yourself. All you need to do right now is be comfortable with where you are and continue to be curious about life. It's all supposed to be exactly as it happens. Don't fight your reality; rather, embrace and grow out of it.

You see, my little one, you are worthy of love just as you are. This means that there is absolutely nothing you need to do to deserve love or to be worthy of anything. It's important that you connect with other humans, and as you connect, do it from the place of fullness and completeness.

Don't seek love; rather love yourself fully and pamper yourself always. The more you love yourself, the better you will connect with other humans. And when you get married, as you will, don't make the other person the centre of your life. You are the centre of your own life; others are simply co-creators of your life. If you disconnect from yourself, you will also disconnect from your husband because you will be looking for him to make you feel worthy, and as much as he loves you, he can never do that because that is your work to do.

Another thing you lost that night is your connection with your body; you were so afraid you might be bleeding that you stopped touching your body, disconnected from it. I want you to take a good look at that fantastic body – let it be your friend. Don't just admire it from a distance; it's yours to touch, to cherish, and to play with. Connect with it, trust it, love it. Let the body, mind, and spirit be together. It's a divine trinity: If you separate them, you come off balance.

In fact, I want to leave you with this word. Connect. Don't just be with other humans; connect with them. There is no danger that you cannot overcome; people love you, and you know you also love them. Connect!

Love, me @50!

CHAPTER 6

The Power of You

Dr Catherine Jones

To my dear Catherine,

Hello. It's me. I mean, you. I'm you, but writing from the future, about 30 years from now. I hope that it's okay for me to write to you. It must be a bit confronting to get a letter from your future self, but I think you'll be okay reading it.

I don't really know why I've chosen now to write to you. It's been a period of reflection for me lately, and for a lot of others as well. It's been a funny few months here, with lots of things going on around the world right now which I won't bore you with. It's probably best that you don't know too many details – after all, it could mess up that space-time continuum that you saw in *Back to the Future*. I know you know that those movies aren't real, but I still felt cheated not to have a hoverboard when 2015 rolled around. Even without hoverboards, though, there are some unbelievable things coming up that you can't even imagine.

Right now, I'm sitting in my house here in Brisbane, actually not very far from where you are reading this letter. Argh, I hear you think. Why am I still in Brisbane?! It's okay – we've had quite a journey to other places in the last three decades; you can't possibly imagine it. Looking back on it, it's been a pretty fun ride. I look at where I am now and often find myself wondering how I ended up back where I started. It feels familiar and comforting, and so different, all at the same time.

You're probably in your room, sitting cross-legged on the bed in T-shirt and shorts, listening to the noise of the other kids floating in from the living room. The glass louvres in the windows are half open to let in a breeze, but it's barely moving the warm air in the room. There are no electronic things in your room, no TV because it's out in the living room for the family to use. All four channels! Exciting. If you listen carefully you can hear the crickets outside, or the neighbours' kids running through the sprinklers in their back yard.

You could be out in your own back yard, messing around in your own sprinklers with your brothers or your sister, but you like to read. The quiet is soothing, some precious time to yourself. You don't say very much generally. So much so that last year your teacher called your parents to discuss your lack of speaking. They asked you afterwards why you don't talk much in the classroom. It's the same reason you don't say much at home, isn't it? Watching what happens around you and listening to what people say ... it's so much more rewarding, yielding so much information, to be stored away in organised folders in your brain for future contemplation.

If you look around your room, you'd see the topological model of the United States you made last week from modelling clay (that was really cool, even if nobody else appreciated it). I can tell you, now that I've been there, that the mountains are majestic, and the rolling plains seem to extend forever. There's that book in Japanese you've been reading every evening and the Japanese dictionary next to it. You'll make good use of that skill later on.

And your desk, a proper full-sized pine one, the only desk in the house and the one Dad uses when he needs to write a letter or do his tax return. That desk is your sanctuary, each of the drawers carefully organised with stationery and interesting papers, a dictionary, a few old school books, your library loans, and some old *National Geographic* magazines that you rescued from the bin at school.

The edge of the desk, near the bed, is where you put your glasses at night. They're still new, those big blue plastic frames covering half your face. I still have the photo Dad took of you wearing those glasses, which is a big thing because there aren't a lot of photos taken in our house. I remember so clearly the day that you finally persuaded Mum and Dad that you needed your eyes tested, because you really couldn't see the blackboard at school. You were still getting everything right on your exams, and your homework was a breeze. But suddenly – you could see things clearly! It was such a revelation! The blackboard was readable. It was like a fog had been lifted from your eyes. Try not to be upset that the other kids call you 'four eyes.' They really won't matter to you in your life; I can hardly remember their names. I've worn glasses every day since then, and I can assure you – wearing glasses does NOT stop boys from making passes, AND you can see the passes coming waaaay better.

And then there's the wardrobe near the window. That wardrobe holds so many things. Your clothes, obviously, mostly well worn. Clothes don't really matter much to you; you've never had many to choose from, and even now I don't pay attention to them. Your school uniforms, constantly too short as you're getting so tall. You're the tallest in the class now, taller than all the boys as well, and the teachers don't like that the dresses are above your knees. Ah well, there's not much you can do about that, is there? You'll get some new ones next year, after the summer holidays; no point getting them now. At least your shoes fit and look nice, since you use Dad's black shoe polish every week to hide any scuffs.

But it's not just clothes in there. The clothes are the boring bits. You've got your box of special things. I've still got that box. I've added to it, of course, but your things are all still here. I know, I know … it's sentimental isn't it? You had a few strange ideas about things to keep, but hey – who else keeps all their baby teeth in a small wooden box? You never know when you might need to wear a necklace of your own teeth!

There's the small porcelain Peter Rabbit ornament from Nanna, given to you when you were a baby. You can't remember her very well, but everyone always says you look and sound like her. Your stuffed mouse baby toy – yep, that's still here, too. A silver photo frame, too nice to use. The children's reading book sent from England, from a relative you've never met. (Don't worry, you'll be off to England yourself.) The small Japanese bookmark given to you by the Japanese exchange student we had.

And the globe, sitting on the floor of the wardrobe. A cheap plastic globe, with strips of paper glued to the ball showing the outlines of the different countries. Some of the names of those countries have changed now, and the borders as well. You spin the globe when you're alone in your room, memorising the capital cities and looking to see where the lakes and mountains are. There's so much more out there, isn't there? You know there is.

You know you've always been a bit different to the other kids at school. All the places you've read about in the library, spending your lunch times flying round the world, through history, into different cultures and languages, you're desperate to go experience for yourself. You've always been the 'clever one,' getting perfect report cards every semester. Mum and Dad proudly tell all their friends how well you are doing, which embarrasses you. They're always pushing you to be the best, and yeah, I know that that can be pretty annoying. Be grateful for their support, though; without them, your life choices would be much more limited. They've always encouraged you to be your best, wherever that may take you, and given you a push when you've needed it.

You're a bit younger than your classmates, but even when you start high school, you float through with high marks in everything. It's strange, though, to be surrounded at school by kids who have overseas holidays and all the latest gadgets, when there's no holidays or fancy clothes for us. We both know how awkward it is on free-dress days at school. You intermittently listen to the murmurings of the teachers, daydreaming out the window as they talk about calculus, chemistry, the laws of physics, and differential equations for blah blah blah. It's hard to imagine how everyone else doesn't understand it, too? But school is more than grades; there's sports, and music, and spending time with your friends. Their excitement over boys and school dances, and you not having a clue what to wear or how to put on makeup. Looking back now, there were so many social things I was blissfully unaware of (like boys!), and there's no need to tell you about them now.

In six short years, you'll be starting university. It must seem an eternity to you now, but to me it feels like a brief interlude between childhood and adulthood. It's amazing how perception of time changes, the longer you travel through it ... Your friends are going off into all sorts of directions, but don't worry, you won't lose them. You'll naively wander onto campus, the arrogance of youth propelling you into every field you're interested in. Physics, maths, engineering, chemistry ... there's just so much to choose from. An all-girls school didn't really prepare you for being a 16-year-old girl surrounded by older people, most of them competitive males. Your abilities will help you with the coursework, but your age and gender will be against you in many ways. You'll wonder whether you're really supposed to be there. Dad will talk to you about how to deal with it, so listen carefully – Dad knows a lot about how the world works. He will sit you down and explain that he can't help you with choosing your path anymore. He has no experience with university or studying, but he's pretty smart and you'll start to appreciate his advice.

You'll be just fine, by the way. Even though you don't fit the mould, you will shine. Trust in yourself and your abilities. You're still a quiet girl, and the sudden realities of boys, relationships, drinking, and peer pressure will come as a shock. Your first campus party – who knew alcohol had such an effect on the ability to walk? Certainly not you. Socially it's all a bit of a mystery ... why are the other girls so much more polished? So fashionable, with the latest clothes and shoes? And why are they so sure of themselves around boys? Who knows ... it's still a mystery to me now, if I'm honest. You'll find your people, though, the ones who understand you, and you'll have those friends for life. Together you'll grow into young adults, keeping watch over each other as you explore all the opportunities on campus. There's the occasional moment where you stray too close to danger, sensing the unpredictability of other young people emboldened by sudden freedom and impetuosity, but you'll escape unscathed.

I want you to know that there's much more to life than mathematics and physics. People are far more interesting than numbers and equations. More soul searching awaits you, my clever girl; you'll have every option to choose from when you finish your maths degree. Medicine ... well, that's a real challenge, and somewhat naively you'll change the direction of your career path. You're still a quiet girl, observing the world around you, reading textbooks and choosing friends who understand you. There are many more moments of social uncertainty, of wondering whether you should be out clubbing more often, or getting drunk at parties. It's awkward and confronting to be out in those places, so you mostly avoid them. You carry on being yourself, and university rolls on, until at 23 you find yourself a doctor. Well, on paper, at least, with no experience of the job itself. It's only 13 years away, but I guess you're only 10, so that must seem a very long time to wait.

And still, you can achieve anything you want, Dr Jones. The world is your oyster. But what to choose ... what to do next? These are questions I still ask myself today. You know that opportunities exist out there in the world. Embrace that inner enthusiasm and just go. Trust me – go, and take every opportunity that presents itself. Be fierce in a world where you won't always be encouraged to succeed.

Those feelings of excitement, anticipation, and mild apprehension, as you board the plane to England, condensing your life into two suitcases, waving goodbye to your friends at the airport, and kissing your family farewell. The shock at seeing Mum and Dad cry as you go through the departure zone – Dad never cries, and it makes you pause. But you carry on, with excitement which will drive you through the years of long hours, constant study, unpaid research, job interviews, so many specialty examinations … it never seems to end. There are many times when being female is a disadvantage, but you still have so many advantages compared to others, and more than enough inside you to succeed.

It has been tiring, at times exhausting, and there are moments when I've wondered why I'm working so hard, and whether it's all worth it. The desperately tragic outcomes at work I've tried so hard to avert, which left me crying alone. But eventually, in a couple of decades, you'll find yourself finishing training, examinations, and job applications. You'll be a consultant specialist, forging your own pathway, confident in your skills and taking responsibility for your work. You'll have a husband by then, one who supports you in your career, and you'll move around the world again a few more times before finally you move back home.

I have lived and worked in other countries, making friends everywhere I go. You'll meet your future husband in one of these places … but I won't spoil the surprise any further. I've travelled to lots of those places on the globe, and my eyes have been opened to the challenges faced by so many across the world. Then one day, a few years ago, I felt a nudge towards home. That nudge became a tug, then a pull, growing more powerful until the day I arrived back. Then it was replaced … by a sense of familiarity, of security and the comfort of knowing that I'm home.

Along the way, there will be loss and grief, as there is for everyone. Dad isn't with me anymore, but I can see and hear him so clearly as I write this. He always loved you so much, and his work ethic and sense of values are inside you, too. Mum is nearby, still in the same house; I saw her just this morning. Grandpa and Gran are such a special part of your life: spend as much time with them as you can. Your brothers and your sister are all nearby, too. You missed them a lot while you were away (surprising, I know), and now you can see them again.

There will be moments that you do not meet your own expectations for yourself. Moments when you act badly, and later regret your words. You'll absorb that regret, internalise it, and try to correct your mistakes. There will be periods of uncertainty, where your self-belief wavers. There's a lot of great stuff too, though. Lots of fun times, laughter, moments when you are proud of who you are and what you're doing. Now I'm comfortable with who I am, and I don't care anymore if the clothes I'm wearing aren't the current season. I don't need to appeal to everyone, and I have the confidence to express myself. I look back on all those times and see that they have made me the person I am now – no longer the quiet one, but still the same person as you, my 10-year-old me.

So, that's how I ended up back here, so close to where you are now. My life is so different to yours, with responsibilities of a job, bills to pay, my own tax returns to file (and I have a bigger desk now, too). I have my own children, nearly as old as you are, and Mum is now a nanna herself. My confidence in myself is greater, and I'm not the quiet girl anymore. I have my own voice, and I'm not afraid to say what I think.

It's startling to look back at the time when I was 10, where you are right now, and realise how much the world has changed since you're reading this letter. My awareness of the world around me has grown, but there's still so much I don't know. In some ways, we have made much progress across our society. And yet in others, it seems that we have made no progress at all. All we can do is keep doing our best to be a positive change for the world.

I don't know what the future will hold. There is much ahead of us, and I don't know which way it will go. I'm not old yet, so this letter to you isn't the end of our story. Far from it. But I do know that the self-belief which has carried us through four decades of living, despite the setbacks and the disappointments, will be with us forever. We are constantly growing, and I know now that it's okay to be a bit different from everyone else. It's okay to have your own thoughts on things, and it's more than okay to stand up and be heard.

Keep spinning that globe. Wear those glasses; be the clever one. Observe and listen; read all the books. Have your own opinions, and don't be afraid to have a voice. Be true to yourself. Be kind and respectful. Work hard, and strive to be a better person.

Keep dreaming of the person you want to be, of the life story you want to write, and you'll accomplish your goals. We all have a worthy story. And although the world is a vastly complicated place, it is better for having you in it.

Love you always,

Me

CHAPTER 7

Own your Light, Own your Life

Mary Wong

Dear Mary,

Hi me, it's me ... plus 45 years!

Listen up, pumpkin. I have some stuff to tell you that I think will make the next 45 years a bit easier. Although, I hesitate. This journey has made you so multifaceted and taught you so much, I don't want you to change any of it.

I guess what I would rather do is to help you understand some stuff – give you hope, so you don't feel so lost along the way.

I bet you are wondering why I wouldn't want to protect you from anything bad that might be around the corner by warning you not to do certain things.

I could do that, but it wouldn't help you grow.

You see, there is a huge gift in the difficult times. A gift that teaches you how to become strong. All the big stuff that happens to you along the way makes you every bit more amazing than you already are – and you REALLY ARE AMAZING already.

I know you don't believe that – you don't think you are amazing at all. In fact, you feel pretty bad right now. A lot of people are unkind to you and you feel very alone and unloved.

I want you to know you are not alone.

There are lots of people who really love you, and plenty who like you a lot but are afraid to say so, for fear the bullies will pick on them, too. Some of them just don't know how to say what they feel, so they don't speak out. And others don't realise how sad you feel. You'll find out in years to come, when you get together as adults – they'll tell you they didn't know what you went through.

They are all busy in their own lives, learning to find their own way through.

Those people who aren't kind to you now (those who exclude you, saying you aren't good enough; the mean kids you have to hide from so they don't punch you; the popular girl who makes your life a misery with her taunts) – all of them have their own problems and have no idea how amazing you really are.

You're different – you know that already, but see it as a problem, a weakness.

In truth, your differences are what make you amazing. They are your light ... your strengths.

The people who are unkind speak from a place of weakness, trying to make themselves feel stronger in their small lives. They see your strength and fear it. Don't let them hurt you – they are simply scared and weak people who need love, and for some twisted reason think they will get that by putting others down.

That's not how it works.

Love will find them, and one day they will realise what they do is wrong and will live with your pain on their conscience.

As for you, just keep being you – even when they don't like it.

There is only one person you must live with for the rest of your life – that is you.

You must never own the words the bullies use when they speak to you. They are not your words, so never think those things about yourself. Be your own best friend and stop worrying about them.

So, who are you, really?

You are someone who would give anything to make other people happy. You always have been that way, and you will always be that way.

It is part of your nature – one of your special strengths. Part of the light that shines from within you.

You got it from Mum – she is the perfect, shining example of a selfless giver.

I must warn you, though. There's a fine line between giving and over-giving.

You know how Mum gets upset because she feels used sometimes? That's what happens when you step into over-giving and people-pleasing. It makes you feel worthless, like you are less than those people around you.

You are not!

Every person on this planet has value. We are all part of a big jigsaw puzzle – one that, like all jigsaw puzzles, is not complete so long as pieces are missing. Every piece is equally important, and no person is less than any other person.

Believe in the value you bring.

When it comes to over-giving, here is what I have learned.

The urge to give or be kind comes from deep inside – it's part of what we hold dear, as something that makes life more beautiful and whole. When we give and our gift is received gratefully, it makes us feel good inside.

When we feel bad, it makes us inclined to give more in an effort to feel better.

That is how it gets out of control and we become over-givers.

Once that happens, people often turn away from us, deciding we are 'try-hards' or 'desperate.'

Over-giving can embarrass the receiver – they may not feel worthy of what you are giving them, or find it too much, feeling they can never repay you, so they respond by either attacking or stepping away.

Others will take advantage of your generosity, pretending to be friends simply because they want to receive from you, and in the end, you will feel used up and even more unloved, bitter and regretful, and you might even feel you should stop giving.

That won't work.

Giving is part of you. You won't feel complete if you can't be generous. The question is, how can you do that without getting into a mess?

You can give anonymously.

Or, if someone needs your help but feels embarrassed because they can't repay you, ask them to pay it forward to someone else when they can. That way they will also get the warmth and comfort that giving provides and your gift will create a ripple of kindness. (There is an amazing movie that will come out in about 25 years, called *Pay It Forward*. You must watch it – it explains this perfectly ... but be warned, you will need tissues!)

Be aware that giving can take away someone's personal power. The wise Chinese philosopher, Confucius, knew what he was talking about when he said, 'Give a man a fish and feed him for a day. Teach a man to fish and feed him for life.' Be wise when you choose how to help. Try to give in a way that helps the person for more than just that moment in time.

Give without expectation of a return.

Before you go about being kind or helpful, understand that if you give with an expectation of return – whether that is to be loved, appreciated, or given something else as a thank you – you will find the feeling of having done something good will not be anywhere near as wonderful as it is when you give without expecting anything in return. Pay attention to how you feel when you give – if you feel flat, there is a good chance you're over-giving.

Don't stop giving; just don't over-give.

Oh ... and here's another aspect to giving that might take a bit of getting your head around.

Receiving.

You know how Mum never asks for help (but feels unloved because she hardly ever gets help)? Be careful that you do not go repeating that pattern.

Being prepared to ask for help shows you are also prepared to receive.

When you are prepared to receive, you create a balance. Giving and receiving are two parts of a whole. When you do one without the other, the imbalance leaves you feeling unworthy and undervalued – like nobody cares about you.

Give because it is who you are; receive because you are worthy.

You will find this balance lifts and satisfies you. You will discover it feels good to receive – it feels like you value yourself, not just others.

Caring about yourself is super important – it gives other people permission to care about you, too. When you don't care about yourself, it makes it hard for others to care about you, too.

So, ask for help.

And be specific about what you need, because people will not know unless you tell them. We still cannot read minds 45 years into the future!

When you are grown up, you will find a way to give as part of your career ... and you will feel totally amazing, because your work will help people to connect and communicate to find peace and support in their lives and their businesses. You're going to make such a difference for the people you work with.

But back to today ... Let's see, what other advice do I have for you?

Oh yes, the road to success.

You are not great at sport. But that doesn't mean you shouldn't keep playing.

Here is the thing. It's not about winning – it's about the benefit of the exercise and the enjoyment of the game.

Don't get me wrong – it's lovely to win, and you will win at some things as you go along, but you'll be surprised to realise that there are some people who are far more talented than you who won't be successful, because talent alone isn't enough.

Determination and hard work, sticking to it through good and bad, are often more important than talent. The people who win at the Olympics were not always the best in their group when they were kids. Work hard, learn as much as you can, strive for excellence, and stay determined ... These are the things that create success.

That doesn't sound like a lot of fun, does it? I mean, who likes hard work, right?

Here is a secret ... choose to spend your time doing things you love, and you won't feel like it's hard work.

That doesn't mean there won't be hard times. Oh, my darling girl, there will be plenty of them! Everyone goes through hard times, because there are things we can't control in life. Here are a couple more secrets to dealing with stuff along the way.

Love what you do and do it because you have a strong connection to the result; you'll find it a whole lot easier to keep going on the difficult days.

And choose your battles. Focus your energy on fixing the things you can control, and accept when you cannot change something. That way you will keep your energy up.

Speaking of battles, pumpkin, I know there are some you are fighting right now.

As the youngest of a large family, it often feels like you have no say in what happens around you, so you fight against it. You're not a bad person, but sometimes you don't behave so well because you feel overwhelmed by control. The problem is, when you do that, they try to control you even more.

As a kid, it's hard when you have parents who don't believe in letting you explore or take risks. As the youngest in a family where the older ones have been tasked to keep an eye on you, there are even more restrictions. It may help to know that this is not because Mum and Dad don't trust you – it's because of the bad stuff that has happened to them along the way. What they went through hurt them, and they don't want you to go through the same pain they did – they're trying to protect you.

You don't know this yet, but Mum's dad died when she was little, and her little brother died from tetanus two years later. Then, when you were small, she lost her stepdad, too. She has lost so many people she loves; she lives in fear of it happening again. That's why she is afraid for you to take risks.

Sometimes Mum seems way too strict and you see that as her being mean. I remember how it feels. When you grow up, you'll discover it's because she loves you, and she wants you to grow up to be all you can be.

She doesn't realise that by stopping you from taking risks, she is creating a block to being all you can be. You'll have to learn how to step away from fear as a grown-up. Because it has been ingrained into you as a little one, it will stay with you for a long time. You'll need all your courage to step up and speak out, but you will do it anyway. You were born to speak out.

Dad yells a lot, and that gets scary. You need to know this is not about you – it's about him. He worries about stuff like money and works hard to provide for you all, and sometimes the stress comes out as yelling. Underneath the noise he is a big softie! He is so proud of you – he is proud of all of you. But he doesn't know how to say it or how to show it. He was brought up to believe that pride is a sin, and he is trying to make sure you stay humble.

Dad, like many people, learnt to talk, but not to communicate his feelings. He grew up in a time when it was wrong for men to show their feelings. In fact, both he and Mum grew up with parents from what they called the Silent Generation, through the depression years and World War II. Times were super tough, so people learnt to put up and shut up. They didn't share their feelings or talk about what they were going through, because they knew everyone else was going through the same thing. They just got on with it.

And in getting on with it, they didn't teach their children how to talk about hard stuff. They didn't encourage talking about it, either. That is why your parents have trouble talking about stuff with you.

They learned from their upbringing that fear is a good controller of behaviour. That is why they threaten the strap if you are not behaving well – and even use it sometimes. They don't know better. If they knew how to identify what's behind the behaviour and talk you through it instead of threatening pain, they would – they aren't bad people, they just don't know another way.

When you are older and have kids of your own, and you prove to them that this can be done, your parents will tell you they wished they knew, because they never liked hurting you.

I think my biggest discovery about parenting is that being a parent is its own journey of learning – that parents have their own insecurities and shortcomings. They aren't perfect (nor are any of us), and they get stuff wrong sometimes. But the one thing they all do is the best they can with what they know at any given moment. Try not to judge them too harshly. Do what you can to help them, be kind and supportive, and you will discover in time that they are your closest and dearest support.

Your siblings have their own issues, too. When the family is large, the attention is divided, so they feel like they lack attention. They say that you are spoilt as the baby and that you get everything you want. It is not true, but for them it seems like the truth.

That happens a lot in life. When someone believes something is true, they will suggest you are lying. Everyone has their own understanding of what happens in a situation. We all see what we're most concerned with. One person's version of something is often quite different to another's version. It doesn't mean they are lying – it's just what they understood from what they saw and heard. When someone calls you a liar, that is why.

And they WILL call you a liar.

In about a year's time, something will happen that will cause the teacher to say you lied. And you will take that on board and think it means you are a nobody – a nothing. That your voice has no value.

As a result, you will stop speaking up about stuff that is happening to you.

Regardless of the situation, you must always believe in yourself and your value, and you must speak up. That is how you will stop bad things happening to good people.

Like everyone, you were put here on the planet to do something important.

You may think you know what you are going to be when you grow up. And for some people, life seems to follow the path they decide when they are little. For most, it does not.

You will discover your path as you go. If it feels right, then it probably is right. There's a feeling you get in your stomach when it isn't right. You know that feeling – it is the one you get when you tell a white lie or pinch a cookie. Pay attention to that feeling and check if it is there before you act, and it will guide you along your path.

In your life journey, you will make many changes in careers, and there will be times when you judge yourself as not being able to stick to anything.

It may feel like that has truth, but in time you will see that you were being guided to your final career destination. That every career you work in brings value to you and to the people you work with, by giving you a unique combination of skills and experiences that you can apply to a broad range of issues.

In every path you take, you will experience different kinds of conversations. Different cultures. Different issues to deal with. You will combine all of those things in your writing and your speaking (ooh, there's a hint!), and you will get to really make a difference in the lives of others through applying your generosity of spirit and helping them grow through the challenges they face with the conversations they have.

Conversations will help you to help them. They will pay forward the kind teachings you give them, and you will have a big impact on their lives and on the lives they touch.

When you do this, you will realise that everything you are going through right now is for a reason. All the difficulties you have now in speaking up, reaching out for help or support, being heard and acknowledged, will drive you as an adult to seek answers, so that others don't have to live through the pain you now feel.

You will spend your life encouraging people to stop judging others, because you know the pain of deep scrutiny and harsh judgement.

You will pass through this pain, and you will discover that there is great power hiding beneath it.

Remember I said the reason people are unkind is that they are afraid, not of you, but of the light they sense within you?

Your light is so bright! You will share it with the world, and in doing so, will encourage others to share their light as well.

Every person is born with bright light within them.

Think about it. You know how gorgeous babies are? They sit and coo and smile and the world coos and smiles with them. Everybody is drawn to them.

What they are drawn to is the light. It radiates from babies with a pureness that is rarely seen in adults.

We are all born perfect, with all the gifts required for our own unique purpose and journey.

As you grow, you'll have experiences that make you want to hide your light. There are times when others will say you're not good enough, or that you're just too much to handle so you'll try to fit in, chipping off bits of yourself as you go along. You want to be liked. You don't want to be too much. You want to be good enough. So, you'll hide your light to try to fit in.

When you do that, you are trying to be someone other than you.

What is most important in life is to be yourself. For your special gifts are hidden within you – not within anyone else. When you try to be someone else, you are trying to follow someone else's purpose and journey without the gifts you need for that journey.

So, stop listening to other people when they say you are not enough (or too much). What matters is how you see yourself, not how others see you.

Listen to yourself. You will know when you are on track. Feel that feeling in your gut – if it is a stolen cookie feeling, you are off track.

This is especially true when you choose who to be friends with. You'll know in your gut if the person you are being friends with is wrong for you. When that happens, don't ignore it. Don't become friends with someone who isn't right for you just because you feel lonely. Those kinds of people will take advantage of you and your innocence, and you will suffer for it.

Protect yourself by making good choices, being your own friend, and giving yourself permission to be you – the kind, caring and generous soul that you are.

Be yourself, and you will discover a power and a purpose that will blow your mind!

And when you make mistakes, or go off track (you will, pumpkin, so many times!), be kind to yourself.

We all get it wrong sometimes, and that is okay!

You are human, and every human makes mistakes – daily, often many times a day.

Use the mistakes as lessons. Look for the gift that is there in the darkness of the bad times. It is always there. It may be learning to be strong. It may be learning to be brave. It may be learning to appreciate what you had already.

It will always serve you if you choose to find it.

I love you, pumpkin. For a long time, I didn't, because I didn't know this stuff. I was way too hard on you, and so very unkind to you.

Now that I know, I had to pass it on to you.

I love you. Deeply, fully, and without reserve.

When you love and accept yourself, you get to step into your light and power and do what you're here for.

Remember this. Apply it. Stop judging yourself and instead love and be kind to yourself.

This is your life.

Yours.

Love it, live it. Honour it.

With all my heart,

Mary xx

PS. Pay attention in Geography class – I know you don't think you will ever go to any of those places, but you will, my darling. You are going all over the place! And you need to know that it does not get cold in Malaysia! Don't wear a fleecy-lined tracksuit for your first time there – unless, of course, you want to faint from the heat!

CHAPTER 8

Choices

Anna Ball

Dear Anna,

I see you, Anna, a 10-year-old standing in your boarding school dormitory. You're just outside of London, but the Home Counties countryside makes it appear as though you're far from the bright lights of a big city. You're even further from your home in Canada.

You're gazing out onto what you'll later appreciate as being lush green lawns; with the expansive tennis courts and the cherry blossom trees outside your window, you're fortunate to attend such a beautiful school. Even if it doesn't feel like it now. Your long blonde hair is hanging down your back, your slim frame draped in a sports uniform after a long, muddy run around the cross-country course. The windows are fogged up with condensation; it's cold outside, and inside, for that matter. It wouldn't be an English boarding school if it wasn't.

The dormitory is sparsely decorated, with 8 bunk beds and 16 beds, the top of each dressing table with no more than the allowed seven items. You're surrounded by friends, but Mummy and Daddy are thousands of miles away in Ontario, Canada, on a military posting. You'll stand looking out the window at your fellow students skipping along the long drive, listening to chatter in the background, and thinking about the week ahead. If truth be told, you're somewhat envious of the day girls, who get to return to their cosy homes and families each night, while you only get that privilege once every six weeks.

Right now, it's spring, and you're looking forward to summer and the long break when you can return to Canada and your parents. It's been a big year for you. You're only 10, but things have happened to you that happen so seldom, that you're a mix of emotions right now. Luckily for you, they're good things – amazing things, in fact. When you became part of the school choir and performed in *Joseph and His Amazing Technicolour Dreamcoat* with Jason Donovan in London's West End, you somehow, beyond your wildest dreams, managed to get talent scouted – and now have an upcoming audition for Cosette in *Les Misérables* in the West End. At the moment, you're taking it all in stride; you don't seem to understand the gravity of it all, the experiences that could unfold if you perform well. It's probably lucky for you, as it takes the pressure off as you amble through the extensive medicals needed to perform – the only derisory comment from the doctor being on the state of your bitten nails. She makes you feel ashamed, and you can't help wondering why she's so miserable and grumpy. Years later, you'll realise it wasn't personal and was more a reflection of her own unhappiness. You'll come to realise later on in life, Anna, that you're responsible for making your own life choices as an adult – being accountable to yourself, more than anyone else, is important.

You head home for holidays pre-audition; I can see you sitting on the stairs, music score in hand, frantically singing, re-singing, and singing again your lines. Your beautiful daddy, a military fast-jet navigator, patiently sits with you, singing the part of Jean Valjean to give you practice, confidence, and reassurance that it'll be okay. He's not a natural singer (that's an understatement), but the whole moment feels warm, cosy, and supportive. I see the pink carpet, the gaps in the stairs, the just-in-the-1990s décor. That night, you sit watching the British election on TV, on a tiny little colour TV that your 40-year-old self will laugh at. You'll remember your return to school in years to come. Daddy was travelling out to the Middle East to fight in the Gulf War. He hands you a Biggles teddy, leather suit, and googles, sprayed with Fahrenheit, his aftershave, which makes you sick with love and hope in the weeks to come. You diligently, week after week, write 'blueys' to Daddy, the wafer-thin airmail paper folding perfectly each time, always adorned with 'SWALK' (sealed with a loving kiss), and have to restrain yourself from using your usual colourful stickers all over it, as they aren't allowed on blueys.

Meanwhile, your singing rehearsals continue, and a teacher chaperones you into London to audition in front of a panel. Miraculously, you stay calm, far too immature to understand what's at stake, and two days later, have a surprise in the school playground. It was an unusually sunny day and each class was lined up meticulously, ready to return to class. Your music teacher, always effervescent with energy, starts to make an announcement to the entire playground and you suddenly realise she's talking about you. You've somehow done it. You'll be Cosette in *Les Misérables*.

Everyone starts cheering – you feel elated, but you feel sad, because all you want to do is share it with your family. Some girls are mean. Matron tells you they're jealous, but their taunts are spiteful and it hurts. You're a sensitive soul underneath your tough, confident exterior and wish they'd just stop. As people are growing up, Anna, they're so often insecure – they're finding their own path in life, discovering who they are, just as you are now. Just know that it's not your fault they're being mean. Growing up can be confusing; they want to be like everyone else and fit in and so tease you to make themselves feel better – but what you'll learn later on is that being different is so much more fun! You want to become the exotic lemon tart that tingles on the tongue, not the common, relatively bland vanilla slice.

Fast forward a few weeks and you're on stage in the West End – you love the buzz of being on stage, but the dry ice still makes you cough and the Stage Manager tells you off, as the audience can hear your nervous hacking away in the background. You feel like the total novice you are. But you weren't to know. You remember finishing singing 'Castle on a Cloud' and receiving a standing ovation, the first one that same Stage Manager had ever seen. The lights are intoxicating, the sights and aromas are stimulating, and your senses are alive. Each day, your patient teachers take it in turn to chaperone you the hour's tube ride to the theatre and back to school again late at night, and you return, tired, to the classroom the next day. You start imagining your future, progressing your singing career – but even at the tender age of 10, somehow it doesn't feel like the ideal fit for you. One day you'll realise the enormity of what you're currently taking in stride, and you'll understand why you make the life choices you do.

You see, Anna, one day, you'll realise that each choice you make leads to an outcome. You'll understand that you're human and life, with all of its twists and turns, can't be perfectly plotted out. It has a funny way of turning situations on their head – and you'll become so much of a richer person for all these wonderful life experiences.

Even at 10, you're already dreaming of one day marrying and living the perfect family life, white picket fence and all. You already know that stage life can waylay that dream, and when you look back as an adult, you will realise you were right. You're the kid that had your wedding dress designed and drawn up before you reached high school; you had already started to work out who you are as a person. Subconsciously, you make a decision which will alter the course of your life – you decide to stop pursuing acting and singing, as much as you love the energy and vivacity of stage life, and instead choose to focus on your school work, on building your dream. You'll find it funny, looking back, as this wasn't a conscious decision on your part; there's no way you had the emotional intelligence at 10 to understand the implications, but I'm proud of you, Anna, for one of your first steps in standing up for who you are.

As an adult, you'll see that life is like a series of doors; when one opens, you enter into a new destination – but what might have happened if you'd opened the other door? Would you still be living in the same city? Be married to the same person? Have the career you have as an adult? The truth is, you'll just never know. It's impossible to say. What I can tell you, Anna, is that being comfortable with your own choices in life is more important than you'll ever know. The world is full of people who blame their unhappy lives on others, when in fact, it's important to realise that you're responsible for yourself. For how you treat others with kindness, how you see the silver lining in every cloud, for how much hope you have for the future.

Bad stuff will happen. That's just life, and no amount of cotton wool protection can protect you. What you can do, Anna, is change your reaction. Change your stance. When the school bully threatens to smash you with a hockey stick, over a minor incident of poor playing on your part, you should know that she'll do no such thing. She's all bravado, all talk, and underneath she's deeply insecure. You'll meet many of these people in life, Anna. You'll come to recognise them pretty quickly – and they're not worth your time or energy. They're the ones with road rage, the bullying bosses at work, the cliquey groups around the school gates who are all shades of grey and you never quite know where you stand with them.

What you should understand is that you think in black and white, which is one of the traits your future husband will love about you. You're a say-it-as-you-see-it girl, making time for those you love, with no pretence when it comes to those you don't. You've got a big heart, which unfortunately can also make you a bit of a yes puppet, wanting to please everyone. If I can give you one piece of advice, Anna, it's to kick this habit quickly – it's one which positively invites people to take advantage of you. You'll see it happening as you get older, yet be powerless to stop it.

You see, when you're 10, you think you know it all. Your burgeoning confidence and your desire to start making your own way in life sometimes overtakes what's sensible. As much as you don't want to, try to listen to those you trust. They're normally, and annoyingly, right.

You see, it comes back to life experience – the more our lives are woven with the rich tapestries of life's highlights, lessons, and challenges, the better you can use this knowledge to make future stages of your life even better. Take the highlights and lowlights from others' reels, Anna; store them away in your memory and call them up when you're making decisions as you grow older. Trust me, they'll help.

Your decision, at the tender age of 10, sees you turn away from a possible career on the stage, exerting your right to choose, even unconsciously. Your stubborn refusal to continue with weekly choir rehearsals, to engage with the theatre agency, has seen you silently celebrate one of your first real life choices. A life choice which, unknowingly, will take you on a totally different path in life. There's no telling if you'd have made a successful adult career out of it (it's a pretty competitive field); what's important is that you know your own mind. The path you eventually choose will see you fall madly in love and move to the other side of the world, to a place you've dreamt of going to – Australia. Its expansive oceans, kangaroos, and cuddly koalas crop up repeatedly in the vivid stories Matron tells in the dormitory at night, before lights out. The 'tri tri tricycle' from the stories has been zooming around Australia, firing up your imagination. Twenty years later, your own little boy will be speeding around on his own tricycle in Australia, leaving you to wonder at the irony of those little seeds planted in childhood that later become a self-fulfilling prophecy. Don't stress about how you'll get there; you just will. You'll make mistakes, but it'll all work out, and nothing is unsolvable. As Mummy and Daddy always tell you, 'You're a Horwood. There's nothing you can't do – don't give up' at those times when life throws a challenge at you. Instead, break it down into small steps and hurdle over it.

Life is a journey, as they say, not just a destination. Your tribe of friends are good ones, Anna. Friends are the family you've chosen; make sure as you get older that you continue to prioritise them. You'll regret it if you don't. You're learning about great friendship right now; your best friend will come out to stay during the holidays in Canada. You'll go bear hunting in the forests on long lazy days, eat ice cream by Lake Ontario, and write each other letters covered in stickers and sellotaped cut outs. In days to come, you'll realise that these simple but beautiful friendships in childhood are to be admired; they're robust, all-consuming, and fun. Keep in touch with the friends you have now. Later on in life, there's not always an ability to capture so much time together, but you should choose to prioritise friendship. Always. During your university years, Anna, you'll meet some special people who'll become your friends for life. They'll become the crew who stick by you through thick and thin, who'll become godparents to your boys and you to theirs. You'll travel and party hard with them in Italy, where you'll live for the year as a part of your degree. Oh, what a year! The daunting start – arriving late evening to Italian halls of residence to check in, not speaking a word of Italian, the stares (you'll stay very blonde until much later), and the stomach-churning nerves at being left in a country where you don't know a soul – is just the start of what will be a rich part of life's experience in independence. You'll see that your tiny little room isn't the prison it feels, where you want to hide for the first few days; it becomes a beautiful sanctuary overlooking the rural Marche hills. You'll find your tribe in those halls of residence – they'll be the friends you march into the tiny medieval hilltop town of Urbino with, armed with empty coke bottles to head to the vinoteca and refill them with delicious Montepulciano wine. You'll spend lazy days travelling around Italy on your student budget, giggling at the nude statues (don't worry, you will become more cultured), and admiring beautiful Italian works of art. During this year, you'll discover what makes you happy – and what doesn't. You'll gain independence you've not had before and mind-opening experiences which will shape the much older Anna.

It's said that we become the sum of the five people we spend the most time with. Use your experiences to find the right five people, Anna – your friends will set you up for success. Choosing the wrong friends can be a hurtful and time-consuming process.

That's another point I should mention – success. It means totally different things to every adult you'll speak to. Many people will mention money –which is of course important to have, but true success isn't based on your assets. It definitely makes life easier, but what it can't replace is love, happiness, friendship, building your own family, taking time to do the things you love. I know that school can seem like a giant race – to win the academic prize, to place in cross-country, to be the best at everything you do. You know that feeling when you're not selected for the rounders team by your peers, that crushing disappointment you knew was coming as you're not one of the best players? It really does suck not to be everything to everyone. Run your own race, Anna; that should be your only true barometer of success. Otherwise, you'll spend the rest of your life disappointed, as there will always be someone seemingly wealthier and more popular than you are.

Remember, you're only 10. You have your whole life ahead of you. Literally millions of choices, tiny ones, all perfectly interwoven to shape your life now and as an adult. Stay in the driver's seat, Anna; by all means take directions from others, but remember that it's your choice where you steer and how fast you drive there.

You're doing just great.

Hugs to 10-year-old you,
Anna

CHAPTER 9

Peeling Onions

Makaela Moore

Dear Makaela J.,

Hi Mak! You don't know this nickname yet, but you will in years to come, and you'll love it. How do I know? Because I'm you. This is your 'official time-travelling letter' from you at age 48. Yep, this is so cool and special because not everyone gets one of these.

There is so much I want you to know, to give you the best possible opportunities in life. I'm going to talk about life as if it were an onion, because onions have many layers, all tightly held together. Each time you peel back a layer of the onion, there is always another underneath waiting, until you finally get to the heart of it. Human beings are just like onions, with many, many emotional layers to peel back.

Throughout your life, you will look back on this letter every now and then, and every time you do, you'll peel back another layer of your onion, discovering and identifying the story of your life.

When we are born, we're like a blank book, ready to be written. In our first seven years of life, our sponge-like brains soak up every ounce of information available to us, but not always with the right meaning, and it all ends up as things we falsely believe and stories that we live our life by. This means that even if things are not true, we can convince ourselves they are and so make decisions based on them. Like the time Mum and Dad gave away your dog, Amber, when you were 4. Even though you knew it was because Mum couldn't look after the dog and all three kids while Dad was away at work, it felt like punishment for not being good enough after your brother and sister were born, and so your brain has convinced you that you are not good enough or important enough.

My darling girl, this is the biggest lie you will ever believe in your life, because you are in fact worthy of everything and loved despite everything.

As adults, if we're lucky, we discover there is more to life than how we are living. We get to peel back those layers and find all those false beliefs and stories that we've carried since childhood. We can change who we are and create a new identity by recognising those stories, and we can choose to think new and different thoughts, which creates a new way of being for ourselves. A bit like an actor playing a different person in a movie, we can be whoever we want to be.

This is where the onion peeling happens, because with every layer that we peel back, we discover more old stories and things that we tell ourselves, which are often not true. When each layer is peeled and revealed, there is always another layer waiting to be peeled back.

While peeling each of those layers is the first step, the second step is to get rid of that peel altogether, throwing it away, never to be seen or felt again, which isn't as easy as it seems.

Much like humans, onions also have a tough outer shell; it is designed to protect the inner layers and can be hard to crack at first. Once inside that shell, each layer can really stick to the next, and they can be difficult to peel. Always be willing to peel back your own layers, because getting down to your core and connecting with your heart will help you to make the right decisions as you navigate life.

When we peel onions, there is usually some crying. Uncovering your layers, as a human, can lead to a lot of emotion. Don't ever be afraid to feel emotions; whether they're good or bad, they are all there to be felt.

But what if we humans didn't have to be like onions? What if we could tell our brains from childhood all the true and important things, so that we could avoid all the fear, frustration, anxiety, and self-doubt that adults experience? At 10 years old, you already believe a tonne of stories that are not true, and you will continue to view your life and the world based on these stories until you can peel back the onion layers and find the truth.

Like, how you think that you can't do hard things, or that you don't belong anywhere, because that is something you really believe in your heart ... but it is just not true.

You are in the very special position of receiving the information that I'm about to share with you, as you enter one of the most difficult times of anyone's life: the teen years. These years will shape you even further than your younger years, so it's completely up to you to be the person you want to be and to create the life you want to create. No-one else will do this for you. Knights on white horses do not exist, and we are 100 hundred percent responsible for everything that is, or isn't, in our life.

Your brain is going to trick you throughout your life; this I know for sure. Its job is to keep you safe from what it thinks are threats to you. Even if you don't think these things are threats, your subconscious brain will, and it will sabotage you by tricking you into things like feeling fear and anxiety, making you believe that you can't, or shouldn't, be or do certain things in life.

With each layer of the onion, you will experience fear and resistance; you just need to remember it's your brain keeping you safe – and that with every layer comes growth. To get through life and achieve your dreams, you need a certain amount of bravery, a vision, and an understanding of what is going on in that brain of yours.

At every stage of your life, you will become comfortable with the things in and about you. You will feel like things are how they're supposed to be. But what you don't see at each stage of life is that there is another stage or phase waiting just around the corner for you, even bigger and brighter than the life you know now. But it can look scary. It can look like you don't belong there. I want you to always remember that nothing is ever as scary as it seems, and you belong anywhere you want to belong. That fear is just your brain, once again trying to keep you safe. This will happen to you with every new phase or stage of your life.

Reaching for the next big thing will always feel scary, because fear is a natural response from our brain when we face something new. You'll be tempted to avoid challenges, convince yourself that it's not for you or that you don't belong there. But that's just the anxiety and fear that your brain experiences when faced with new situations and challenges.

You've already faced the difficulties of moving interstate several times, changing schools regularly, trying to make friends and then having to move all over again. Being the new kid at school sucks, but what I want you to realise is there is a whole other side to the regular interstate moves and constant changing of schools that you haven't seen yet. You will develop an interwoven depth to your character that probably wouldn't have developed without all that change. You may see it as constantly being the new kid, the outsider, or as a disadvantage. But you will see it's an opportunity to develop relationship-building skills, to build connections and create a network of friends that could last into adulthood. It's an amazing opportunity for growth.

Fear and self-doubt became the theme of life into adulthood for me, right alongside not feeling like I was good enough or that I belonged anywhere. I let it hold me back from chasing dreams and believing in myself and my possibilities. You have the chance to change all that. You have the chance to take what I've learned in my 48 years of life and forge your own path, free of all that self-doubt, fear, and negativity. You have every reason in the world to live a confident life of freedom, fun, happiness, love, and abundance, but first you must recognise that some things that you firmly believe to be true are not; they are just stories made up by your subconscious brain to keep you safe. Everything you know is an interpretation, a story made up by your subconscious brain, based on the life you have lived so far.

Right now, you are feeling the weight of the world on your shoulders. You go to school every day too scared to speak up for yourself, too afraid to put your hand up in class, feeling a bit lost. You're sitting on the outskirts at school, so stuck in your head about being the outsider that you've made yourself even more of an outsider. The key here is to dig deep, listen to your heart, not your head, and know that you are worthy of friendships; other people do want to be friends with you; just open up and be a friend.

You aren't alone; you'd be surprised just how many people feel like they're not good enough or don't belong in life. Most human beings have the same insecurities, so don't ever feel like they are better than you, or that you're not good enough.

You are a cosmic being, here to have a human experience, and your purpose here is to grow and evolve your spiritual self – and you my dear, are just as special as anyone else here on this planet and in this life.

You have gifts that are not easily seen, because they need to be felt. It is in the silence that you will begin to hear and feel these. So, while everyone else is riding the next wave or following the latest trend, listen to your heart, sit in the silence and connect with your intuition, and stay true to yourself, because you are special. You are a writer, a creator, an ideas machine. You have a wonderful imagination that will take you far in life and in business. Your heart is bigger than most people's, and you are compassionate, loving, and super-inspirational to many people.

One of the most important lessons I've learned in life, which I only wish I had learned when I was your age, is that we have personal power, and when we allow other people to overstep our personal boundaries or to take advantage of us, we give away that power. When we allow someone else's actions to 'make us' angry or sad, we give them our power. No-one can actually 'make' you feel anything, because your feelings are yours alone and are created by your thoughts. So, when you're in a situation, you can choose to either react and give away your power, getting caught up in emotions you'd rather not feel, or you can choose to be in your power, by thinking and choosing how to respond to any given situation or person. Setting boundaries and standing in your personal power will take you so much further in life than allowing people to control you or walk all over you.

One of the biggest things that holds people back in life is the fear of judgement: worrying about what other people will think or say about us. It is honestly so crippling for many people, me included. While I am now an Intuitive Leadership Coach, helping women in business to shift their identities to overcome things like lack of self-confidence, procrastination, and fear, including the fear of judgement, I wasn't always confident. I worried way too much about what other people thought of me, and it stopped me in my tracks for many years.

One of the wisest things a mentor has ever said to me was *what other people think of me is none of my business*. This one statement blew my mind and changed my life. I was surprised and wanted to disagree, because I believed I needed to know everything that everyone thought and said about me. But trust me, you don't.

If you take nothing else away from this letter, let it be this: Do not worry about what other people think of you. Go and run your own race, in your own lane, in a way that only you know how. If people want to be in your life, they will be. Those who will love you, will love you fiercely, and those who don't are not worth you leaking any of that precious personal power over. Not everyone will like you – and that is perfectly fine.

You will have times in your life when you don't feel confident. When you feel anxiety, that sickening butterfly feeling in your stomach, just know that it will not kill you. Ironically, that feeling is almost identical to the feeling of excitement, so turn it around and instead choose to think of that feeling as excitement, and fear won't run your life.

Feelings are not something to be avoided, pushed down, or ignored. All feelings, both positive and negative, serve a purpose in our lives, and we all need a balance of both positive and negative emotions, almost in equal servings. It's just like light and dark; we can't have one without the other. We need to feel the negative emotions so we appreciate the positives. Please don't do what I did and stuff those emotions way down low, burying them for decades, because they fester and manifest as physical pain or illness. Know right now that it is just as okay to feel fear, anger, sadness, or disappointment as it is to feel happiness, joy, and love. None of them are wrong or right; they just are what they are. Emotions are there to be felt, and once felt, recognised, and allowed, then they will dissolve away.

There are so many things in this world that you will not see. You'll be told that many things simply do not exist because we can't see them, like the energies of the universe and their magical effects. We can't see the air that we breathe, either, but we all believe it exists. Trust your intuition on this. You know that feeling in your gut? Trust that feeling. When you tune into your intuition and trust it, you will never be steered the wrong way. You will always end up exactly where you need to be. Although you may not see it straight away, you will later.

You are destined for an amazing life, but like everyone, you'll have ups and downs. Learn to lean into the hard times and learn from them. Don't despair and believe it's your forever situation, because I promise you, it's not. Not unless you allow it to be. You can be and do anything you want in life, but YOU will be the creator of it, because you are more powerful than you know. Between tuning into your heart and learning how to manage your subconscious brain, you have the perfect guides and maps for your life, right within YOU!

Don't be afraid to have clear visions for your life. Write them in your journal and plan them out with clarity and precision. To overcome the fear that pops up its ugly head anytime you want to try something new or difficult, just know that our brains need to see and almost feel things before they can become real for us. So, use your wonderful imagination to its full potential to place yourself in that winning position. Be there in your mind, already having achieved your big goals. Feel into the excitement, joy, and pride, smell the taste of victory, hear the sounds of celebration. You love writing stories, and your future dreams need to be documented in intricate detail, but for your eyes only at this stage. Your imagination is a wonderful thing, my dear; don't ever lose that. Your imagination and your journal will be your biggest allies in life.

I know you're feeling less than a priority at home right now, not being encouraged by Mum and Dad to achieve things, and just feel unimportant. They want you to be a good person, do the right thing and use your manners, etc., but they're not the best cheerleaders. It's not their fault; it's just the way they were brought up, and they're doing the best they can with what they know. They don't realise that allowing you to quit everything isn't the best way to teach you commitment, so you're going to need to take some initiative and responsibility in your life to make things happen for yourself.

You have the power within you to be your own cheerleader, to take control of your life and achieve things that, right now, you don't even know exist. And trust me, you do achieve them! You go on to have achievements of all sorts of things in life because, as it turns out, you are actually super-smart; you just don't know it yet. The advantage you will have is that you'll go through your teen years and into adulthood with much more confidence than I did. You'll be armed with more information, more certainty, and more intuitive abilities than I ever knew when I was younger. You have the power to change the world, and despite what you may think of yourself, you were born a leader; you just need to find that within yourself.

What you are called to do in this life will be uniquely your experience and won't be the same as other people. Don't spend your whole life trying to be like everyone else. This is YOUR life, not theirs, so you do 'you' and let them be themselves. The world needs unique snowflakes just like, but different from, you. If everyone were the same, the world would be boring.

When running your own race, be willing to be unliked. Don't try to be everything to everyone, or you'll end up being nothing to anyone, and most of all nothing to yourself. No-one else is going to achieve your goals for you, so you need to get out there and make things happen for yourself. Things will be frightening and hard, but you can do hard things; we all can if we put our mind to it. Be willing to fail and to be criticised, because if you aren't out there having a go at things, then you can't possibly succeed.

When failure does occur, and it will, find the gratitude in the failure, take the lessons, and remember them moving forward.

Always be the person who does the things and takes the actions of the person you are aspiring to be. If you're always taking the actions of the person who doesn't have or do the things you want in life, then you can't possibly expect to be the person who does actually have those things. Your identity is your way of being in this world. You get to choose what that will be and, therefore, how you will be.

Not all relationships will work out the way you think they will, but in heartache, you will find enormous gratitude and profound life lessons which will only become apparent to you later. Just know that everything that is in or out of your life is meant to be. This includes people, opportunities, money, health, everything. You can be, do, and have anything you want in life, but the key to that is understanding how our subconscious brain and the energies of the universe work, and believing and really knowing you already have everything within you.

Often in life when we're peeling back those onion layers, we find things we don't like, don't want to face, or simply don't want to let go of. We can become very attached to ideas, thoughts, beliefs, people, and places, and we can be very reluctant to let some things go, even when we know that life can be better without them. They are like our security blanket, and without them, we can feel exposed, raw, and vulnerable.

We can also be attached to our expectations of other people; we attach meaning to those expectations that is rarely true. You'll go far in life if you can remember that everything is a story and that nothing has any meaning except the meaning you attach to it. Don't believe everything you hear, and definitely don't believe everything you think, because don't forget, your brain will try to play tricks on you.

Observe your thoughts and take notice of the thoughts that are true for you and the thoughts that are stories created with meanings and expectations attached to them. When you get attached to expectations, you will often be disappointed.

I've peeled back most of my onion, but this took 48 years and I'm still going. Your mission now is to start early and not grow many of the layers that I peeled back for myself. You have so many tools right here in this letter to help you grow and evolve far more smoothly than I have. You can live a life standing in your power, using your voice, fully knowing and understanding your worth and your purpose in this life.

This life, this human experience, is special, and we look after things that are special. We look after things that we love. Love yourself like your life depends on it, because it honestly does. Look after that body of yours as fiercely as you can, because it's the only one you get in this life. The more you can look after your body now, the healthier you'll be later, and you'll definitely thank yourself for that one!

When you think all is lost in any situation, you'll discover that everything is a phase and something else will be along soon to divert your attention. Everything has a way of working out, even without stress and worry, and you'll find yourself working through things in life with ease and grace. Just always, *always* look for the lessons and the benefits of every situation, because it all happens for you to grow and evolve – then you can let them go and be free of them.

Everything always has been, and always will be, just fine. You are so loved, by me and everyone around you; never forget that. You matter in this world.

You've got this, MJ.
Love, Makaela M. xx

P.S. Be picky and wait for THE right man in your life. Trust me, this one was worth the long wait. Your soul will recognise his soul the moment you both meet. xx

CHAPTER 10

Perfect in All Its Imperfection

Lisa Boorer

Hey Lisa,

You are now 10 years old, and so many events have already taken place in your life. I know you are feeling lost and confused, but I want to reassure you that the life ahead of you will be amazing. You will have great friends and share insane adventures; you will love, laugh, and cry a few times. You will learn and share so much – and end up being the person you want to be. In spite of your beginnings, you'll ultimately dictate the way you live yourself.

Right now, you are standing here in your dress, all frills and lace, long, white, lace-topped socks and black patent leather shoes, long blonde hair pulled into a bun decorated with small flowers … and a tear-stained face.

Mother is happy with the look, but you feel betrayed that they make you look like a girl. A girl, of all things. She knows you want to be a boy.

Smile on command: it's photo time. Your mother informs you that you're off to hear about Jehovah today, about living in the new system where you can play with lions. Your daily life is full of a world full of the horror of gruesome Bible stories and the fear of

Armageddon and the destruction of the world. You hate it. These people are nuts, and you really, really hate this.

You're are the eternal tomboy. You don't believe in god, because if he existed, you would be a boy and you're not. You're a girl, and you damn well hate girls! You hate women! You hate makeup and lace and boobs – and anything else girly!

To travel the road of life, some few lessons are learnt the hard way, and others the fun way. The following are the things you need to know to guard your heart, to light your path, to project you into the woman you are going to be.

The idea of perfection was created to enslave people, forever seeking an unattainable state that is nevertheless freely promised. You are perfect in your imperfection – that means that you are what you need to be, nothing more, nothing less.

Believe your instincts and trust your intuition. When your tummy knots, it's a sign from your higher self that something is off. Listen to your gut. Do not be swayed by those around you.

Parents aren't always friends; sometimes they aren't even good people. They don't always do what is right by you or for you. As much as that hurts your heart, it is also a lesson on trust. Just because someone says 'I love you,' it doesn't mean they do. Just because they shouldn't hurt you, it doesn't mean they won't.

Be aware of the manipulation and games of the people around you, and train your eyes to see their hidden agendas. Not everyone has good intentions. Some people see the value or the vulnerability in others and exploit this or use them. This is always damaging. If what they want doesn't benefit you, don't engage.

Respect and trust are earned; be wary of giving them freely, as they are often and easily abused.

Build sandcastles and collect shells for all your days. They will forever link your present to your past and lay forward your future. You already have quite the collection from amazing places and safe places you've escaped to. At times in the future, when the sea is too far, you will allow your mind to wander to those locations, as your fingers stroke the shells to calm your inner turmoil and reconnect you with your freedom and your dreams.

Travel the road of life lightly, with a sense of adventure and wonderment; be sure to leave in your wake compassion, kindness, and love for everyone you encounter. Even though at times people will take advantage of these traits, remember that their actions don't diminish who you are, but instead highlight those they themselves are lacking.

You will spend so many hours worrying that people will like you or that they won't like you. The truth is, you probably won't remember their names in the future, as they really have little to no effect on where you are heading in life.

Education is important. Work hard at school; do your own research and ask questions. Be inquisitive and thoughtful and use reasoning and logic when sifting through information. Once the what, where, why, how, and what are considered, then make your own decisions.

Equally important are experiences. These can be alone, with friends, or with a partner. Experiences are always best when shared, so read loads of interesting books and travel to exotic destinations. Take the time to experience the culture and understand the people. Take loads of amazing photos and turn those great memories into books on your return. Sit still for a moment and absorb your surroundings. As you read, allow your imagination to create the scene, to smell your surroundings; allow the story to live and to take you to the places you are reading about. Lastly, share what you are reading with others and inspire them to read.

Live in different cities in different countries; immerse yourself in different cultures and embrace everything they have to offer. This will add a richness to the tapestry of your life.

Don't just accept opportunities; instead, seek them out, look for them, put yourself with likeminded people that walk their talk and don't just talk their talk. Say yes when an opportunity is useful to your progress, or is in line with your beliefs and values or will benefit mankind. Even if you don't know how to do some of the things required, say yes and then figure it out as you go along. You know you are far more resilient and resourceful than you could ever imagine, so remember to never second guess yourself.

Ask yourself what the worst that can happen is, and then decide on your course of action. If the joy it will bring you outweighs the consequences you may face, then don't hold back. Life is meant to be lived.

Possessions help us feel like we have achieved, yet it is through the people we meet and the connections we have that our true achievements are measured. A home full of nice things will not ultimately make us happy or keep us company. They are ornate objects, whereas people fill our lives with wonder, and challenges, friendships and company. I'm not saying don't have nice things, just that it shouldn't be your main focus.

You have noticed that many people hide their true self behind their hair, makeup, and the clothing they wear. These do not define you; think of these as wrapping paper and yourself as the gift. It's on the that where your true value lies. This is not an excuse to get out of doing your hair or dressing appropriately; rather, it is to remind you that what you see is not all there is.

Design the life you want. We can do this by identifying the person we want to be. Do we want to join the circus or be a politician? It's already inside us; spend some quiet time allowing your self to still and find it.

Identify and study the qualities you admire in people and identify why you're drawn to them. Seek these individuals out and learn from them. Who do they admire? Who inspired them? How do they think? What is their decision-making strategy? What do they read? How do they apply the traits you are drawn to?

In doing this, you will learn new ways of thinking, reasoning, decision making; these will add to the qualities you already have by expanding your knowledge and vision and adding depth to your experiences.

Embrace truth, embrace honesty; always speak these with a gentle tongue. Sometimes truth does not need to be spoken; if it's not going to improve the situation, then maybe hold your own counsel.

Never hold back being honest with yourself; it's important that you remain true to you and use this truth to help you navigate through life. Many people are frightened of the truth and lie to themselves; this compounds your problems and creates much distress in life. Learn to love your own truth, as it is a great measuring stick when decisions need to be made.

Learn to respect your own counsel and trust your own beliefs; this is how you build confidence and self-worth. It is important that you don't share your beliefs with those who will not appreciate or respect your beliefs and boundaries, or who will try to undermine your confidence and self-worth, those who try to force their own beliefs on you.

As you age, your mind will play games with you, to remind you of lessons taught when you need them. You will hear her voice; she is in the kitchen. You will see yourself sitting stubborn and determined, holding onto your own point of view; you will smile. Nan looks at you and shakes her head and tells you, 'Lisa, they say pride comes before a fall.' You'll see yourself shrug, thinking, *typical Nan*. Pop looks at you and smiles, saying, 'Lisa, practice patience, humility, and acceptance, as they will soothe your soul.' You will be thankful that the strength he had still holds true, that his voice soothes your soul and his lessons carry much weight. You'll recall them long after he has gone. You will allow his lessons to direct you all the days of your life.

It is appropriate to say 'NO' if it doesn't feel right. Don't allow yourself to be pressured into something you don't feel comfortable with it. If you just don't want to do something, don't do it. Learn to be comfortable with this process; it will stop you from feeling used and being taken advantage of.

Think of the leaves in winter as they blow from place to place, wherever the wind takes them: no direction, no identity ... This is also is the life of a 'people pleaser'; with no personal direction or destination, they are at the mercy of others' decisions and directions.

Learn to be your own person. Set your course and harness the wind to direct the sail; enjoy the journey, bask in the sunlight, and batten down during the storms. The destination will be all the more appreciated for the effort put in.

Walk to the beat of your own drum. The world is full of sheeple; it's fine to be different, unique, to have different views and beliefs.

You will meet people in life who have beliefs that you don't understand, whether religious, racial, sexual, or political, to name a few, then those who hate meat or sugar ... and even those who love things like snakes. (Eww.) Respectfully allow them to have and hold their beliefs; if we all thought the same, life would be very dull.

Never lose your inner child in your quest to be an adult. Still look for the pot of gold at the end of rainbows, see fairies in the garden, chase leprechauns; let the spirit of Santa, the Tooth Fairy, and the Easter bunny fill your heart. As silly as these may sound, they symbolise love, acceptance, values, kindness, warmth, and belonging. Embrace these as part of your essence.

The simple things are truly the best things in life: good friends, camping, melting marshmallows in the fire, singing songs and sitting under the stars, telling scary stories before bedtime ... There is no age at which this stops.

In life, it is always easy to see the big achievements one makes and to celebrate these. Yet we should celebrate every success, no matter how small. Consider a building: it is made up of many parts, some really small, others huge; without each of the parts, the integrity of the structure would be compromised. The same is true of your life. Every part, no matter how small, is an accomplishment and a necessity to the overall success of your life. Celebrate every one of those achievements. Celebrations are fuel that inspires you to keep going, to keep striving, that it is all worthwhile in the end.

Practice gratitude every day, in every aspect of your life; you do this by saying out loud or writing down the things you are thankful for. Start by being grateful for your life, the lessons you've learnt so far, the people who bring you joy or the people who challenge you. Be grateful for the opportunity to explore the world, to explore different views and philosophies. Be grateful for the small things – a smile from a stranger, a compliment from your boss. Being grateful is for ourselves; a person who lives in an attitude of gratitude attracts like. Such as people who appreciate you and your efforts, people who have a higher vision than their present circumstances. It is enriching and drives us to be peaceful, accepting, calm, humorous, visionaries, benefiting ourselves as well as those around us.

When challenges arise, and they will, don't shy away. Don't feel defeated. Identify the best course of action and face those challenges like a warrior: grab your armour of bravado and bravery, pull out your arsenal, and never say never. Fight until victory is assured.

At times in life we are hit with situations or judgements that can hurt or raise questions about your own beliefs, that can create confusion and anxiety. Learning the skill of reframing will put you back in the driver's seat. The ability to reframe takes you out of being directed by emotions often attached to being a victim and into you directing through clear, balanced decision making, and into the mindset of control and confidence.

When you don't understand another person's actions or speech, be slow to judge; you never know the battles a person is living through. Be kind, for they are doing what they know how to do. It may be important to be supportive from a distance, to ensure that the tender heart is kept safe from hurt and drama.

If a job is worth doing, it's worth doing properly. See things through to completion and bask in satisfaction.

Above all else, be kind to yourself; nurture yourself. Spend time adding to your emotional piggy bank. You can do this by having positive self-talk. Work on creating more of the things you find enjoyment from, attending classes or reading books, adding to your talents, nurturing your creative side, valuing your own opinion. The most important thing here is to not feel selfish because of putting your own needs first – never, ever, ever ignore your needs to win over another.

Embrace peace and calmness; connect with the earth and the sea as often as possible. This will nourish the inner self and mend broken thoughts.

You will have boyfriends, and boy friends who will want to be more than friends – they will want to spend time with you, hold your hand, even kiss you. Eww. What a yucky thought, right? But you will engage in the dance of love and lust and all things physical; do so with integrity and honesty and only at a pace that is comfortable. Don't let anyone force you to do things faster than you are ready for.

Choose a partner for love, for their generous spirit, their kind heart, their sense of humour. Do not choose by their looks, the size of their wallet, their silver tongue, or their fancy car. A body deteriorates, cars rust, a silver tongue grows weak – a genuine person lasts forever. If the person you fall in love with does not treat us as a queen, then we cannot treat them like a king, and it is only time before we are nursing a broken heart.

As you mature, many pretty boys will catch your attention. Some are just for looking and others you will be drawn to engage with mentally, emotionally, and physically. At times this will be exciting and breath-taking, and at other times horrible and heart-breaking. Celebrate each of these, as they will help you to identify areas of yourself that you didn't know existed and prepare you for your true love. You will find the love of your life when you least expect it; yours will be a love story that will make the hearts of those around you melt.

With love, when creating a union with another, *ask what am I bringing to this relationship? Ask what are they bringing to this relationship?* Logically weigh the pros and cons. Don't ignore the niggling doubts or the ah-ha moments; if you ignore these, the cost in the long run will be great.

Your best friend betrays you, you just lost your favourite jumper, your boss yelled and screamed, your father has cut you out. You will be hurt and angry and resentful. At times, you won't know which way to turn. You will rake your mind for a solution. Sometimes the best option is to remember, with every difficulty you face in life, that these four words will get you through: This too shall pass. It will help you cope with the many challenges and hurts in life.

Like who you are, change for no one; we are who we are due to the life we've travelled and the experiences we've had.

Embrace a love of music. Your hand will reach for the guitar at times of deep sadness and at times of celebration. Playing and singing will provide a safe, peaceful place.

Develop a great sense of humour; it softens the challenges we face during times of adversity.

A truly amazing gift is the ability to tell stories, those that teach lessons through morals, adventures, humour, and relatability. Develop your story-telling ability. People love a story; we connect by sharing stories. It's the best teaching tool you will have in your arsenal.

Life will go in stages. Each will have success; each will have failures. Learn from these as you transition into the next phase. Be grateful for these lessons. Without them, you will not move forward; instead, you'll be like a dog chasing its tail.

To become the person you are destined to be, you'll need to understand the way growth happens in life. One grows through feelings of discomfort and pain; don't shy away from things that are uncomfortable or frightening. Instead, grab that beast by the horns and ride out the other side, bigger, wiser, stronger, and more resilient than before.

You will laugh one day looking back at those dresses your mother thought were pretty, you will own jeans and dress pants and many fancy shirts, and your wardrobe will be a dress free zone.

You will end up working in the same industry as your mum, at times in collaboration and at other times in competition. Your career will need you to bring all your courage and strength, insight and wisdom, acceptance and kindness. It will take many twists and turns and you will find yourself mothering many hundreds of girls in the adult industry. Through judgements and abuse, loss and fear, you give these girls direction and hope. You will see them develop into the best version of themselves. You will feel pride, compassion, gratitude and love much like a mother does when their child accomplishes their dreams.

And one day motherhood will arrive. The thought is horrifying: you don't even like the look of babies – they have no hair, no teeth, they just eat and cry. But, alas, it will happen, and it is through these children that the greatest lessons, adventures, and realisations about life will take place. They will teach you more than any other event or person has or will.

The first-born son will bring out traits of determination and stir emotions. This will be a struggle for you; how to show these emotions outwardly will be a new experience. His birth will force you to refocus and will create the need to make choices you didn't realise existed. He will be one half of your soul; through his birth, you will grow up in many ways. You will grow up together as you will still be a child when he is born. Together you will go fishing and camping, watch documentaries and wag school; you'll read to him out loud well into his adult life. He will be your best friend.

The second son will try your patience; he is smart and wilful, obstinate and determined, creative and funny. You will travel the world together and share a love of libraries, reading, theatre, and art. He will be your greatest advocate, your rock in stormy seas. By the time he is born, you are more confident and determined to embrace his uniqueness. He is the second half of your soul.

Then, many years later, a little girl will arrive, a special gift at the right time. She will teach you that showing your soft side is okay. Thanks to her, you will learn to cry and laugh publicly; she will remind you to chase butterflies and to see fairies, insist that the leprechaun door in her room transports her to Ireland at night when you sleep, that ice cream for breakfast is perfectly normal ... and that in our forties, your world will be very different than what you thought it should be. Through this little girl, inch by inch the shackles of expectation and perfectionism that have impounded you all our life will be removed.

So, my precious child, I surround you with white light and blue light and send you into the world, to learn and grow and chase rainbows. Hold that innocence close to your heart, for it is a precious gift that will see you manage many challenges and adventures with good heart and great humour.

THAT LIFE IS PERFECT IN ALL ITS IMPERFECTIONS, JUST THE WAY IT IS.

Love, grown up you.

CHAPTER 11

Tiggerliscious & Boomerang Wishes

Taryn Claire Le Nu

Dearest Tigger Ten,

Oh, gorgeous cub, how you bounce through life. You have finally reached the ever-magical double digits at last. Oh, what a glorious age to be! Every fibre of your being is vibrating excitedly about life and the endless opportunities that will fall at your feet.

Your long-awaited Chinese dress-up themed party celebration last night was so much fun; shoving your face full of marshmallows and giggling your way through trying to say 'Chubby Bunny' was hysterical. With an ever-increasing load of pink mallow clouds in your mouths, and general silliness in the chocolate eating game, this party holds a strong emotional feeling that will last a long time in your vault of favourite memories.

I'd love to give your old soul a sneak peak of what is to come. I'd love to share with you the gems that I wish I had understood sooner. When I think of all the possible things that I could impart to you, what would create the greatest impact in the shortest amount of time if you were to know them now … it would create a few volumes, for sure.

I've had to be ruthless, deleting my ever-expanding list of 'Golden Nuggets You Must Know,' as it spilled over into pages and pages. You and I both know that you're not much into following rules, and you most certainly wouldn't end up reading this letter if it were overwhelmingly extensive. At your core, you are an information junkie who loves your information in bite-sized pieces.

I have devised a plan – and I know you love it when a plan comes together (to quote your current favourite, *The A-Team!*).

You can either read this letter in one hit, or break it up and immerse yourself daily in measured learning, dished out for each day of the month. Nothing here is stated in any particular order of importance for you to know – and the list is certainly not all encompassing, either. Here are some incredible, useful, powerful jewels I have lived long enough to discover, and to wish I'd known about earlier in life. I now have a daughter who is a few years past your age, and like you, she too is an old soul. I will speak to you in this letter the same way you think ... sometimes cryptic, sometimes quirky, and with a few metaphors thrown in, as you love those!

Day 1

Peace. Make it your personal priority. While you are trying to make sense of things in life, may you equally learn to make peace with those things you can't control along the way. Making peace with things comes from a place of acceptance and surrendering. This is a lesson you will struggle with because you simply want things to be your way, straight up.

Day 2

Live your life by leaving footprints of love wherever you go. No matter how old the person, everyone is sitting in a state of being thirsty to feel love and to be loved. You can never make a mistake in life if you live it from a place of intentional love. People crave to be loved and to feel love. Some people are unaccustomed to being shown love and will reject your love along the way. This does not indicate that you ought to back off. These people often require more love from you, not less.

Day 3

Sparkle like nobody's business. Not everyone can see your sparkle, and that's okay. You don't need anyone's permission to

SPARKLE. Keep shining in your own special way, because you are always making a difference, even if you can't immediately see it! Your impact will ripple out far and wide to people you don't even know. You will touch people beyond what you can imagine: When you receive written messages of gratitude from strangers, saying that their lives have been saved as a result of hearing you speak about breast cancer, you are humbled. Or when you receive deep appreciation from those who read your book and felt less alone as a result of you sharing your story in a humorous, positive, and uplifting way.

Day 4

Take the ultimate trip from head-space to heart-space. The answer to all mysteries lies in your heart. We have three brains. A head brain, a heart brain, and a gut brain. These three brains are like an impressive orchestra, with billions of neurons cooperating to produce a harmonic symphony. The ever-changing network of neurons needs to be harnessed to work in synchronicity. Your job, Agent 99, is to practice getting out of your head and back into your heart. Over and over again. The mind can be a drama machine, but you don't have to buy into any of the stories it comes up with. Sometimes your mind tricks you into taking the easy road. Sometimes your mind fabricates some great excuses for you not to do something. You have choice: The opportunity to choose to step out of your mind and into your heart and feel what is right for you. Solely using your mind will ultimately limit you. Overthinking things can make you find excuses NOT to love longer, harder, and deeper. When you approach your problems from your heart-space, you will find and feel greater inner peace. Your sense of satisfaction in life will explode, and you will create a ripple of love in your wake as you walk through life.

Day 5

Be a gardener of the soul. Let your heart bloom. I know ... am I still harping on about love? You bet! You will discover this is a recurring theme. Love will be an important message that you will live and breathe in years to come; it will become a failsafe, a fallback, no matter the occasion. Allow yourself to love unconditionally without expectation. It will be rewarding in its own right. Love without sitting in anticipation of receiving another person's happiness in return. Make your ability to love independent of what you receive in return. When you sow the seeds of love for a flower garden in your own heart, they will bloom all year round, even through a cold, dark winter.

Day 6

Be brave. Choose love. Be the one who chooses love over and over. Am I sounding repetitive yet? That's okay. I will keep saying it till the story is embedded heart and soul in your subconscious. When someone hurts you, it is because hurt people hurt others. You may not see or understand their hurt, as people will do anything to hide their vulnerability. Stop before you respond and react from your place of hurt. Break the cycle of creating more hurt for that person. Take a deep breath and reset yourself back into your heart-space. Choose to respond from a place of understanding. Observe their hurt without attachment to responding with your hurt. Respond with love. You will resolve things faster from a place where people feel seen, heard, and felt when you respond with the intention of love.

Day 7

When in doubt, choose love. It's kind of a failproof way of leading your life. Even when others around you are falling into reacting to situations and you're tempted to do the same because it is so much easier. Try not to fall for the short, easy road, as the big picture rewards will be less fulfilling for you. See it as a game with challenges and play all out. Choose to believe in the good of the person, for what you focus on grows. It would be a much better world if we all did this.

Day 8

Forgive yourself, and do it often. If you can't treat yourself with compassion, understanding, and forgiveness, then you will struggle to do the same for others. Know that you are always doing the best you can with who you are at the time. You will never stop learning in life, growing through things, and improving upon your level of self-awareness, so tread the road of self-forgiveness regularly. Self-forgiveness liberates you from heavy shackles that serve only to hold you back and keep you stuck in cycles that don't serve you.

Day 9

Stop. Be Still. Within you, there is potential for great stillness. You chase things outside of you to fulfil your desire for peace. You have the magic within you already, the ability to decompress and disconnect from external chaos, but you need to work on your patience and tenacity for practicing to go there. Within you lies your very own accessible sanctuary, to which you can retreat at any time. Visit this place often, for it is your own spring of pure soul reinvigoration. Learn how to meditate from a younger age; continue to do the breathwork taught to you in drama at school and slow down using yin yoga or somatic body as soon as a yoga teacher steps in your direction. All this foundational work will help you to access this place of stillness faster, so you can reap the rewards quicker. You will discover that a rich life has nothing to do with money. When you activate, harness, and live with meditation, breath, and yoga, your life will be rich beyond measure.

Day 10

Recalibrate your compass. You're in charge, darling girl. It's totally up to you. When you feel that you cannot change your *destination* overnight, you most certainly can change your *direction* overnight. If you feel like things aren't going in the right direction and you are getting results you don't want, or are surrounded by people you don't like, YOU ultimately hold more power than you think you do. You may not be able to change others, but you do have the opportunity to change you. You have the power to engage in simple, miniscule changes along the way that will compound the interest on the outcome over time. There will be times where you will be overwhelmed, feeling that too big a change is needed to change your course and direction. Focusing on making a few simple changes at a time will build momentum. You only need to alter your behaviour, thoughts, feelings, or beliefs by one painless degree at a time, to discover that one simple degree over time will totally change where you land. Keep working on those incremental changes. That is indeed where the magic lies.

Day 11

You are so loved! Everyone feels alone, scared, or misunderstood by others from time to time, but ultimately you are well and truly loved by people you know and also by people who know of you. So long as you keep living your life with your beautiful servant's heart, you will continue to be a magnet to other people's love. People will shower you with healing love during your times of greatest need. On many an occasion, you will use love to soften the edges of life's inevitable sharp corners. Warning: Spoiler alert. What I reveal next may feel like a shock to your pure, innocent 10-year-old ears, but by the time you experience these traumas, you are already on your way to being a far stronger woman than anyone could possibly imagine. You have an old head on those young shoulders and have resilience, tenacity, and determination in spades. By the time your eldest son develops cancer at 3½, you will feel the full impact of all the love you have ever shown to others be returned to you tenfold. This will reconfirm that showing love never robs you in the process. When you are diagnosed with breast cancer at age 41, you will not only feel this love once again to the power of ten, but you will also experience the gift of love from just as many strangers, too. This love will be used by you to help you heal. It is incredibly powerful.

Day 12

SELFcare SOULcare. We are made up of body, mind, and soul. Your own soul is your guru, and as you quiet your mind through the process of binaural beats and meditation, you will discover the power of being able to tap into listening to the wisdom of your higher self. Society teaches you that self-care is all about facials, pedicures, and massages, but true self-care is ensuring that you don't do things that insult your soul. Your soul is part of you and governs who you are. Staying in alignment with your highest good keeps you in a good rhythm for creating flow in your life. Your higher self cares deeply for you in human form, and she guides your intuition in ways beyond what you're currently able to conceive of. Those little voices that speak to you are on your side, supporting you, guiding you, and giving you hints about what is right for your soul. Listen to them. Practice good soul hygiene by following your gut instinct, practicing active listening to the infinite intuitive advice being offered to you from your soul in an act of ultimate self-trust.

Day 13

Be brave for your own growth. Be brave enough to suck at something new. While you are young, you are constantly in a state of learning something new. It keeps your mind busy and keeps your ego in check. As you get older, you will gravitate towards things that come easy to you. When you try something new, you won't like the feeling of not being accomplished at it. Remember that that uncomfortable feeling won't last forever, and you will soon pass out of this zone with time, too. When you dare to be brave, you will be rewarded, and you will love the experiences that follow on from that decision to be brave.

Day 14

Pause. Reset. Restart. Press the pause button when you find yourself thinking about your problems. You have already over achieved at being an overthinker. Energy flows where attention goes. Problems can be like sinking sand and will suck you in before you know it. POOF! You'll be trapped in a negative mindset. Rather, reset your centre of attention. Recalibrate your locus of focus. *But how?* you ask, with a mild air of irritation and impatience. Simply reboot your process by appreciating all the blessings in your life, particularly the ones that you take for granted. It will shift the energy in you and around you. When you turn your attitude to one of gratitude, it shifts the frequency that you're operating in and the frequency of what you are attracting back into your life. Daily Gratitude Journaling is the fastest route to rewiring positive electrical energy in your direction. Fill an entire page with 'I am grateful for ...' and fill in the blanks. It's not exactly what you are grateful for as such, so don't get too hell-bent on running out of honourable things to mention in your list. It's more about harnessing the frequency of gratitude, not being all high and mighty about being grateful only for things of real value. The secret is to tap into the frequency and feel of it.

Day 15

Your anxiety is lying to you. Your anxiety doesn't look like other people's, so you won't appreciate that is what it is. It will take you a long time to realise that you even have anxiety. Anxiety for you is not the panic attack you witness in other people. Anxiety for you is the drive to do something at 150 percent when 100 percent is actually okay for society in general. When anxiety arises, see it as a form of fear. Fear is a learned state that your body puts you in, to keep you safe. Speak to yourself. Tell your body that you are safe. Thank your body for looking out for you and wanting to protect you and that you can handle it from here. You are already loved and you are going to be okay. And some of the time your body is programmed to be extra cautious and will hold you back from fully achieving what life has to offer. This is your 50 percent zone from which you operate, too. Now that you are aware of your far pendulum swings driven by anxiety, choose to strive for the balance of 100 percent!

Day 16

Boomerang wishes. From the place of wishing someone well, you will fill your own bucket! What you wish for others, you are indeed wishing for yourself, so be true to who you really are today. Keep following your heart's longing and eagerness to be kind to everyone. The compounding interest will pay out dividends and it is contagious. I promise. Your Grandma Del lives her life from the premise of never thinking or speaking a harsh word towards another. As you start to put this into practice for yourself, you will notice that many unexpected forms of kindness start to flow your way from others. You soon learn through experience that when you pass judgement, the lesson returns quickly to you, to experience what it is like to sit on the side of feeling judged. I daresay it takes you a while to learn this harsh lesson, despite the pain you experience during it. Take the time to teach others what you have learnt about this as a concept on the way.

Day 17

Look in the direction you are going. Don't stumble over something behind you. When your mum is driving you to school, she is looking forward, ahead of her, and for good reason. If she were to focus her eyes on the rear-view mirror constantly while she was driving forward, she would soon crash. This little analogy will support you well in the way in which you live your life. Don't let the things in your past be your focus, trip you up, or make you crash. You are not ever going to go backwards in life. Time by nature moves forwards. Take your cue and move forward, too.

Day 18

The only difference between a flower and a weed is a judgement. You are in charge of your perception of things, so strive to see things from the higher frequency of acceptance and love. When you pass judgement on people, situations, and things, you are not serving yourself well. Practice seeing things from a place of observation instead. Notice what is, without buying into the feeling and emotion of it. If you're starting your sentence with

'You're so xyz (e.g. stubborn, opinionated, self-righteous),' know that you're probably sitting too comfortably in your judgement groove. When you start swapping your thought patterns out for 'I can see that this means a lot to you, that you are hurting, it's important that you are acknowledged' you start to name the behaviour as opposed to name-calling the person. When you name the behaviour, you take the emotion out of it and are able to observe and state the facts.

Day 19

You've totally got this. Just in case you are feeling a little overwhelmed by all this information right now, remember that you are braver than you believe, stronger than you seem, and smarter than you think.

Day 20

Live with a sense of connection and community. You will come to understand that we are not on this earth to see through one another, but to see one another through. When you witness someone who is struggling, reach out with a helping hand. There will be times when you will prefer to see right past them because you won't feel like helping. Go within and ask if you have the ability to be of service to them, and if the answer is no ... still acknowledge them and offer to hold space for them. Everyone appreciates feeling seen and heard.

Day 21

You will win over more bees with honey than vinegar. There is a saying that 'kind words will unlock an iron door.' Leave your bulldozer at home and win people over with kindness, compassion, empathy, and understanding. Everyone is struggling; even those who appear to be flying high will experience their own struggles. Kindness is the high road. Choose it every time.

Day 22

You're a full-price, rare, high-end item. Every unique individual in this world holds this title, but many fail to appreciate their own worth. When you fail to appreciate your own worth, it can be tricky to see it in others. You will meet many people on the road of life who can't see your worth – just don't let it be you. Believe in yourself and what you have to offer to the world, and do so with unparalleled conviction from here on in. When you value who you are and see and feel your worth, you are honouring your soul. You are equally setting the tone for others to do the same, as it will be easier for others to believe in your worth from you leading by example.

Day 23

Sometimes you win and sometimes you learn. Winning is nice, of course! But we have come down to Earth School to learn, so there will be many lessons along the way. You are slowly progressing from kindergarten to grade 12 in Earth School, and as sure as you inhale and exhale, there will be more lessons than wins along the way. Knowing that we learn through our mistakes is a healthy attitude to begin with.

Day 24

Talk about your joys. You'll meet many people in life who are addicted to talking about their problems. Be a beacon of light to others and lead by example. Focus on the things you want to draw more of into your life. Speak things into existence. Be unafraid to be called a delusional 'Tigger' in life, who bounces around speaking about all the 'fun fun fun,' as you will be growing the Frequency of FUN. Consciously choose to be a Tigger as opposed to the monotone Eeyore who views his glass as half empty, focusing on lack. The more you speak about your joys, the more you will attract people around you who want to be part of the Joyeux Movement. The more you mix with joyous souls, the more joy you will create in your life.

Day 25

Love yourself enough to forgive others daily. I know I touched on self-forgiveness earlier in my letter, but forgiveness of others is an equally tough aspect to manoeuvre. Forgive, even when you're hurt. I know. This is tough. This is hard. You won't feel like doing it because it is much easier at the time to carry your hurt in a rucksack over your shoulder, lugging it around with you each and every day. Over time, holding onto hurt and not letting it go will take its toll on you in both physical and emotional ways.

Don't take your resentments to bed with you, for they make a prickly partner. When you forgive others, you free yourself. Daily practicing of the Hawaiian Forgiveness Prayer, 'Ho-oponopono,' will work wonders in your life:

I am sorry
Please forgive me
I thank you
I love you

Day 26

Passion and purpose hot tip. It's an adult conversation that you will happen upon soon enough. At some point you will be worried that you can't figure out your purpose, your exact reason for being on this earth, why you were born and what you were meant to do while living here. Perhaps try switching things up and figure out what you are passionate about first, and then your passion will lead you directly to your purpose. Voila!

Day 27

You are not your age; you are your energy. Keep your energy high by eating high vibrational living foods. I can see your sugared-up eyeballs rolling already. All that sugar is dead food. Dirty carbs are empty foods that aren't fuelling your body in vibrant ways. When you eat food that is not nutritionally dense, you never feel truly sated. There is a gnawing feeling inside of you that still craves something more. When you swap things out for whole foods, you will notice a difference that makes your heart sing.

Day 28

In a nutshell. A quick recap over the themes already covered in this letter, just in case your concentration is starting to wane. Here's a few more punchy statements to add to the list.

More observing, less judging.
More responding, less reacting.
More self-love, less self-sabotage.
More inner peace, less outer chaos.
More clarity, less confusion.
More being, less doing.
More faith, less fear.

Day 29

This world needs you to be you. Don't give up when things seem beyond you. Keep showing up. Keep loving. Keep giving back. Keep being kind. Keep being brave. Keep caring. Keep trying new things. Keep showing grace. Keep on.

Day 30

Vibe high. Your DNA is being created every single day and is therefore stamped with the history of your emotions. Take the time to be a gatekeeper to which emotions you allow to unpack their bags in your space. You are allowed to fully feel and express all the emotions; however, some emotions need to have an expiry date stamped on them, as they won't serve you well played out at full volume for extended periods of time. Take personal responsibility for the energy you bring to a space. Bring this to your conscious choosing each day. Get your vibe right before you proceed forward.

And now my love, I realise there's a bit to digest among these pages. I suggest you take as long as you need to immerse yourself in the principles that have been put forward. There is no pressure to perfect these suggestions; rather, see it as a suggested map of favourable places to visit to ensure you get the best out of travelling in this lifetime.

Remember that I love you, and that I won't ever stop loving you. You can always count on me. I am entirely grateful to you for this first decade round the sun you have travelled. Your creative energy and time spent in the garden has laid the foundation for some truly glorious memories.

Much love,

Tiger Taryn

(your four-and-a-half decades round the sun older self)

CHAPTER 12

Be the Champion Over Your Inner Anxiety Monster

Courtney Kynaston

Dear little me,

Your life is fun, easy, and simple right now, with your mum watching out for and looking after you. Spend lots of time with her; you'll never have a best friend that matches who she is in your life.

As you get older, your perspective about life, growing up, and being an adult will change. No matter what, your mum will be there, supporting you every step of your journey. Always explore your creativity with her, as she will keep teaching you everything you need to know to succeed as you move through life.

You will face lots of challenges that you won't see coming. When they hit you, it will feel like it is unbearable, and the weight of it can make it hard to breathe.

In those moments, the world feels impossible. You don't know how to navigate it. Here is something that, at 33, I want you to know and remember:

YOU ARE STRONGER THAN YOU THINK

No matter what, never forget this. Keep this thought with you and remember it always.

Everything you face you can and will get through, even when you feel like you can't.

Through it all, you have a 100 percent survival rate, and you even come out the other side of those moments with lessons and strength you never thought possible.

Keep working hard for everything you want in life: the hard work pays off. No matter what other people say and do, live exactly how you want to moment to moment and everything will fall into place.

Right now, you go to school, you have friends, you play sports – and it is fun. What you don't know yet is that there is a mind monster out there called anxiety. It takes over your thoughts, makes you feel like everything and everyone is working against you. It will take your appetite and make you feel light-headed. Over time you will learn to fight through it, and you will be your own champion in this battle.

Ahead of this battle, here are some ways you can prepare for potential anxiety triggers:

It's okay if people don't like you. People will come in and out of your life, and it's okay if they go. Don't hang onto the sadness for too long; it's not your fault. It's okay to grieve the loss of a friendship and relationship, but they were only meant to be there for a season. Look for the lesson you've learnt; have you discovered something about yourself you didn't see before? Do you know more about what you do and don't like about the characteristics of people now?

There are amazing people waiting in your future who will be part of your life for a much longer period of time.

Boys. They aren't all great, but some will be. You will find nice ones and you will find some crazy ones. Don't be afraid to walk away if it is not healthy, especially if you enter into a romantic relationship. If they make you sad, if they make you cry or feel scared – you can walk away. Don't feel bad; your family will be there for you, and it is safe to leave, no matter how scary it seems.

Some guys make the best of friends, and they are so much more down to earth than girls. Don't chase this; just let them grow organically and you will settle into a group of really great people.

Jobs. Try anything and everything. Explore every opportunity and figure out what you enjoy and what you don't. It's okay to decide it's not working and walk away. There's no shame or any reason to be embarrassed or anxious about quitting a job to do something else.

Most of all, don't let a toxic work environment consume you. You're supposed to wake up and be excited for each new day, not scared about what might happen. The moment you stop waking up ready and keen for what is coming, get out and start the next journey in a new environment.

Workmates. In the working environment, people won't always like you, and that's okay. When you're good at your job, some people become threatened by your talents and try to bring you down. Know yourself and who you are, and they will hold no power over you. Don't give them the power to tear you down.

People gain energy from you by making you feel like you are less than them. These aren't your people; they aren't your tribe. So, step away and start a new adventure where you can find the people that suit you.

Family. People say you can't choose your family, but you can. You can choose who you connect with, and they may be more like a brother or a sister or aunt or uncle. You can choose to walk away from toxic personalities and not interact with them. You can do this with no shame or guilt. You have permission to walk away because there are bigger and brighter opportunities in the world ahead of you.

The family you find along the way will be more amazing than you can imagine. Through sport, you will find your hockey family, and through creative adventures, you find your sisters and inspiration for your art and creativity. You will find people that fan your flame and make you shine brighter. Don't fear the 'loss' of your blood family, as you will find great strength in your soul family.

Friends. Friends will come and go, and different moments in your life will highlight your lifelong friends and your short-term friends.

At times it hurts when they become distant and you lose touch, and you will feel like you did something wrong. Life just moves people into new directions or paths; sometimes this makes it hard for them to keep in touch and see you as often as they used to.

Human nature is to change and adapt, so if people move into and then out of your orbit, it's okay to accept this for what it is and move on to your next opportunity.

You don't have to be perfect. People will pick at you over petty and pathetic things. This will make you feel like you need to be perfect, but when this happens, just take a breath, fix up whatever is wrong, and move forward, knowing they have nothing better to complain about because you are doing a good job. If the only thing they can say is something small and petty, then take that as a compliment, because everything else you are doing is strong and good.

You will learn quickly that silence is the greatest compliment; if you are not being fussed over or corrected, allow this to increase your confidence to know that you are doing a great job.

Hold onto these thoughts, because this is an area that can come up in any aspect of life. If someone starts picking at little things in one environment, you will start to notice it in others. Breathe through it and keep moving forward.

There is no such thing as the right time. People around you will try to tell you that you need to have things done by a certain age. They couldn't be more wrong.

Everyone's timeline is different and unique.

You don't have to choose a career chosen by 18, you don't have to be a mum at 25, and you don't have to own property or a car by 30. These things take time and discipline to achieve.

The most important thing you need to accomplish and reflect on at each birthday is that you've had fun and experienced life. You need to stop and do things you enjoy – even better if you can make an income from those things (but it's not always possible). Don't get caught up in a career you don't enjoy or trying to live up to everyone else's deadlines and expectations. Give yourself permission to find your own way.

Shine your light. The world needs it. There is a great saying: 'To the world you might be one person, but to one person, you are the world.' You don't need to change the entire world, but if you connect to a few special people in your life, that is all that matters. Don't let anyone bring you down or make you feel like you are unworthy. If they do, move on from them; you do not need them in your life.

Anxiety feels like butterflies in your stomach, flying around so fast that you lose your appetite. It feels like you want to go back to bed and sleep for a week. It feels like if you curl up and hide, you'll be safer. Anxiety is mean.

It makes you imagine things that are not true and creates stories that don't exist. What's worse – they feel real. Each moment feels like it is actually happening, and it is so hard to break through. All aspects of life can present an opportunity for anxiety to take hold, but if you follow the steps above, you will be greater than the anxiety.

Creativity is key, as it is one of the best outlets and inlets for all kinds of emotions, in all different lights. When you're happy, sad, or anxious, use creativity to move through those feelings.

Never lose your creativity. Growing up, you will explore all kinds of projects, so don't hold back from trying all different types and methods. Draw, paint, write, crochet, journal – do anything and everything you can think of. Explore ways to evolve each creative journey and build on them. Never forget all the things your mum teaches you, and ask her to show you more. Spend hours and days just doing any and all types of art styles: find the things you love the most.

Over time, creativity can become the way you calm the anxiety and clear the fog. In the worst moments, when you can't eat, breathe, drink, or think, you need to find that way to control your mind so you can focus. Mindful breathing exercises are something you will learn about as you grow up. You can practice now by sitting with your feet on the floor; as you breathe in and out, think about how your feet feel on the floor and how each part of your body feels where it comes into contact with your seat and anything you are touching.

Don't forget – all those creative projects focus your mind onto something that can make you happy, and you can then re-focus on the problem at hand and find your way.

There is always a way to get control back over your mind, so in your good moments spend time exploring and creating ideas;

when your hard moments arise, you can lean on these positive experiences no matter where you are or what you're doing.

You can always be the champion of the battle with your anxiety. You are never alone, and you aren't a burden to those you choose to reach out to and talk about it with. As you face your challenges, your anxiety will speak lies into your mind. So, as you reach out for support, it's easy to feel like people around you don't want to hear it, and you will think that you need to keep it to yourself. The people that care about you, and support you, will always want to know when you aren't okay and want you to reach out when you need them.

YOU ARE STRONGER THAN YOU THINK

With all my Love, not so little me

CHAPTER 13

Health and Healing

Rebecca Lang

**I FEEL THE STONES THAT ARE ALONE;
I FEEL THE LEAVES THAT BREATHE.**

Dear Rebecca,

I've had this amazing opportunity to write a letter to you. I am you in 30 years' time, so I can give you some words of wisdom from my life experience. This will be a gift to you and will help to guide you in your life. All of those entries in your diaries ... this is a letter back to you. It is magical.

At 10 years old, you only have another six years that you'll be living at home with your mum, step-father, and brother. You'll never be able to get this time back, so I'm going to try to help you to realise a few things, to make your life easier.

At this age, you are feeling so sad and lonely, even when you have people around you. I have some good news for you: You might want to make the most of this quiet time. In two years' time, your family will start to grow, with three new sisters and another brother.

Your extended family is going to fill your life with so much extra joy and happiness. It will be like having four more best friends that stay with you for life and love you always.

Your love of dolls and teddies has prepared you to be the big sister, to nurture and be close to your sisters and brothers. Your older brother, Jason, and you will always be close, and will only become closer as you get older. He will be your mentor and spiritual support. You will continue having long conversations with him over the course of your lives.

The uneasiness you feel inside yourself is called anxiety. I know it's crippling for you at times and that it can make you feel physically sick. Anxiety is actually very common, but right now, in your time, people don't talk about it. Many of your friends also feel this uneasiness, but they don't know how to talk about it, either.

When you are older, you will realise that you are not the only person in the world that feels anxious. But that won't be until you are about 30 years of age. What I can tell you is that your anxiety is there for a reason. It's what will lead you into your life's work as a naturopath and nutritionist. You will be able to help many people with anxiety, as you will have a full understanding of how they are feeling. This is when you'll start to realise that you aren't the only person in the world that suffers from this.

For now, you really need to know that it's very normal. It doesn't need to hold you back from trying new things and meeting new people. You don't have to feel depressed because you think there must be something wrong with you. And you won't ever take medication for it, because you'll learn to deal with it and work through your physical and mental responses. Then you'll teach others and use natural medicine to help at times.

The anxiety is why you can't sleep at night and also part of where the continuous nightmares come from. I know your mum has said that you can't keep waking her up every single night with your nightmares now because you're getting older. You need to understand that she loves you, but she needs her sleep to be able to function and work the next day. Your bond with Jason will build even more now that you wake him up every night. He'll help you to understand your nightmares more, and you will both start writing a dream journal each morning of your good dreams. This is where the healing begins and your nightmares ease. You'll start focusing on the good dreams and creating them before you even go to sleep. This also allows you to start seeing how your good dreams are giving you guidance, especially when you ask before going to sleep.

It is around this time that you and Jason will receive red telephones for Christmas. Jason wires them all up over the top of the door frames and under the carpet so no one can see them, and you talk to each other at night. It's very reassuring for you to know that you can pick up the phone and talk to your brother. Over your lives you may not live physically close to each other, but you will talk for hours on the phone, sharing your lives and loving each other.

One thing you will learn as a naturopath is that gut health can affect mental health, including anxiety. You will tell your clients that you were born bloated and with anxiety, and you will laugh. I know that at this point in time, though, it is no laughing matter for you.

Your brother has created 'Bec's Book of Excuses,' for all the reasons you make up about why you can't eat dinner. You will later make your little sisters laugh by telling them bedtime stories about how you used to say you had to go to the toilet, but would actually go outside and throw food over the back fence and into the alleyway. Or into the toilet and flushed. You once tried to flush a whole lamb chop down the toilet, and you didn't realise it didn't flush until your mum found it. You did get in trouble, but later on your little sisters will say, 'Bec, Bec, please tell us the story about the lamb chop in the toilet again.'

Notice how when you do eat, you only like to have one food type at a time. You don't mix your protein and starches. You don't like two proteins together. This is to do with the enzymes that break down different foods – starches, proteins, and fatty acids. Your body is deficient in these, so you aren't digesting properly, and this is why as soon as you eat you become so bloated and uncomfortable. When you have to stay sitting at the dinner table for hours, just try and continue to eat small amounts slowly, and chew really well. It's also best not to have water when you're eating.

The other issue that you're suffering with is called Irritable Bowel Syndrome. You have diarrhoea some days and constipation other days. Initially, you won't realise that not all people suffer like this – not until Jason points out to you it's not normal, because he's not like that. You laugh years later about how you said to him, 'It's all milky' – if only you knew that was an indicator of what was going on.

When you were around 5, you suffered constant ear infections and would wake up screaming in pain. You had many courses of antibiotics, until they eventually removed your adenoids. Your gut has never really recovered from the antibiotics. I know that you don't eat any yoghurt ... but that would actually be a good start to repairing your gut and helping you to digest better.

When you are 18, you will do a detox, and when it's finished, you'll go back to your normal diet. This includes Just Right cereal with cow's milk. You become very sick, and the doctors can't work out what is wrong with you. They do all the tests and tell you that you don't have a parasite, and that there's nothing else they can do.

You go to bed one night completely nutrient depleted, dehydrated, and exhausted. You pray to anyone who is listening to please tell you what's wrong with your body. That night, you have a powerful and profound dream of a lady with beautiful long black hair. She looks you straight in the eye and says, 'Don't drink the milk,' and you wake up straight away. From that day onwards you stop drinking cow's milk ... and you become well again.

Later on, as a naturopath and nutritionist, you'll look back and realise you can relate many of your childhood ear infections and digestive issues to drinking cow's milk. It's okay for some people, but for your body, it just doesn't work. From the morning of the dream, you'll never again touch a glass of cow's milk ... though you will eventually only have goat's milk.

These digestive issues are also why you are so skinny and borderline underweight. You will be teased for many years at primary school, and even at the all girls' high school. You'll hear variations on *Rebecca, you're so skinny* and *Rebecca, you're anorexic* for years. Try not to let this upset you too much, as it really starts to affect your self-worth and increases your anxiety. You start to feel ugly and that no one will like you because you are too skinny.

Kids can say things and be mean, but they are also going through their own issues as well. You are no angel, either. You're sick of the insults and lash out at that boy in your class, call him fat. That isn't very nice of you; he must have gone home and been very upset, too. I'm glad that you later apologised to him and became friends.

So, while you're working with digestive issues and anxiety, your mum tries to help you by suggesting your thin, lanky hair needs an improvement. She decides to update you with the fashion and takes you to get a perm. You don't really know what this is, but you have this vision of long, soft curls flowing beautifully down your back. When the hairdresser finishes your hair, though ...

you will cry. It will look exactly like the hairdresser's – but you're *10*.

You get yourself so worked up that you wake up the next morning with your first bout of tonsillitis, which lasts three and a half weeks – throwing more antibiotics to go into that already vulnerable digestive system of yours. And then your break out in psoriasis all over your scalp. This is … really not a good year for your health.

But don't worry – as an adult your health will improve!

Your mum takes you to a specialist in Fremantle, who writes out a script for special shampoo and conditioner. There isn't much they can do because it's on the scalp. There is no tablet to fix it – but they give you another course of antibiotics, just in case it helps. But the antibiotics only seem to make it worse, and your digestion suffers even more. Your brother's 'Bec's Book of Excuses,' about why you don't want to eat dinner each night, is becoming a very thick book by this point.

You do still have to eat dinner, though, as Mum's trying to help you to be healthy and put on weight.

The chemical smell of the psoriasis shampoo and conditioner will stay with you forever. It makes you want to vomit each time you wash your hair, and it really doesn't make any difference. This psoriasis on the scalp will stick around for about a year, no matter what chemical is put on it.

The psoriasis eventually just goes on its own, but very slowly. Sunlight and saltwater seem to help it. When you are a naturopath, though, you will love helping people in this area. You will be especially good at treating psoriasis in the scalp with natural oils. You will get it back every now and again yourself, but as soon as it appears, you treat it with your natural oils and fix it. You'll have many discussions with your clients about your own experience, and you'll be able to look back and laugh.

These health issues may also be part of why you are obsessed with the show Young Doctors – and you know 100 percent that you want to be a nurse. That is your plan. You really want to help people, and you know that this is what you were born to do. You will work in doctor's surgeries and hospitals, and you'll start studying nursing … but it will be the natural medicine that leads you into a degree in health science, majoring in naturopathy, herbs, and nutrition. You work out that is your best way to help people. It's important, though, that you start your studies in nursing and learn from the doctors so you can have an understanding of the medical system.

You have been very blessed at this age to have some strong and powerful women around you, women who will help to guide you on your path as a healer. Your great-grandmother, a strong and independent woman who lives by herself, reads tea leaves. You and Jason will love listening to her tea leaf readings and will just think it is so magical when things come true. Great-grandma will always give you and your brother 50 cents at each visit. This shows her generosity – that was a lot of money when your pocket money was 80 cents a week!

Your Nanna (Dad's mum) and you will be very close, too. She is Catholic, and she will take you to church; she'll be glad that you go to a Catholic primary and high school, and will teach you about God and religion in the most beautiful way. You'll sit together for hours reading books. Nanna is another woman living on her own after her husband died, strong and independent. She studies Latin, history, and English literature at a school in the city, and teaches you about other countries and cultures. She teaches herself how to paint and tries to teach you. Your time together is precious, and you spend a week or so with her often in the school holidays.

Nanna will really help you in many ways. Being the child of divorced parents who've remarried, while also attending Catholic school, is very challenging. As far as you know, you are the only child of divorced parents in your whole primary school ... though in the future, one in two people will be from divorced families.

The fact that your mum gets remarried is actually even more unacceptable in the Catholic religion. Nanna helps you to feel less judged about this. She loves your mum as her own daughter and has a lot of respect for her. Nanna teaches you that God does not judge; its only humans that judge. She always tells you that God loves you, that you can pray to him to help you with anything that you're struggling with. It's a relief to know that there is someone or something out there that might be able to help you with your issues. Your Nanna's words of wisdom and strength will stay with you for the rest of your life.

Your religious upbringing will give you good grounding. It will lead you into a more spiritual belief system which will support you throughout your life.

Grandma, your mum's mum, has been in a nursing home for three years now. You visit her every week. She was diagnosed with epilepsy at the age of 2. She was on a cocktail of medications throughout her life ... many of which were banned due to the side-effects. Part of Grandma's sickness was no doubt from these many side-effects.

You will have memories of when you were younger and stayed the night at Grandma's; she'd let you and your brother and cousins stay up until midnight playing cards and board games. She was always very loving and affectionate.

Seeing her in the hospital, shaking and struggling to talk, is hard – but your visits bring her so much joy, just from helping her to eat her food and holding her hand while your mum talks with her.

Aunty Dot was an older friend of your mum's, the mother of your mum's best friend, Marie, who lived in the country. Aunty Dot lived in a little house near Fremantle. Visits to her house were always special, as she treated and talked to you and Jason as adults. She was very spiritual. She would set up her organ, and you'd learn to play Christmas carols. She had a black cat named Shad and a small dog named Goldie.

Many of your happy memories will be with your cousins. Your cousin Vanessa is two years older, and it's like being blessed with a big sister. She'll teach you about many things when you're young, and again when you reconnect when you are older. You will sleep over at Vanessa's regularly, and you'll both lay and talk for hours. She'll remind you, many years from now, that your favourite topic was Jesus. You wanted to know everything about him. You received a lot of comfort from knowing there was someone always there for you. You also missed your dad a lot, and so you found comfort in Jesus.

Your time with Vanessa and your other cousins will be treasured memories. When you are older, your work will be on the other side of the country from Perth, and you'll lose contact with your cousins. There will still be a treasured time when you're older, though, as you reconnect with Vanessa.

Your obsession with the Helen Keller movie, with learning sign language and walking around the house constantly blindfolded – to make sure that if you went blind you could still find everything – is part of your preparation to be a healer and naturopath. Your mum wearing a hearing aid now doesn't seem to affect you too much, thought it does affect her on a daily basis, and her hearing will continue to decline. She knows she'll lose more hearing with each pregnancy – and she still has two more children to go. Eventually, as she gets older, she'll be completely deaf in one ear and wear a hearing aid in the other.

Your son will also be completely deaf in one ear. It isn't hereditary, and it's not connected to your mum's hearing problems. You'll find out when your son is 5, when you are serendipitously working for an audiologist and an ear, nose, and throat surgeon. All they can assume is that he's been deaf in his left ear from birth. Having a good understanding from growing up with a hearing-impaired mum will help you with your son.

Although you take your mum for granted at this age, you'll become closer to her over time, and she'll come to be your best friend. At the moment you get upset with her because you miss your dad ... but your mum is really doing everything she can to give you a good life. It won't be until you're older that you'll understand more about her life – supporting her own mum, who's in a nursing home, bringing up two kids and then choosing to have two more ... all the while trying to work and manage finances.

There is a time, at this age, where you see your mum step forward and really see her for the person she is. You'll have been at your new school for less than two years, but your mum becomes the president of the school P&C. She sets up fundraising events and brings many parents together. She networks and builds a dynamic association. She's a wonderful example for you of a confident and strong woman standing in her own power – and this will be very influential in your life.

You see your dad sometimes, and you totally idolise him. It's this year, though, that he'll pick you and your brother up from school for the first time. He'll tell you both that he's done his will and that your brother will inherit all the properties. You are shocked, and ask why. He explains that this is the way it is; Jason will keep the family name, while you'll get married and change your name. From this day onwards, you promise yourself to never change your family name. And you never do. This wasn't your dad being unfair; it was just the way people used to do things back then. Everything changes later on anyway, so don't let this upset you. You may not see your dad much now ... but as an adult, you become very close.

Your sensitivity will always stay with you. When your brother kicks a rock on the footpath and you have to pick it up and put it back from when it came from, this is your sensitivity. When you feel sorry for ants and all creatures and people laugh at you, know that this is your sensitive nature ... which will also be your guidance. When you are 18, you'll read a book by Louise Hay called The Power Is Within You, and it will confirm everything you've felt. You will be so happy. You've known all along that everything is energy and that we can create our own reality. That everything happens for a reason.

I FEEL THE STONES THAT ARE ALONE; I FEEL THE LEAVES THAT BREATHE.

To end this special letter to you, which is surrounded by magic and love, I want to tell you this. Everything that you are going through with health issues, mentally, emotionally, and spiritually, is going to create you and lead you into your life purpose – to be a naturopath, nutritionist, and healer. Influential and independent women will lead you to become a successful business entrepreneur. You will look back one day, and it will make sense that it had to happen this way. You have made a commitment at 10 years old to help and serve in this lifetime, and this is what you will do. Your own experiences have paved the way for you to truly be able to help others. You are blessed.

Love from your older self,
Rebecca Louise Lang

CHAPTER 14

The World Is
Your Oyster

Tara Nelson

Dear Tara,

I want to savour you at 10 ... so carefree, loving life. You're totally yourself right now, unencumbered by life's worries and responsibilities, an absolute cutie, little and blonde and hazel eyed. Growing up in a country seaside town, the beach – only a block away – will become your sanctuary. Still is your sanctuary today, even as I write this.

You learn early on to enjoy friendships where they arise, knowing that one day they might be gone. Mrs Malaise, for instance, the little 80-year-old who called out to you from her balcony one day on your way back from the beach, and who you enjoyed tea parties and Minties with ... Mrs Malaise, who wasn't well and needed to rest with oxygen, a service you became accustomed to performing for her. Mrs Malaise, who one day in your future will be gone, devastating you.

Many people will come and go in your life, Tara, and it's really a life privilege to have these experiences. They will prepare you to relate to and have empathy for the many people you will one day come to help, to be able to understand them as they go through their own lives.

You've had such a blessed life so far – what some might believe a *perfect* childhood. I want you to stay like this forever. To be free and unencumbered and able to say whatever you'd like to say – but perhaps with a tad more tact. At the moment, saying what you want to say always seems to come out wrong and get you into trouble, but I promise, Tara, that particular 'gift' is one you'll develop over time. You'll be 50 years old and still upsetting people with your words. The difference is that now, at this age, you'll know your truth, that your words come from your heart, and if someone is offended, well, that's just a life lesson for them. Knowing this wisdom will make life so very much easier. In fact, you'll use this unique gift of yours in your line of work; people will actually come to you, seeking your directness and honesty and wanting to be told what they need to do.

You see, Tara, everyone sees you as this outspoken, strong force to be reckoned with – and you are! Your brother often tells you that, though you're little, you carry a big stick – and it's true, and it's who you truly are. Believe in yourself and your strength. You can stand up for yourself and speak your truth, even though sometimes, it doesn't feel that way, deep inside.

If you ever feel like this, Tara, talk to someone. It will make life so much easier.

Because life is going to get tough.

Somewhere along the way, you'll lose your self-confidence, your strength, and your ability to speak your strong opinions when desired. I wish I knew at your age how beautiful you are, how unique and amazing. How perfect your body is, just the way it is. How many people envy that cute little body of yours. But it's going to be years before you recognise this, my love, and in the intervening time, from, oh, about age 14 to about age 24, you're going to go through a very tough period of your life.

It starts with your good friend. She tells you about a way to control food intake and how much you weigh. It's something she's doing – she eats, and then she makes herself sick, and voila! No weight gain. You think it's a great idea; why not give it a go?

And then it becomes an obsession, especially when people tell you how great you look, how skinny. Once you start, you'll be consumed by it, for many years – it's all you think about. Your body image will be ruined. What you see in the mirror is distorted, foreign to you. You see a girl you hate – she's short, fat, ugly, has big calves ... There's nothing you like about her, and you will do everything to try to change her. The drive and strive for perfection is pounded into your head so early, making you believe that your own, beautiful body is wrong, bad, imperfect. You see imperfection where there's perfection, feel lost despite being surrounded by love and support.

Eating disorders are real illnesses. Even once you break free, it will take a toll on you for much of the rest of your life. Destroyed teeth enamel, poor gut health, blood sugar issues, a thyroid condition ... I wish I could give you the strength not to do it, but I know that it becomes a way to handle the stressors in your life, to release your emotions, your fears, and your frustrations. I know. I remember. You're all too good at hiding things, my girl, at putting on a brave, impenetrable façade.

But when you overcome this illness – and you will, soon – you'll develop other ways to deal with stress, like meditation. Even better, meditation will become a passion of yours, something you use to help others. And, too, overcoming this illness gives you an amazing strength of character and helps you to develop empathy – your experience will allow you to help so many people later on in life.

I wish so much that you didn't have to go through all the pain, Tara, but now at 50, I wouldn't change a thing. You'll emerge from your troubles stronger, with wisdom and strength and compassion to serve many people. Your life experiences will shape your very core; you'll face down every challenge life throws at you, and come out the other side victorious, able to face the world and live a wonderful life. At the time, things will feel cruel and unfair, but your love for life, and your love of helping other people, requires life experience – pain, compassion, understanding. Believe you'll come out the other side okay. After all, you are such a tough little cookie!

Even better, once you get past this particular decade of turbulence, you're going to live a charmed life. Almost like you needed to go through this time to prepare you for your life's purpose – and how to deal with your own kids' teenage years! Your children will be such a blessing, such a gift; I can't wait until you get to meet the beautiful souls that choose you as their mother.

While your teen and early adult years will be challenging, they will also be some of the best years of your life! You will make friends with some amazing people who you will stay close to your whole life. You will have so much fun and many wonderful experiences that you'll never forget. In Year 7, you'll take a trip around Australia – your second! And while it's a great trip, it does mean you miss out on your Year 7 camp to Kalgoorlie, but just think about how lucky you are to see and explore this big, beautiful country of yours. All of that time travelling will instil in you a passion to see the world, to travel further abroad – as you will years later, with your kids and your partner.

After year 12 and TEE, you'll leave home to move to Perth and with your best friend. Freedom at last! Moving from the country to the big smoke is a bit daunting, but life will open up for you. It'll be the start of your independence. You'll meet a man who will shape your life in so many ways and give you your first real taste of falling in love; you'll never forget the first love of your life. He will also teach you a valuable lesson in love, one that everyone should learn in life: the type of person and the kind of values you really want to be with.

Then, one day, you'll be standing in an airport book shop when you see an advertisement on the back of a *Wellbeing* magazine ... and you'll have a light-bulb moment. Then you find out that there's a course, starting the next year, called Naturopathy. This four-year degree will change your life. It's like coming home. You'll meet the most extraordinary humans of your life, people who become lifelong friends. You'll seek and get the help you need for your eating disorder, and slowly emerge from your illness. That strong, powerful girl you lost sight of as a teen?

She's back.

This is your life's calling and purpose, Tara, and you will rock this world with it. This path will bring you many years of joy and happiness; over the years, you will rise as a leader in your niche, achieving success and fulfilment. You'll be an educator and a speaker – pretty awesome, right? You'll be asked to speak at events about your passion for health and wellbeing, and will find yourself helping and serving many people from all around the world. You'll find a tribe of likeminded women, and learn from and grow thanks to some amazing mentors. The opportunities are endless – especially since you're amazing, little one!

These are some of the best years of your life, Tara. In these years, you'll find yourself attracted to all things spiritual. Mrs Malaise, your childhood imaginary friend Mrs Magilicarty, and your beautiful Nan will each appear to you later in life as spiritual guides you can tune into and ask for guidance. I know at 10 this seems like a really weird concept, but you'll develop a strong spiritual practice in your forties. Crystals, tarot cards, spiritual readings ... each of these will bring a level of healing into your life. You'll embrace the woo woo – even if you can't imagine yourself as a crystal-wearing hippie right now! – and it will bring you such peace and clarity. You'll fall in love with herbal medicine, iridology, and nutrition. Finally: a way to heal yourself and also help others.

From all the struggles and challenges you encounter along your way, you'll emerge with strength and love and compassion, and you'll carry these forward into your career as a naturopath. You get through everything life throws at you because of your amazing strength of character. Even though your road will be rocky for a while, know that you will emerge on the other side a stronger and better you, with all of your life experiences a gift that enables you to better relate to all of the people you help in your career. You get through this because of your amazing strength of character, your desire to make a difference in the world – to be the change and guidance that people seek.

And so, my dear Tara, looking back … I wouldn't change a single thing.

I'm right here beside you, dear one.

Know this:

I LOVE YOU.

xx Tara

P.S. It might not seem like it right now, but your mum is your biggest fan. You and your brothers – three kids in three years! – are a wild bunch, and Mum's dealing with her own life experiences. She puts up with a lot … and she's doing her best. Besides, you have this to look forward to in *your* future, from your *own* daughters. One day she'll be your best friend, but she will always be your mum.

CHAPTER 15

What's Your Philosophy?

Donna Gabriel

Hey, Little D.

It's 2020, and 52 years have passed since you turned 10. A lot has happened since then, and even more importantly, you've *learned* a lot! I don't want to change your journey, but you should know that I think you're awesome and uniquely you – so please be kind to yourself.

There's a day in your future, when you're in your twenties, that you are asked, *What's your philosophy?*

This question never goes away.

Over time, as the years roll on from the first time you heard that question, you collect what you call *learnings* – and those *learnings* will eventually, magically morph into one kick-ass *philosophy*. I know how much you hate yourself and your life right now, but – and this is really important – you will grow to be someone you can love!

Hang in there, Little D. I promise that life improves.

The first nine

How lucky were you to get through those first nine years? Your life was so full of food allergies, asthma, bronchitis, and eczema – caused by stress, diet, and every product you touched. Mum would warn you – 'Donna, that's got peanuts in it'; 'Someone's mowing the lawn; go inside'; 'Sit in the front or you'll get carsick!' – but despite her warnings, she was up most nights, calling the midnight doctor when there was nothing more she could do. You'd pass out in Children's Emergency, waking in the ward, drip in arm, and peering through an oxygen tent.

Remember, the massive, painful boils that came from the Chinese medicine man that Mum took you to see? You hated him for them, and hated her, too ... for a minute. The good news, Little D, is that years later, other natural therapists will agree that the boils were a turning point; once you've had them, never again. Yay!

Such a deep thinker, full of bravado and cheek – you'll learn to bluff your way into, and out of, so many exciting and even scary situations. But you can also be incredibly sensitive; how many times were you crushed by one acid comment, or even a look? It could set your head chatter back miles. In an effort to understand what happened, you might re-enact for hours, and then prepare for every imaginable future scenario. All in front of the mirror. Though this playacting is useful sometimes, please know there are still worlds out there that you've never imagined.

Be careful, Little D. Listen to your heart.

Grade 4 takes you from perfect student, hungry for learning, to cynical rebel finding any opportunity to distract and entertain. The education system let you down; Miss Read, for instance, was frightening, and definitely shouldn't have been allowed near children. Leave Miss Read behind – new school, new beginnings!

People will say you have great legs; hear them, even if all you see is how short they are. No, they'll never be Shirley MacLaine or Cyd Cherise legs, but they stand you well and keep you dancing; love them. You can list your faults so easily, it has you worrying if you'll make any new friends at Kilvington. Please, D, hear me; other people won't care about the things you worry about. They will enjoy your smile and energy, your interest in people and life. And you won't be the only one with head chatter; many will also be busy worrying through their own.

Did you know that you breathe all wrong? It's creating a barrel chest and all of your shoulder and neck tension. Not sure how

Mum or Dad found Vijay Yogendra, but he sure grows you. Thick with sandalwood and sitar, his Yoga Education Centre is the only yoga school in Melbourne. A truly gentle, smiling Indian Adonis, Vijay teaches you to breathe, and learning to breathe will help in so many ways ... although it's the junk food that makes you ping off the rails in hyperactive rants! Please practise *'Thanks, I'll have water.'* It becomes easier; you'll never really be happy, or well, until you do. When you hear, *'What a lovely smile!'* That's a compliment, say thank you.

Vijay also instils in you an ability to listen to your body – true understanding of why you return to the breath and posture, yoga and stillness, for resilience and calm. The yoga comes easy, complimenting your calisthenics and dance. The new culture is fascinating. It works.

Best thing? You feel asthma coming on ... and then you meditate, and it's gone. It's like a miracle!

Psst, secret! Dad's taking you to see *The Monkees*, live at Festival Hall really soon! You are going to love it so much!

LEARN TO BREATHE; HEAL YOURSELF

Wellness = catch up

Yoga plus Ventolin = WELL! The more 'well' you feel, the more you want to do. After all those years of eczema and asthma and allergies and bronchitis, you've finally got a life to live and plenty of lost time to catch up on.

You're forever mingling two lives into one; as a teenager, it's a week full of dance, drama, calisthenics, and learnings before a coastal weekend of sun, surf, mischief – and some different kinds of learnings. With a dose of puberty, you find heaps of new interests: Boys! Music! Theatre! Parties! Boys! Art! Boys!

If life is a line-graph, yours is a roller-coaster. You love to ask why, to rock the boat, keep it fair. Be that rebel ... but always be kind. A couple of defining moments are coming up, where you hate yourself to a new level, for being mean; it's not worth it. Give love. Be kind. Help others.

Also, let go of perfection. All the 'perfect' people you love will be beamed up to heaven way too soon. If the good die young, then stay a bit grubby, to hang around a whole lot longer. Leave the stress of straight A's to your sis – B+ is awesome.

BREATHE AND BE LIKE YOUR BLOOD TYPE: B+

Baptist school

At Kilvington, you think it's funny that you and your sister are 'the girls from the broken home,' because it now seems normal for you. Dad was never home, anyway, so when he left, it made no difference. In fact, "Every second Sunday" outings are cool! Living the '70's dream, Dad thinks he's James Bond; good fun, just not fatherly. More a friend? Apparently, his Dad was really mean, so you are doing fine. You've blamed yourself for breaking up Mum and Dad. Then you blamed Nana. Then NanaG. A Scottish Protestant and a Sicilian Catholic, both colourful, hilarious, and interfering ... but neither broke up Mum and Dad. No one did. Dad was brave enough to live his truth and leave, rather than pretending. And isn't Mum amazing? You never saw her cry or complain ... though you did hear her crying on the phone sometimes, after bedtime.

Your school's values are not your own, in any case. You already know Mum is all you need in a parent.

And, funnily enough, by Year 10, half your mate's parents have broken up; you show them that life goes on!

It's a long eight years at Kilvington, not least because you're allergic to the wool uniform – plus, Baptists don't dance! In pursuit of modesty, even cartwheels are curtailed, lest travellers on passing trains sight your undies.

During those long years, Miss Sampson's art room is your saviour. If you didn't talk so much and keep getting thrown out each year, the Choir might have been, too. Keep singing anyway; you love it, and it's great for your lungs.

KEEP BREATHING AND LEARNING

Year 12

By the end of Year 12, you've found your groove between naughty and entertaining, cheeky but not offensive. It's fun! Play there, Donna! You can make social comment and instigate new learnings, even positive change, when your head is in this place. Here, you take on real responsibility for the first time. No thank you to Prefect status; instead, you run with House Captain and magazine editor, both fun creative *learnings*. Training all your house teams to incredible success, you even conduct the Choir to blitz the first House Chorals!

And it's the end of Year 12 when you find purpose; a degree exists for Drama and Dance! Finally, head down in class; there's no time for homework! Work Friday night and Saturday morning, ballroom (or should I say boyroom) Thursday, Calisthenics Tuesday and Saturday. Then, IF AT ALL POSSIBLE, straight to Pt Lonsdale for sun, surf, and sex!

(Whoops ... did I say that out loud?)

BREATHE AND GROW ME INTO THE ME I LOVE

Bachelor of Education

Studying Drama and Dance in the seventies is an experience like no other, and you'll find yourself challenged more than you could have imagined. You squeeze in as many productions and theatrical experiences as possible, unwilling to waste a moment. The Packer Wacker Tracker tour, through Victoria is a hilarious, wonderful highlight; running dance programs in schools during the day, then performing the Pub Show at night; lots of comedy routines followed by the band; which you're in, of course. Such good fun.

Some major takeaways?

You choose excellence and leave competition behind.

You are way too sensitive to dance all day into mirrors.

You prefer the coast to inland.

When you don't live by your word, your head chatter is punishing.

You dance yourself a degree!

BREATHE AND REMEMBER YOUR LEARNINGS

All is well in my world

Not sure if you remember that someone once told you that you were the sum of your thoughts. You were furious, because it just isn't fair that you can't even think whatever you want!

But when you accept this learning, you'll set out on a journey to actively choose positive head chatter words. I know, it takes time, a bit like when you train yourself to change your handwriting. And it can be hard. But in the end, I have to tell you, changing habits and things you don't like about yourself will become a favourite pastime, because it's about learning to like yourself.

And it's pretty exciting.

BREATHE: I AM CONFIDENT, STRONG, CREATIVE, HAPPY, HEALTHY, WEALTHY, KIND, AND BEAUTIFUL

I CAN be, do, have anything... just not everything

Life in your twenties, Ms Social Animal, is full on! Allergies to makeup, hairspray, and tan take away the fun of performing. Instead, you turn to teaching, choreographing, directing, MC, coaching, stage managing ... and then you'll drive to Lonnie for parties, late nights, parties, early morns, parties, missed meals, parties, boys, parties, love triangles, and more, if that's even possible!

Over and over you will learn that while you might want to do it all – you can't.

Yes, you prioritise and manage your time incredibly well, but nothing can replace taking time out to rest and re-fuel. Be gentle on yourself, Donna. It's not a race. You can take your time.

There's a point in your twenties where you'll have the gut-wrenching realisation that what people think about your friends ... is also likely what people think of you. The idea that people might think poorly of you, when you feel that you're much nicer than quite a few of your friends, prompts you to get fussier around who you spend your time with. And what your idea of 'fun' is.

Great idea, Little D!

Realising it's not about fate, but rather about choice, you begin to look at others more for their values than what they do or say. Over time, you gravitate towards incredibly diverse and wonderful people; many become treasured lifelong friends. They are like a cocoon, a buffer between you and that enormous unknown world out there. Lucky and blessed are you.

BREATHE AND CHOOSE FRIENDS WISELY

Be here now

Over time, as you learn from naturopaths, kinesiologists, and many other '-ists' how to understand your allergies, intolerances, and overall *weirdo-ness*, you discover your ability to choose *positive change*: training your brain to love people, foods, and lifestyles that suit you, while leaving behind those that make you itch.

Living in the now is a revelation.

Instead of: *What went wrong? What will happen next?*

Let's use: *What went right? What's my next exciting adventure?*

Leaving behind your guilt for the past and your fear of the future, you find joy and stillness in the now.

What if? What if you choose fun, fulfilling futures, now?

Well, you'll find yourself in Europe on your own terms, flying solo with the motto of 'no guilt, no fear' and taking some real risks – mostly heart-centred and wonderful.

BREATHE: NOW IS MY POINT OF POWER; LIVE WITHOUT JUDGMENT; NO GUILT, NO FEAR; LISTEN TO YOUR HEART

Love

Learn about boys while you're little, D. Boys are just people - so completely different from you and yet just the same, all at once. It's not just about their different bits. In your ten years, you've known so few boys … sisters, cousins (all girls), both Nans (no grandfathers). And calisthenics is all-girls, as is your school. That's a lot of feminine energy! So do try to get to know more boys before you start dating – easier said than done, but give it a go!

Falling in love is amazing, wondrous and indescribable; you'll fall in love twice in your twenties! Both times, it feels like there's nothing else of importance in your life – enjoy it while you can!

And then remind yourself that life does, actually go on when relationships end.

Imagine something for me. Imagine your life as a pizza. (I know, it sounds silly!) In this pizza-shaped life, love is only one slice. It's not your entire life. There are so many more slices: your physical, spiritual, and social health; your *learnings*; our *earnings*. When you 'specialise,' some pizza slices are neglected; your head chatter doubles and your health and inner happiness plummet. For a full and complete life, we all need to regularly nurture ALL slices of our pizza.

As you learn to choose your words more wisely, and ask much more useful questions, Dad's words finally ring true:

No bastard will look after you but you, Donna.

No one but you knows if you are happy or living your truth. Be kind – especially to yourself.

BREATHE: FEED ALL PIZZA SLICES; CHOOSE EACH DIRECTION; ONLY UP FROM HERE!

Two worlds marry and collide

Okay. This is the hardest bit for me to write. When your beach romance comes to the city. And never leaves. You clearly needed *learnings* from this marriage experience, but gaining them ... it's harder than you could ever imagine from where you are now.

I can tell you that it won't all be bad; after all, you'll celebrate your son's first year with joy. Your beautiful son and his younger sister change your life beyond your most wondrous imagination. It's pure joy, like popping a bow atop your parenting journey.

Nothing can ever prepare you for being a mother: it's its own incomparable experience. The love and lifetime commitment come without a blink. It's hard, and you will make mistakes, just as all parents do, but please know, your love and determination get you through when times are overwhelming. And never one regret – just two beautiful bubs and heaps of new learnings.

BREATHE: YOU DON'T KNOW WHAT YOU DON'T KNOW; WE DON'T ALL THINK THE SAME

YOU CAN ONLY CHANGE YOURSELF; BE YOUR BEST 'DONNA'

Single mum, healing

Strength and tenacity save you and your two rabbits from a marriage of total insanity, heading further down your *Graph of Life*. Despite never having imagined yourself as a mother, you were clearly born to be one. Your two children, both individually and collectively, change your world for the better, even with the pain and worry. As a parent, you are a lifer, just like your mum, Dawnie. Who is still going strong at 90, by the way! Rejecting the guilt of religion, she is still humble, true, and good in every way; I believe she WILL go to heaven. She says she took the Ten Commandments and left the rest. Not a bad idea? The inspiration from and gratitude you continue to hold for Dawnie is indescribable. You know already, what she has put up with! Sorry Mum! Thanks Mum!

Wait until you meet Vito! Your kids still think he was your boyfriend; he isn't, but the love is real. A dear friend and mentor, thanks to him, you add *BEAUTIFUL* to your *I am*; you dance through days, not just class. Early on, he comments with surprise, that you're quite educated; his honesty doesn't offend. Appearing 'educated' isn't your priority; clarity for connection is. Vito introduces you to the world of incarcerated women. Yes, really! You teach in our women's max-security prison – zoning in on your *why* to *touch your truth*. Each class recipe is clear. To attend:

> *We agree to read, write, share, listen, consider,*
> *learn and leave feeling better than when we arrived.*

Inspired by author Louise Hay, you spend evenings writing a recipe for a man – your man.

And would you look at that – a man appeared, so fast! Exactly what you asked for … and also *married*. Noooo! Start again!!

A tweak of the recipe, with the all-important 'AND SINGLE!' scrawled across the bottom of the page. BANG! Introducing Peter! Less than a year later comes the merging of your families – with two kids each, you're nearly the Brady Bunch.

And, Little D, this is important: 25 years and we're still going strong.

BREATHE, DANCE; WRITE VERY CLEAR RECIPES

Calisthenics

You never stop! But why?

I think it was my life force.

No matter what, you'll be there. Passion keeps you tidy, even saves you: the people, teams, performances, forever friendships, unwavering dedication. For 34 years, you eat, breathe, and sleep Emmanuel Calisthenics, coaching teams into the elite Championship Grade, as an alien non-champ gal! You are deemed naughtiest coach to cleverest, and back again, many times, shunned or adored for radical choreography, costumes, and song choices.

At Royal South Street Eisteddfod, when you arrive with a ghetto blaster and ask for a power point, the stage crew stare blankly at you as they ask, 'Where is your pianist?!'

Priceless.

BREATHE: ENJOY THE RIDE

Gold

Enough, you say. No more Cals. But a year later, you miss it more than imagined. You miss it enough that, on a whim, you and Ronice Ritter, open GOLD Cali Masters, aligning yourselves with a local existing club, Kingston Calisthenics.

For 10 years now, you and Roni together have attracted a divine calibre of woman: your Goldies, who bring home more medals from the PanPacific Masters Games than you could have imagined! What a way to move and groove into your Golden years! You'll love the RoniDoni Thing, Little D!

BREATHE AND BELIEVE: WE ARE THE SUM OF OUR PARTS

Teach, create, motivate

Yes, things get better. You won't always be sitting at your window, watching people pass by while improvising scenarios in your room for the social life and entertainment you dream of. You're building resilience, patience, an ability to find the positive that motivates you and others, forever!

Teaching drama 'Down in Monterey' High makes a woman out of you. A bunch of divine students run with your crazy ideas; it just works! These treasures flood back into your life, years later, with the invention of a crazy thing called Facebook – but that's another story.

'Retiring' from Monday to Friday, you head off, carving out your 'Donna' career, which is always project-based and enormous fun, if at all possible. Just as your early days were split between city and beach, you blend careers between education, theatre, and events.

Head chatter and playing out every possibility in mirrors finally becomes useful in The Doris Ice Cream Show – the one-woman play that YOU write and tour through schools! Doris rehearses her life in her bedroom and then barges out into the world to stuff it up with over-excitement and expectation. Yes, Donna, you know Doris well. You thrive creatively in supportive environments but shrivel into babbling head chatter when plans go pear-shaped. If someone is mean about you or wants your job, you tend to back off, let them have it, find something else.

Pure arts feel somehow indulgent; you prefer melding creativity into learning to build happier lives.

BREATHE; DANCE EACH MOMENT

When you are invited to create a relationship program, Social Impact, for adults with special needs, your careers finally and wonderfully combine. Your days pass with training and events based on meeting people, making friends, even finding love. You joke that you have a PhD in partying, and so of course it's your duty to share your knowledge! Social situations play out dramatically; ethics are debated. As your confidence builds, new friends are made.

You can play here forever.

BREATHE; TEACH TO REMEMBER

DGC stands alone

These days, now that you're grown up, you live to nourish all slices of your pizza, encouraging others to do the same. You write, teach, produce events, choreograph, coach one-on-one, and consult. Your regular events – After Hours, the Social Club, and precious Beaui Beach Dancers – have a life of their own.

Daily, you aim to *feed the animal you are*. Nourish, be kind, learn, and grow. You love your garden, the salty, sandy beach, sweaty dance classes, and the joy of a home-cooked meal. You never stop consciously looking for balance. A fire walk experience doubles your *I can* attitude. And, adding Russian Creator Knowledge and 'conscious concentration' to your *bag of tricks*, you can't help but feel grateful for the diverse life that is yours.

BREATHE; CHOOSE LIFELONG LEARNING

One life, this life

Little D, you're gonna FLY! The bad bits, the good bits – you need to experience them all. Life is still a roller-coaster, but as you grow, your Doris chatter chooses to be YOUR BEST FRIEND, and you come to enjoy the ride. Feeling more capable, happy and healthy through the years, appreciating the beautiful people weaving through the worlds you choose – well. It's a blessed journey.

BREATHE; LIVE IT; LOVE IT; DANCE IT

Finally, in 2020, what's your philosophy?

BREATHE 'N FLOURISH IN HARMONY

Xx Bigger D / Donna Gabriel

CHAPTER 16

Your Dad, Your Hero
Charlie Giles

Dear 10-year-old Charlie,

I see you, I hear you, I know you …

I would love to wrap my arms around you and give you a big squeeze, one of those hugs that almost hurts but feels so good.

I've wanted to let you know for a long time now that you are loved, that everything really will be okay, even if right now it seems a bit scary. You aren't a baby anymore; you are a grown-up girl. Well, at least you feel like it every time you announce how old you are to the world. But now that I look at you, I see how young and innocent you still are and how brave you have already been for such a little human. I want you to know that I am so very proud of you, and this letter is written with an open heart with so much love for who you've become.

You're missing your dad right now and feeling so alone without your big brothers around. It's just you and mum and the new dad, right? It's not the family you grew up with and definitely not the family you wanted.

Let's go back to when you were just 5 years old …

You were so little, but there was a moment you remember so vividly because it changed everything. You came running into the lounge room from playing outside. Mum was sitting on the lounge, hunched over, her head cradled over a large porcelain dish that she was holding up to her face. You were curious to see what she was doing, so you hitched yourself up on your tippy toes to look inside and saw a river of bright red blood, filling up the bowl as it flowed from Mum's face. You look straight into her eyes with a wide-eyed stare, and she looks straight back at you without words, wincing at a swollen smile.

As your eyes searched her face for answers, you were suddenly whisked away by Aunty Marie, who threw you over her shoulder and said, 'Come on, you, let's go to my house.' As she brushed past your dad, you remember he turned his back on you, burying his head in his hands ...

And that was the day that became etched in your memory as the day your dad went away.

But now you're ten, and here you are reading this letter ...

Wondering why your dad left and why he doesn't want to see you anymore ...

And I know it haunts you.

You're wondering what you did wrong to make him go away.

I know that you cry into your pillow at night so Mum doesn't hear. She would be upset if you didn't call this new man 'Dad' like she says you have to.

You don't want to start fresh with a new life, when you were happy with the one you had. You miss your friends and your old home and yes, I know, you really miss your dad.

The hardest part about being 10 is that everyone keeps telling you how grown up you are now, but nobody really tells you what's going on because you're too young.

You know just enough to know something is wrong, but nobody tells you the truth in any detail. So you end up making up the story in your head, based only on what you assume to be accurate.

And Charlie ... this is exactly why I wanted to write this letter to you ...

So that you know the truth.

First of all, you WILL see your dad again one day.

It won't be the magical moment you dream about, but it will happen. You're going to have to wait another six long years to see him, which isn't going to be easy, but you will make it through ...

And, eventually, you will understand why all this had to happen the way it did.

Listen to me, Charlie ... I want you to understand something very important ...

I don't want you to think for a second that there is ever an 'okay reason' for a man to hit a woman.

In fact, for anyone to hit anyone.

But it happens. It can be the event that changes everything, and, sometimes, it can just keep being chaos. Either way it's **never** okay ... I know you are going to struggle with this thought pattern for many years to come, so this is my way of settling something for you.

During those six years of not knowing why your dad didn't call, you will make yourself believe that it's because he didn't love you ...

You'll make yourself believe that you're not worth the visit, and you'll continue to think that you're not worth much to anyone for a really big part of your life.

This thought pattern you create for yourself will become a belief that stays with you and infects every part of how you view yourself in the world.

How much effort you put into your school work, what kind of jobs you put yourself forward for, even the kind of boys you end up 'going around with.'

I know the idea of having a boyfriend is gross at the moment, but that will change. Sadly, you don't do so well at picking ones that are good for you.

Eventually, you'll rebuild your relationship with your dad, but it'll be hard work. He doesn't make it easy for you, but I know how much you love him and how he is your hero.

And I know you are conflicted with your values ...

After all, he did hit your mum ...

But for now, let's just put this away and be kind to yourself.

There is no guilt or shame in loving someone who has made mistakes. You will make plenty yourself, and it won't do you any good to hold grudges, so you might as well let that go.

Your dad was born into a very tough generation and the only thing he was taught well was to fight his way out of any challenging situation.

He was born during a time when Aboriginal people were not yet accepted as citizens of this country, and his mum was a 16-year-old 'half-caste' Aboriginal girl, terminology that was derogatory then and still is now, so don't ever use it, please.

His father (your granddad) was 23 years old; you must understand, this was not an ideal relationship and it meant Dad was born into a double whammy world of shame.

He doesn't have very good memories of how his father treated his mother, either ...

In fact, by the time he was 5 years old, they both copped a beating which resulted in them both being thrown out onto the street, with literally all their belongings and nowhere to go.

It was because of this and his mother's last beating that he decided he wanted to learn how to fight, so he could protect his mother.

And at 5 years old he felt helpless ...

But he was determined to start training as quickly as he could.

By the time he was 12 years old, he decided he couldn't wait any longer, so he walked into the local police station and asked to get his licence (you were meant to be 15).

The policeman gave him a wink, signed his piece of paper, and just like that, he was 15 years old. Until the day he died he kept that secret from the authorities and was always three years younger than his driver's license said.

He loves that story, and I can assure you that you will hear it many times over when you start visiting him in his senior years ...

Just pretend to be surprised every single time he tells it because you love how he chuckles at himself for getting away with it.

The very same day he got his illegal piece of paper, he walked into the local PCYC and jumped into the boxing ring.

He couldn't wait to learn how to fight, and his strongest motivation was to protect his family. The only family he had was his mother.

Imagine a wiry 12-year-old kid jumping into the ring and boxing with 15- and 16-year-old boys.

The way he tells the story, he would sometimes get knocked down but always got up and kept fighting. Nobody could knock him out.

Charlie, if there's one thing you get from this story, let it be this …

Don't let anyone knock you out. Always get back up.

Well, guess what?

His mother eventually did meet a lovely man who became your dad's stepfather, who you now know as Pop.

And it wasn't long before he had a new family of his own as well …

He had a new sister (your aunty Jax) and a new brother (your uncle Michael).

But your dad would never really feel like he fit in or belonged anywhere.

This era held a long-time hostility towards anyone of Aboriginal descent, and this kind of shame can't help but get handed down to your children.

Intergenerational trauma sounds like a big bunch of words now, but it's a real thing that you'll go on to learn more about – and it will be something which helps you heal as you get much older.

His mother used to bleach her skin white to fit in and was forbidden to see her own mother because she was so black.

His father threw him out on the street like garbage, and his mother is not even classed as a citizen.

All these events are going to have a traumatic effect on what you think of yourself, and so Dad wasn't able to be the best role model as a father.

Your dad's luck eventually changed, and he was raised to become a strong, hard-working, tough-as-nails kind of guy. He judged everyone by how hard they worked and how much money they made. But he hated people who tried to bullshit him.

One of his favourite sayings was always, "You can't bullshit a bullshitter.'

Your dad could detect the slightest whiff of BS from miles away, and he would call you out or shut you down, depending on how many beers he'd already had.

While he was harmless in many ways, his death stare could kill a zombie.

He was one of the most misunderstood humans I've ever had the pleasure of knowing.

And the reason why I'm telling you all this . . .

Because you spend way too much of your life desperately wanting him to be proud of you, desperately wondering if he loved you, and always feeling crazy guilty for loving him and respecting him despite how terrible he was as a husband and a father.

It's going to take you years of heartache, tears, and, eventually, his death before you realise that despite his inability to know love, show love, or even understand what being a good father was meant to look like ...

He loved you so much it scared him.

The emotion of love was so foreign to him that it's the very reason he distanced himself from all of us and why he used alcohol to numb the loss of it.

It was he who thought he wasn't good enough for you.

It was he who felt the shame of what he had done.

It was he who was consumed by guilt because he had broken his own promise to himself and become the exact version of his dad that he himself despised.

He ends up never forgiving himself and literally drinks himself to death.

Again – his actions and behaviours towards your mum are never okay, but that event isn't who your dad was.

He was an incredible human with a big heart – bigger than Phar Lap.

And I miss him now even while I'm writing this to you.

I know you miss him, too, but you will spend so much precious time together – I promise.

And he will love you for every second of effort you put into making that happen.

Whenever you hug him, make sure you hang on just a little tighter than the time before.

Make sure you tell him that you love him because it will make him squirm and grizzle but warm his heart.

Make sure you listen to all his crazy stories, even though you have heard them all before, because one day you will be sitting down to type yourself a letter ...

Just wishing that you could hear one of those crazy stories all over again.

But most of all, tell him that he was the best dad he could be …

And, given time all over again, you wouldn't want any other dad but him.

Forgive him – because he really did the best job he could.

And he loved you the best way he knew how.

Most of all – forgive yourself for all the guilt you're feeling now and will feel in the future …

Because despite what you're thinking right now …

And what you will struggle with as you grow up …

Remember that he didn't do such a bad job of raising you after all –

Because as I look in the mirror …

It looks like you turned out okay to me.

Lots of love,
Charlie x

CHAPTER 17

Magic Outside the Square

Maria McDonald

Dear Maria,

Wow, 10! Yay! You made it! You have been counting down to this age for some time, as having two digits really is growing up.

Your new home is beautiful. You have recently moved to a new farm, far away from where you lived your whole life, away from family and your friends. This is quite a change for you, and you miss everyone. Your parents moved you from a very isolated community to give you kids the opportunities that they never had. They didn't want you to have to go to boarding school. Heads up – don't get too excited about the possibility of boarding school after reading the Malory Towers or St Clare's books by Enid Blyton; this won't be your path!

Your parents work for everything they have, and as you get older, you have a strong sense of honour in achieving for yourself that sense of independence. You want to do well at school, and in those IQ tests; you want to be a doctor. Or an ambulance driver. Because you like helping people and you want to drive and it seems exciting. And you want to make your parents proud. You do, but you should also be proud of yourself.

You live from food on the land – good, unprocessed food. Your dad milks a cow every day and there are chooks and eggs. You have a cooked breakfast every morning. You ride horses and motorbikes and have a swimming pool and trampoline. When you are older, you work hard to get this lifestyle for your own children so they can enjoy the beautiful childhood that you had.

One day, your dad and brother fall off their motorbikes, get really grazed up on the road and need to go to hospital. They are alright, just cuts and bruises, but it will scare and upset you. This is your first experience of trauma, and when you have your first cup of tea. It is when you learn that a good cup of tea in the kitchen fixes everything. There will be more trauma in the future, and you'll find yourself at the heart of nurturing those around you, making many cups of tea, and providing a lot of wise counsel.

You are happy and grateful. A true little Pollyanna, always seeing the good in life, wanting to be good, wanting to please, and determined to be a success. Keep seeing the positives and wearing your rose-coloured glasses; it is one of your superpowers.

You can't wait to grow up. You want independence. You want your own grown-up life, so you can show how amazing you are going to be. And you want it now. You are impatient and in a hurry. This impatience never leaves you; it's a trait that means you do not suffer fools. You do not tolerate shonky situations and you get out of pickles pretty quickly. Be proud of your impatience. You are here on a mission and you need to win fast, learn fast, and move fast to where you need to be. Actually, more accurately, to move to where you *are needed*. Because you are here to be impactful. Make every contact count, and don't underestimate the impact you have on others.

Your wee country school is cute, and your year has seven girls and seven boys. There are great games like bullrush and candlesticks on the field, and there's monkey bars to hang on and swing from. The biggest challenge for you is in the friendship space. Seven girls is a difficult number, as however you break up the number seven, there is always one girl left over, on the outer, and it's a bit unfair because that is usually you.

Being on the outer – whether you like it or not – will remain with you. Don't see this as a bad thing. Magic happens outside the square. People think the magic is by being in the in-crowd, but it's not. Magic needs space and freedom. You don't create your own magic when you stay safe and meet the expectations of others. You have a life of magic ahead. Believe in yourself, and the magic will follow.

While experiencing being an outer of the crowd, you discovered an escape place within yourself. You will spend increasing time in your life inside your head, like a movie ... you call it daydreaming; you know it as nothing else. This is the most delicious place in the world, and it will remain so forever. The more mundane the activity the better, as it is easier to flick into this place. You can float away into a beautiful make-believe world, with visions and homemade movie scenes and scenarios of full colour that you can follow and be content in. You can even set the question or focus for the dream. You can unwind bits and reset it. Doing the dishes, in the shearing shed, picking or packing fruit, riding the horse, playing the piano. These activities are amazing for this escape. And this is your gift. It is incredibly powerful. You will be afraid of what this is, and of the power of your dreams. You feel its power but don't know what to do with it. Don't be afraid. Trust what this gift is; know that this is your intuitive world, always with you. It is another of your superpowers. The sooner you realise and embrace this, the more amazing your life will be. You will never get more than you can handle; just know that.

And your humming! You don't even realise you're doing it – non-stop humming of music. Whether it's the new music you've learnt at piano lessons, or from an advert on the radio, or the last thing you heard, or the song from music at school. Or just some random song from somewhere. Let me tell you, you will still be humming at 50, and it's beautiful. You get so many intuitive messages from your humming and your visions and daydreaming.

Anyway, back to the friendship thing. Others will follow the crowd, the trends, be led by what others say or think. Don't be like them; don't buy into other people's expectations. You have what you need within you. You don't need to follow anyone else's formula of how to get that job, be successful, or get a boyfriend. Do it your way. Your way is best. Back yourself, listen to your heart and follow it; your heart really does not put you wrong. You are the lead role. This life is your life; you must be you.

You will eventually learn that overthinking things just drags you down. Going over and over, framing things more and more negatively, churning, blaming yourself, getting stuck in self-blame, and making yourself the villain in your life story does not make you happy. So please catch yourself when you do this, and choose to feel love and listen to your heart, not your head. Listening to your heart means feeling emotions with your body, noticing the flutters in your tummy or the tightness in your throat or the tingling of your hands. It means feeling your feelings and noticing when they are reacting.

You, my darling, are unique. You have gifts and are here to create new pathways. You won't realise for some time that being outside the main crowd is a strength. Does it help to know that following this path of your own involves you becoming a trusted advisor and guide to future change makers and global leaders? How amazing is that! You will bring heart, intuition, and healing to help raise the level of humanity. For you to achieve this, you need to be you: The world needs you.

It takes a while to love who you are, what you have, and feel comfy in your shoes. You feel left out for ages from strong female friendships. The barrier you put up strengthens your resolve for independence and operating on your own. That's okay. Some special friends will remain from your teens, and they will be there for you through thick and thin. And as you strengthen your intuitive business networks, you make the most amazing kindred connections that are beyond one lifetime of friendships! So don't even break a sweat worrying about what you can do to change yourself, questioning why you're a bad friend, or thinking anything is wrong with you for not having a girl gang. Nothing is wrong with you! Your girl gang comes along a bit later, and is like a boss-witch gang – watch out world when you meet this sisterhood!

In your teens, you will start to have dreams. Scary as dreams. Out-of-your-body type dreams. Tell yourself that these are cool, not scary, and feel free to tell yourself to have a night off dreams every now and again when you need rest. You can manage yourself – dreams are a tool – but they should not dictate your sleep or make you freak out.

Around this same time, you start being successful, like becoming hockey team captain, being asked to consider doing a scholarship, and getting leadership roles. You are recognised as a leader. This success, along with the dreams, starts to scare you. Not on the surface, but in your head, you are starting to panic about what you wished for; you are not sure you are worthy of this. The dreams start freaking you out. You read late into the night to switch off the dreams.

And not long after the dreams kick in, you start self-sabotaging your success. You don't try as hard. Underneath it, you want to be liked, and you have a belief that successful people are not liked; they are nerds or geeks and are excluded. So, you peg yourself back, trying not to stand out.

And then, you find alcohol. Alcohol makes you feel good, successfully stops the dreams, takes away the success fears, and, would you believe it, provides instant friendships. It's amazing how friendly everyone in a pub is, and how friendly they are after a few drinks. What a eureka moment for you! You have lots of fun, take lots of risks, and you surround yourself with others who are the same, so it's okay, right?

But in reality, you pay a high price. You learn a lot of lessons, as your drinking mantra of Go Hard or Go Home does not always end well for you. And this successfully diverts you from bringing your full self to the world for way too long.

The reason you keep drinking for so long is that, on the face of it, you manage to have it all. Work hard, play hard, and all that the drinking culture values. But eventually, your world crumbles, and you realise that it is not about getting through things by drinking – maybe what you're going through is because of your drinking. You have a lightbulb moment where you realise that there is no amount of drinking that can get you through this one, as you are at the end of the drinking road. Good drinking has gone bad, and your number one priority is just to get through daily life, never mind any major life challenges. You realise that if you choose to take the drinking path to cope, you will lose your family, along with your job, your dignity, and your self-respect. This is not the person you want to be, or the person you are.

You go cold turkey, never to drink again.

You should be super proud of this achievement. It's a silent one. An achievement which receives no awards or publicity, but one that was done by you, for you. The biggest achievements in life are the deeply personal changes we make.

Stopping drinking in the end isn't the hardest part. Once you decide to do it, you have the commitment to stop, and you stop. The challenge really is in the discoveries about yourself after stopping drinking. You realise that drinking has been disguising the fact that you need to rebuild yourself from the foundation, as you are in fact quite emotionally stunted.

You lack the courage to be honest with yourself, let alone others, and to be vulnerable and really express yourself. In fact, it becomes clear that somewhere along the line you stopped loving yourself, and that you questioned whether in fact you were worthy of being loved at all. This is a time of internal despair. But you make the best choice ever. You lean in.

You decide to feel everything rather than numb things with alcohol. You want to experience life fully, with all the ups and downs, and you want to read all the signs and know yourself much more wholly. You meditate, you find your dreams again, and you use your intuition, reconnecting your experiences and skills in a much different way.

You go within to find those answers. You invest in yourself rather than the wine bottle. You take courses to use these skills, and you find your girl gang. They are your life force.

You do this for you. Because you finally realise that you cannot be the best mother, wife, daughter, healer unless you are the best you. And if you are not healed first, you cannot heal others.

Slowly you learn to love you. You learn to express yourself, and to communicate about things that actually matter. You can finally have meaningful connections with others, and you start to see that you are loveable and that people like being with you. You start to feel the love of others, and it feels real. It's felt right in the heart; it's not words. Guess what? This is you being your true self.

Your commitment to a journey of self-development leads you to take responsibility for yourself, and to question what your purpose really is and how you can make a difference to the world. This is hard work. But worth it. It will see you through anything. With every trauma and pain that follows – and believe me, it comes – you face it with heart and grace. Oh, my god, I am so proud of the woman you become, the things you work through, and the heart you have. You are a true goddess.

You take responsibility for your own growth, but you also gather the tools to help others and apply to other situations. Helping other women move from pain to empowerment, and to be their best, too. It's not an easy journey, but things worth fighting for never are easy. You are worth fighting for. So are the changes the world needs.

What an amazing kid you are!

You don't need to prove anything to anyone. You are already cherished and adored, just by being you!! You have such amazing gifts. You, my darling, are unique. Don't hurry, honey. Your journey will come, just as it is meant to be. You just keep on humming and dreaming. Be proud of yourself – you are a goddess. Know that you have your own back, every step of the way. Everything will be okay – more than okay. In fact, it will be perfect, and just for you.

Be in your own corner, have your own back, love yourself.

Love from your future self xxxx

CHAPTER 18

Northern Rivers

Luke Amery

Good morning, young Luke.

Let me shake your hand – and don't be concerned! I'm the grown-up version of yourself., at the ripe old age of 40 and I've come to help you think about some situations you will encounter in life.

Let's take a drive to the small suburb of Palm Vale, on the outer slopes of Murwillumbah in the beautiful Northern Rivers of NSW. This part of your childhood, living on this small farm, will plant the seeds of your life and stay in your mind forever!

As we get closer to your farm gate, look at the little white house on your right. That's where you'll meet Paul and learn how to play Atari. You two will think you're just the best experts at this game! But along with learning video games, within this family, you will also learn the meaning of supporting your neighbours when in need and helping those who are worse off than you.

Lot 88, on your left, is your farm. The timber support posts of the metal gate still need some attention, as they always have, but that's okay. The gate still opens to let us in and out, and on a farm it's what's good for the job at hand that matters, not how pretty something looks.

Across the road is a farmer called Jacko – a lovely old chap. You'll often spend time here after school and weekends, rushing about in the grassy fields and watching the adults tend the cattle, feeding, dipping, and getting them ready for sale. As you watch, you learn that jobs get done more quickly when everyone co-operates and knows their part of the work. This is a good life lesson to learn.

It's a bit of a winding drive uphill to the farmhouse, and the gravel is slippery after the rain. After heavy rain, the only way to the farmhouse is with a 4WD or on foot. So, you'll slip-slide your way up and down this muddy driveway many times. And you'll love those times because, apart from having fun playing in the mud, it helps you to see that there is no such thing as perfect weather. What's good for the grass paddocks isn't so good for the gravel roads.

So here we are at the farmhouse. Before we go in, just stand still and smell the fresh clean air! And listen carefully. Can you hear the creek running after the recent rain? Can you hear the water trickle over the rocks and the wind rushing through those glorious gum trees? You will love this place especially when it gets heavy rain, as all the rainwater rushes down the hills and into the creeks at the bottom. It's a magical spot, full of nature's energy. And the creeks and streams are full of fish and turtles swimming around having an amazing time.

Your Uncle Tom will often take you fishing with your cousins. This is where you will learn how to really 'go fishing.' Even though you may not catch anything, Uncle Tom will make you aware that it's the experience and the company that count, not the number of fish you caught. From these casual, often impromptu outings, you will learn to value good friendship and shared experiences.

Let's check out the house now. Wow! Yes, mate, this place is yours – well, your parents' house, of course! That is, your mum and your stepdad. It looks massive to a little kid, doesn't it? Even though it's not much to look at (it's more like a big open shed with cupboards used to separate the rooms, than it is a house), you're really going to enjoy your time here. You'll develop a love of music from the little family telly in the lounge; this'll help calm you through some troubling times in your later life.

Righto, matey, let's step outside again and into the front yard with its wide views of country, grassy hills, and natural bushland, selectively cleared for cattle and dairy farming. Let's take a seat on the rocks under the shade of these big gums. This will be a private hidey-hole just for you. Here you can chill out, think about what's happening in your life and try to figure out answers to questions for which you won't get any closure for many years.

Sometimes you'll be incredibly sad as you think about your life, and other times you just need some time to yourself to think about things that have happened. Sitting quietly by yourself will become a habit with you as you grow older, a way to sort through some of the frantic thoughts that, at times, go round and round inside your head.

Let's start doing that now, shall we? Let's see if we can sort out some of your questions now – and, of course, the big question for you is your biological father and the real reason he has not been in contact with you.

You know your life started out in Mackay, which is a small sugar cane town up the Queensland coast from Rockhampton. This is where your mum met your biological father, Jimmy. You were born there and lived in a suburb called Slade Point. Mackay is well known for its sugar industry and cattle but is also attached to the coal mining industry, where your dad was working as a boilermaker. There was always good money to be had working in the mines, and it turns out that your father would develop a strong need for this 'good money.'

Luke, my boy, you lived in Mackay for only a short while, and you have little memory of this time. But your mind will immediately jump back to Mackay as you start on your seemingly never-ending wheel of questioning yourself, family, and the universe about what happened in those short years in there. What happened with your father in Mackay that made your mother pack up and leave? What was the truth about your father? What was the real reason that your father never contacted you? Was it because there was something wrong with you? Was it because he didn't love you? So many questions for a young lad, and seemingly no answers available.

You will eventually find that your real father had a dark side.

Let me explain a bit more. They say when a man gets a taste and hunger for alcohol, it grips him to the bone, like an old pirate soaking up his rum to dull the boredom of months at sea. Jimmy loved his alcohol, and it seems he always had a beer in his hands. But oh wow! It all came with a twist of massive hangovers and violence that would wreck him for days. Paying for all this alcohol left us chronically short of money, but he would find ways of solving this problem. There was a time Jimmy lined up a car for a test drive and then paid for it with a cheque, even though he was fully aware there was not enough money in his bank account to cover it. In other words, he wrote a dud cheque.

Shortly after this, Jimmy found out that there was well-paying work available in Western Australia and was soon contracted to work as a boilermaker there. His recent dud cheque for the car hadn't caught up with him yet, but it was soon to blow up in his face. He drove the new car interstate with his family and started working at the local iron ore mine. Your mum, of course, was blissfully unaware of the dud cheque, so she was shocked when debt collectors approached her one day in the town to repossess the car.

'But my husband paid for this car in full!' she insisted.

'That's true,' one of them replied. 'But he paid with a dud cheque and no money in the bank. So, sorry love, but we're here to repossess the car.'

It turns out that, after this little escapade, Jimmy did some jail time for fraud, but nothing would stop him drinking. His love of alcohol was affecting your family more and more, and, even though you were small at the time, you still soaked up all the negative energy in the family that Jimmy's behaviour caused, and could feel it as a knot in your stomach. Why was everyone so angry?

Let's fast forward a few years now and move from WA back to Mackay. Jimmy's addiction had become so strong that there were times he would wake up in a pool of blood. This chronic addiction not only affected his health, but also his work and, of course, your family. Your mum was constantly questioning, 'Should I stay, or should I go?' Thankfully, she finally chose to leave him and head south to Tyalgum where she grew up – another small town, just outside Murwillumbah.

Although the best decision for the family, you were a very small child and didn't understand the family dynamics, and so you began to ask the most challenging question of your life – why didn't your father want to see you anymore? You will never get to know or see your dad again. Luke, I'm sorry to say that your father dies a lonely and broken man – but it'll many years before you find this out. He will be buried in a lonely graveyard which you will probably never get to see in your lifetime.

And all those years of wondering where he was, and why didn't he try to find you, were just a waste of energy and time. But the question seems to consume you as you enter your teenage years. Not knowing if your father is still alive or dead, and why the family call him 'a bad man,' will be a constant frustration, and you will often feel alone and lost.

You come to feel like you're stuck in a bubble, forever asking the same questions of your family and getting the same inadequate answers. You will try your best to seek 'the truth.' But this process will send you into a downward spiral of doubt about your place in the world. Was your father a really bad man? Would you become like your father, or would you be able to rise above his addictions and his shortcomings to live a good life? In your late teens, you will even fancy that you had actually become a bad man just like your father and that everyone could see that about you.

But that's a long way in the future, and here we are now, sitting near the farmhouse at Palm Vale, where your earliest clear memories of your childhood will start to bring some positive – and not so positive – memories into your life.

Okay, Luke, do you have any questions? – Yes, of course you do. So fire away!

Will I live in Palm Vale for a long time, and will I like it?

Well, Luke, that's two questions, but I'll answer them both.

You'll live here for a few years. In the early stages at the farm, you will discover the rhythm and flow of the circle of life for yourself, other people, and especially for the farm animals. You'll be given responsibilities on the farm. You will have to attend to the house cow every day, plus the dogs, and you' have to learn how to chop the wood and make a fire, so that the farmhouse could be heated.

I will have to darken your story a little now, sorry. At this stage in your life, you'll have noticed that life begins with birth, but will have had no experience of death. This will be the first time you will discover the 'meaning of life,' with its cycles of birth and death.

Your favourite farm animal is a pregnant cow called Gertrude. You will watch her give birth to a beautiful baby calf, Dexter – but Gertrude will die suddenly due to complications with the birth. You will be heartbroken. On the heels of witnessing new life come into being, you'll need to dispose of the body of your gentle Gertrude. This will be done by cremation on a bonfire. Watching Gertrude's body burn will not be a pretty sight; the smell and sound of her body burning is almost too awful to bear. This particular moment of your life, encompassing joyous birth, inexplicable death, and gut-wrenching disposal of the body, will stay in your mind until you pass into the next universe.

This will be a traumatic time for you, but now comes the beautiful part of the circle of life. Though it was at the cost of her life, Gertrude brought new life into the world, and now it's your job to focus on Dexter, to acknowledge him as the continuation of Gertrude's life. Dexter is going to need lots of love and attention from you. One of your first tasks is to feed him – and, in a way, to act like his mum and give him the attention and sustenance that his mum cannot.

This will become one of your daily chores, mixing powdered milk and water into a drinkable solution to feed Dexter, which you help him to drink by placing two fingers in the milk solution and then letting the calf suck your fingers to get the milk. Your job is to feed and keep him alive so he can gain enough strength to get on his own four little feet and become independent.

You'll retain a strong connection to Dexter, as you recognise that he and you have a shared experience. You have both lost a parent without knowing why. Little Dexter could not understand that he had lost his mum, but at least there was a finality to Dexter's lost mum; you, on the other hand, continue to question the universe as to what happened to your father and why he hasn't wanted to see you.

Life on the farm will be only a few years, but it will contain some of the grandest and happiest memories of your childhood. So, you will not be particularly happy when your parents decide to move to the Gold Coast. Moving towns also meant new schools, and your experience of school will become more daunting as you grow older. You will discover the meaning behind some of the 'learning difficulties' your parents and teachers talk about, but you'll be an adult before you finally understand that you learn things differently compared to others, that you learn better by 'doing' as an outcome of being a 'visual person.'

Your teenage years will be a struggle and it will be many years before you can find your own way forward. You will feel stupid and left out of the class. Learning how to comprehend what you are reading will not come as a skill until your early twenties. Sorry, Luke, but that's the truth of it.

The move to the new and bigger school will also be the start of your experience of bullying. At the time, it will be nothing too big, nothing you can't handle. But this is only the start of bullying, and your experiences of school and schoolwork will become more and more negative, but then your family will make another move to a new suburb and another school on the Gold Coast called Mudgeeraba. Fortunately, here you will meet some lovely people and make some positive lifetime friendships.

Are you ready now for a dark journey, Luke? Hold onto your hat, because you are about to discover what you'll be doing up to late 1996.

You will have a job in the retail food sector. At first, you think you're going to love this job, and you love the freedom of being away from the classroom and schoolwork. After a while, though, the party life kicks in. But lots of alcohol and wild partying tends not to turn out well. You'll get trapped in a cycle of binge-drinking, and after a while it will dawn on you that this was what your father was like. But this won't stop you drinking, and you become more and more despondent because you still have not resolved the burning issue of finding your father.

Living life like this will become like a never-ending cycle. No matter which way you go, you'll always come back to the point of not knowing where your father is and then drinking because you don't know where he is or how to start finding him. What keeps going round and round in your head is that 'your father was a bad man.' All your relatives said so, and you never wanted to be like that. But at the time there will seem to be no way out of this destructive circle.

Think of this time like a never-healing cut to your leg, where no band-aid could possibly stop the bleeding. Luke, you will one day discover that alcohol is a temporary band-aid that will only last as long as the next urgent need for more. This behaviour will go on for a couple of years, but eventually work managers will notice your slovenly appearance and that you keep turning up late for work with excuse after excuse. There is something deep inside you that connects this type of behaviour with what you've been told of your father's behaviour. Can you see it? Yes, there it is. You're really just like your father after all.

But that's too far into the future just yet. Let's jump back to a younger time and your move to Mudgeeraba. Your neighbours will introduce you to karate and it will come to have a soothing touch on your soul – to the centre of your being. There is something about karate, Luke; you won't be able to put your finger on it, but it will be the main discipline that helps you clean up your act and gain focus in your early twenties. The strong discipline of mind and body necessary to earn a black belt in karate will be called upon many times.

Luke, you're going to have some major setbacks in life. Right now, you may not get what I am talking about – you're only 10 years old. You will go through a global financial crisis in 2007. This will affect the global markets, but it will also put considerable stress on you and what you will need to do for employment. You will feel like you've been kicked into a high functioning mode, thinking, *how on earth am I going to solve this problem?*

And then you'll start to see a better way of supporting your family (you have a wife and a baby daughter now). But guess what? This way of earning better income is in the mining industry. And there again, it feels, is your father, metaphorically tapping on your shoulder and saying, 'Don't stuff this work up like I did.'

A career in the mining sector will hold you steady for the rest of your life, even though there are some steep challenges ahead. You'll discover that the life of a fly-in/fly-out worker can be ridiculously hard on the body – but the life of a drive-in/drive-out worker will be the worst of all. The hardest challenge you'll go through in your mining career will be your health. It will become ironic that, not long after starting mining, you'll get a card reading from a clairvoyant, who in the reading tells you're going to suffer from a health problem that will nearly kill you.

She was right.

An aggressive brain tumour will be the most difficult thing that you have faced so far. But even though you will almost die three times and endure indescribable pain and mental fog, you will feel that it makes you a stronger, better person. Meeting people going through similar processes will not only inspire you but help you to inspire others along the way. Luke, you will find that there's something about your life force that helps people you meet through guiding them with your positivity and energy. Even though these times for you are going to be a fundamental setback, I can assure you that no matter what comes across your path – major setbacks, toxic people, health challenges – you will discover your inner strength. You will feel alone during these times, but the people above have your path clear for future prosperity.

You are going to find that, by almost dying three times, how incredibly lucky you have been to be alive. You will be given three challenges to get back up on your feet, and each time you will understand that you simply need to tighten your belt and suck it up, princess for each challenge that comes along. If you don't try your hardest each time, then this most likely will be the end of you. But right from the moment of your diagnosis, you made it clear: 'I've got this!' And you stuck to your word. But for all the pain and heartache, believe me, you are going to come out the other side of ill-health and near-death with a new respect for life.

Slowly, as you regain your strength, you will begin to see that you are a 'people person' and that all those years of hard slog at school to learn maths, history, and other stuff were never going to prepare you for what you feel you are truly good at doing – connecting with people and sharing your story of struggle and overcoming major life adversities. Your karate training and discipline will be a huge part of your ability to control your mind and body to do the job at hand.

You will finally discover the truth about your dad in your early twenties. The real reason that he never made contact with you is that he was slowly killing himself, and nothing mattered except the next glass of beer. I want to reassure you though, young Luke, that your father was only going through his life and dealing with his addictions the best way he could.

It's best not to hate your father for the outcome which occurred. Hatred and anger breed illness, and it's simply not his fault. Things happen to people in life for a reason. I can't explain; only the universe has the answer there! But parents can become separated from their children by the circumstances of their surroundings, whether work, lifestyle habits, or living environments. It's never the child's fault.

It's not your fault.

As you go through this journey in your young adult life, the hunger for finding your dad will feed your fire. This will help you immensely when it comes to providing fundamental principles for your own children when you become a father.

You will be able to provide a positive, loving, and learning environment for your own children – guiding them throughout their own lives, teaching them the importance of leadership independence and self-esteem … which you yourself so desired when you were young.

Your life, Luke, as I have shown you, will be difficult in many ways, but you will rise above your adversities to become the happy man I am today.

Well, it's been a pleasure talking with you, Luke. Are you ready to get back into my magic car, or shall we sit here for a while longer, under the swaying gums, and let nature wrap her peace around us?

Yours truly,
Luke Amery

CHAPTER 19

You Can Choose a Different Path

Michelle Beauchamp

My dear Michelle,

As I sit down to write this letter to my 10-year-old self and remember that wonderful little girl, I just want to give you the biggest hug. With hindsight, I know how difficult your next years will be and how much you will need the resilience you already demonstrate. Hugs, love, and hope will be your strength as you will go through loss over the next little while.

Family life means that growing up with emotional and physical upset will become difficult. However, you are strong and will get through this time, despite being at the mercy of a dreadful person, disguised as a parent, upon whose trust you should be able to depend. Your decision as a young teenager to grow into an adult different to Dad will become a message you want to share with the world – and you will do this.

Deciding to be a different adult self is not even thought of 10 ten years of age as a rule. To be able to stand up where strangers tread and say out loud *Stop that behaviour* or *Stop being abusive to each other* or *Take a moment to look at yourself and decide to be different* – this is not how you share life with someone you claim to love. Is this what you want for yourselves, your kids, your families, your friends, those around you, in public or private spaces? You'll often will ask this of others, completely hoping their answer is: No.

During your life space as a child, you have the ability to create a very adaptable headspace, one which will see you grow into a unique adult. This is a huge task, a massive burden – and one you should not have had to build around you. You will feel alone, isolated, and abandoned at times. Feel deeper; you often trust your strength, and resilience will get you through the rubbish.

At times there will also be joy, fun, and laughter. Finding the ability to let things go and not hide from your own feelings will be a positive outcome for you as an adult. You'll have days where you feel confident and an inner peace, almost as though the chaos of your life doesn't exist. This will be a really great trait for you, one you'll carry with you for times you need it in the future. Occasionally you will even wonder if you will ever have a bad day again. This will be when Dad isn't at home for a while.

Life will require tenacity, strength, and personal acceptance, along with an enormous amount of courage and endurance. All of these qualities you already have – you're just not completely aware of them yet. Each of these qualities will have a turn at helping you through your teens and young adult life. You'll call upon when you need them, ticking your own boxes to seek help or support yourself. Not just support with your daily perseverance – it'll develop into an innate ability over years, to manage how you cope. Your life stream will allow you to share your stories as you become brave enough to, but these will also be difficult times. Sharing your life stories will bring tears to your face and to the faces of others, along with doubts and possibly renewed fears – and you'll often be left wondering, have you said too much? Or not anywhere near enough? Sharing your stories will become a passion when you are much older, and the journey this leads you on will be amazing. Over time, as an adult, you will become a very inspiring individual to many.

Often, you will wonder why the path you were led down carried you through such a dark corridor, eerily quiet and at times an isolating space. You will realise over the coming years that much of the dark corridor was not your choosing. At times, with you thinking out loud, can this be real. Your life will balance out. Occasionally you will feel like your lot in life seems to screw you over a bit, but you will also realise you have also grown, with much to be thankful for.

During the harder times, you may struggle to see far enough ahead to believe it will ever change. The good news is that you will soon be able to switch off your brain and your heart as a way of being okay with your childhood, and it will also help you to get through those tough times and become an awesome adult. Sharing your message, coupled with a 'want to be heard' attitude, will eventually help you to bring life into perspective for you. Growing into adult life as a forward-thinking person, you will begin to share your stories and build your ability to become staunch in your opinions. A sense of being able to speak out, to allow yourself to be heard, will emerge. Asking others to do the same will eventually become second nature. Days and nights of thought process will allow you to get past these thoughts. A lifetime will seem to pass in a very short space of time. You shall learn positive actions along life's paths, to help you adjust and still be okay. You will leave some negative stuff behind; you will hug lots and be a happier person. This is surely perfectly fine along the way.

As the day to day mental health of your parents deteriorates and Dad's downward spiral, which began years ago, continues, the abuse will escalate beyond any comprehension for you. The cycle of mental and physical trauma will continue. Learning over coming years of the mental and physical abuse your grandmother suffered at the hands of her husband makes you realise that this is a poor trait to carry forward as an adult. Apparently, no-one ever told Dad that. Dad championed the flailing traits of his father for his entire life. You will grow to tell your dad these very things.

Living in various small communities will teach you that people care and want to envelope Mum and each of you children in warm, thoughtful embraces. Small communities will often mean short stays for you all as a family. When Dad becomes an enraged individual and punishes all of you, the community will want to save you all from his terror. And then he demands everyone pack and you all move to another place, an apparent new beginning, and the evil cycle begins again, with no chance of support. No hope of a positive outcome for anyone during these crazy cycles.

Finding safe places at home as a child will become harder, as sadly, Dad doesn't know how to behave in the right way with his daughters. This means that on top of him being angry and mean all the time, sometimes he will want to do other things that he should never, ever do with you. But you are so brave, Michelle. When Dad tries something more, you will be strong enough to kick him and scream at him, and he will leave the room without doing anything. He will never try again.

Because there is so much going on at home, I know it can be hard to be around other people. The voices in your head can be so loud sometimes, and you often feel really sad, or even sick. This means that, as you grow up, you will want to be alone more than some other kids. It's just easier that way.

Every time Dad is not present for a while, life will blossom; the family happiness will make you feel good about each day. Every time Dad returns, life hope plummets for you all. Many times, the cycle will repeat itself – over years to come, seemingly endlessly – and your resolve will weaken and your hope for a better day will fade. But you shall get through and get past these times. Stay as strong as you can during this. Beatings are random; you won't know if it's a good or bad day for him. Hiding will become almost impossible, and the games you create to justify being in your own mental space will feel like another life. The outcomes are varied, and you'll feel the emotional and physical roller-coaster almost continuously. Remember to lean on resilience; seek out your inner self and hug yourself often. You are great at getting yourself to a much nicer place. Keep those thoughts; grow your stronger place within you.

But I really want you to know, beautiful Michelle, that you are so strong, and so brave. You are perfect just as you are, and you are more than enough to love. You deserve love. Your dad just wasn't a good dad, and it was never your fault. The strength you build and your ability to be strong and brave will serve you so well in your future.

During the next little while, your heart shall have to draw on the strength you have built. You'll deal with loss of family and wondering how death actually works. This will happen a couple of times. But you'll still grow strong through the struggles of loss. You can withstand anything life throws at you.

Even when hard things happen, you will know in your heart that your newfound angels are watching over you, even in your darkest hours. As you grow up, you shall often daydream of the happy times with them in the past, of what should have come, and think about what shall never eventuate. Allow time for you. In the coming years, it is something you will crave.

That your parents live in an endless abusive cycle and don't manage their own grief and loss also means the horrendous cycle will continue. Your dad isn't able to cope with the emotional or mental struggle of tragedies that occur in your world. Mum barely gets by, managing family stuff, while fighting off his extreme moods. Over time, they move towards losing all of you, not always to dying; to having had enough, to wanting out, wanting to leave this cycle of abuse. Your spirals, both up and down, will be difficult at times; it will be a foreboding place to be, away from help, support, love, understanding, and comfort. Keep hoping for happier times ahead and hold on. Your inner strength shall support you.

During a night in a women's refuge, hearing a counsellor tell your mum that someone needs to break the cycle of abuse everyone keeps going through, you'll silently promise yourself that you'll become that someone. Armed with this promise to yourself, you'll be able to find your voice. By the time you are 13 years old, you will speak up against the abuse. You will suffer as a result. But your strength and resolve will get you through. You will be able to shout. You will be able to scream. You will be able to say, 'I do not like you doing this to us.'

You will grow past so much adversity in every single day to come. You will become the only adult of all six of your siblings who breaks the chain of emotional and physical abuse, to grow into an adult who will not only refuse to accept that genetics will mould you but will also stay firm on never accepting any level of personal abuse from those around you. You will become a strong advocate for making different decisions, for you and for others.

In your coming adult years, as a parent yourself, loss will again knock on your door. You shall struggle but nevertheless draw on the inner strength, as you have done so before. You will get through this time. Share stories and memories. These things will keep helping you for years to come.

Being decisive as to what is and isn't acceptable as you grow into adolescence and later young adulthood will help you choose the type of people you prefer to have in your life. For a while, you'll become harder emotionally – though really, you're really like a toasted marshmallow, slightly firm and a little crunchy on the outside, but soft inside. This is perfect for you. Stay firm about people you deem optional in your life and move on from having to deal with them; this is healthy for your mind. As you grow into a middle-aged adult, carrying the burden will become tiresome. You continually strive for resilience in your days ahead. Strength and courage will back you up and ensure you have what you need. Keep pushing ahead and sharing your message.

Looking forward, new journeys and a fresh outlook will help to revitalise you. So many grow from hearing your voice and becoming more decided about their own life paths. Grow strong inside, and the world shall become a greater place for you to be.

Share your messages of life lessons as often as you feel brave enough. Many will see you at your best; some will see you at your worst; and lots will see you come into your own. Only you will truly see all of you, and you will open much of your soul for the world to see.

Awesome hugs to your young self.

Michelle

CHAPTER 20

The Oath

Kati Britton

Dearest Kati (aged 10),

With your big bright eyes, your long mousy hair, pulled into a tight ponytail, your tomboy style. That cheeky grin and independent attitude, your constant wonder of how the older generation function in a somewhat perfectly imperfect world. So much to learn. I love the way you will look at life from a social lens, always watching how people in your world are figuring out their lives and wondering why they are making certain choices. At times you will feel unsure of where you fit into your family unit of your parents and older brother. The lack of structure and routine that make you rebellious will provide a future template for your independent little soul, to wander this earth without restrictions or limitations. Your creative spark will be ignited by your mother, a potter and artist, while your grounded attitude will be influenced by your father, a firefighter, who like yourself is committed to a career helping the community.

Kati, your home, although it will be chaotic at times, is a world full of nature. A big willow tree stands proudly outside your bedroom window and, like a huge hug, you take comfort from the tree's long, swooping willow branches, rustling wistfully in the wind. The creek that runs past your home will provide hours of entertainment, developing your curiosity for the natural world. The smell of running water mixed with mud and lizards –

the bushland will provide many places to hide and build cubby houses. You will escape to a world that is not real at times, and maybe this is a way of blocking out the bigger issues going on around you. I want you to know, my love, that around this time your intuition is right; there is unrest brewing within your home. Ultimately, your parents do not want to control you as a young 10-year-old; you will grow up in the seventies, a time of freedom and love. The communication and positive influence between your parents and yourself somehow gets lost. This rupture and disconnect within your relationship is when the trouble begins, and unfortunately it will take years to repair.

Innocent Kati, I am writing this letter to you about the day you had that talk with Mum on the beachfront, the conversation where she shared with you one of those adult choices you did not quite understand –

'I want you to know that your father and I are going to separate; this is going to be the best choice moving forward for all of us.'

The waves crashed onto the shore as this news was delivered to you, dear Kati. The sting of the salty air hit every nerve in your little body. Your eyes started to water as you held back the tears, trying to stay strong as you always do. You found yourself looking away from your Mum, focusing on a seagull trying to steal a hot chip from another child sitting happily with their family. You hoped the ground would swallow you whole so you didn't have to speak. At 10, those words could do nothing but deliver angry feelings, along with confused thoughts to your mind, body, and young soul.

In that moment on the beachfront, you made a decision – a decision that will change your perception on relationships in the future. Kati, you made an oath that only you would be the source of a sense of stability and nurturance in your world. While you are going to want to cling to this oath, made in this moment, the future has a different plan. You'll encounter three curveballs that challenge this decision, making you realise that relying on others is sometimes unavoidable, necessary, and, often, for your own good.

But before I go on, don't panic about what Mum said. I want you to know that your parents stay together. They see the effect that the proposed separation will have on your emotional state, and by working through their issues, your parents will realise their love for one another is still there. Their marriage was still yet to be explored, and the relationship was worth fighting for. Nearly 40 years later they are still married, and own a loving home and art gallery in the Blue Mountains. Kati, I want you to know you have a great relationship with both of your parents and your brother, and now know your place within the family unit. I just wish you knew that this was how your family would end up in the future. But let's not get ahead of ourselves just yet!

The road ahead will see you fighting for your life several times. Every low will bring with it lessons in resilience, trust, and hope, as well as life skills, which will help you commit to a journey of helping others through your own experiences. Young Kati, you will make friends with other troubled souls along your path. The majority of your friends will be from broken families, or have parents suffering from addictions and or mental health conditions. What you don't know is that, ultimately, all these relationships that you experience will lead you into your career. As an adult, you become a professional counsellor and play therapist, and have helped many children and families suffering from trauma.

But let's go back to that first curveball, young Kati.

Only five years after the conversation on the beachfront, your oath to never rely upon others will be challenged, at the ripe old age of 15. This challenge will teach you a fierce lesson about finding inner strength and the will to live and, most importantly, will help place your trust back in people in order to receive the nurturance you are in need of. Dear Kati, it's summer of 1986, and as the headstrong, carefree 15-year-old that you will become, you decide that you are moving out of your family home. Unfortunately, at this age you will start to become reckless in your choices.

One particular decision you make on Boxing Day night proves to be a big one. On that night, at a party, there will be underage drinking, partying, and laughter in the air. Kati you will make a decision to get into a car driven by an older boy who is intoxicated. For a fleeting moment, you will think to yourself 'I want to go home,' but everyone is saying, 'Come on, Kati, let's just go for a drive around the streets before heading home.' You will decide to go along with the crowd, as teenagers do.

Opening your eyes, dear Kati, your mind will be foggy, like in a dream. You will be thinking, *am I still alive? Is this real?* Your nose will fill with the acrid smoke lingering in the air; you'll see folded metal all around you and realise that yes, this is real! Brave Kati, you will see the driver of the vehicle pulling a friend from the car, onto the dark and empty road. You will wait for what seems hours out in that dark, desolate, 'Coal & Candle Creek Road' in Sydney's Ku-ring-gai Chase National Park. You will be scared, but you will be found. Kati, your amazing ability to sink into a meditative state in the hours after this accident allows you to survive the pain. This night gives you remarkable insight into how brave and resilient you will become in the future. This particular night will also provide you with the experience and knowledge that you will eventually pass on to adolescents in the future. A positive will come from this negative, as you will use this story to remind teenagers to listen to that inner voice when it tells you to go home, because that inner voice is trying to keep you safe.

After the accident, you will spend time recovering in hospital, and it will take some time for you to come to terms with this new reality. This will be a time when your oath to yourself on the beachfront will be challenged. In the years leading up to the accident, you will have built a very strong protective wall around yourself. In those crucial years of your young life, dear Kati, you will cut off communication with the most important people in your life, your family, as it will feel easier than maybe being hurt again. This will make it very difficult for family members to break down your walls, allowing communication to flow freely between you. Due to your injuries, Kati, you have no choice but to move back into your parent's new home in Berowra. This house will feel a million miles away from your friends on the Northern Beaches, and this town will definitely feel foreign. You will have to relent, letting your parents provide you with much needed safety, stability, and nurturance in order to heal. Remember, Kati, 'people need people,' in the good times and the bad. You just needed to feel this again in your heart. This experience will bring your family back together again, not entirely, but it will knock a layer off that wall you built around yourself.

Another positive that will come from this car accident is the monetary pay-out you receive. This money will buy you your first car, and life will truly begin. This will spell freedom for you, my love. As soon as your injuries heal, you will move back to the beaches, into the comfort of your own surroundings, and start paving your own path.

Fast forward to 1998, when you will be 25 years old and in the prime of your life, living in the beachside suburb of Manly. Beach, boys, and friendships will abound. You will be free, and that, dear Kati, is all you care about. The live music scene will give you a home at night, and by day you will work hard. You will absolutely love hitting the town to watch live music at any opportunity. I truly believe, Kati, that this is your saviour throughout your teens, twenties, and early thirties. You will find that music gives you a great escape from the real world, a place that makes you feel alive. The music will take away your inhibitions, and you can just be yourself. The people you will surround yourself within this scene become like family. This I know, because you are still friends with these amazingly supportive people in your future.

You are always socially observant and aware, watching people's behaviour everywhere you go. Maybe this makes you feel safe in your own little world. One particular day, Kati, you will become distressed while watching a program on the foster system. This feeling of distress will lead you to make a journal entry that will one day become the prologue to the rest of your life.

'Why do people keep having babies when there are so many babies in this world who are in need of a good home?'

Little did you know that you set your future right there and then. Your second curveball, which will again challenge your oath on the beachfront, would soon arrive.

In March 2000, at the age of 27, you will marry your soulmate, Chris. If you could compare him to an actor, he would be the real-life version of Han Solo from *Star Wars*. This man has confidence like no other. When you meet him you will find him cocky but charismatic, charming but aloof. These qualities draw you both together; you complement one another, and he will be strong enough to match your strength. His charisma and ability to draw in a crowd will lead him to become the front man of many bands you see over the years. Your future husband is a good listener; he is wise with his words. He will help you break down the walls of communication you've built – and this, dear Kati, is a good thing. And guess what, Kati – 20 years later, you're still happily married. You allow a deep trusting relationship to grow with your husband, which will provide you safety and stability like no other. Dear Kati, there are no words to describe the strength, love, and friendship you will experience together. You will travel the world, laugh, and go through some extremely difficult health issues together, but, most importantly, you will communicate effectively with one another.

Seven years into your marriage, you will start your inter-country adoption journey. Dear Kati, this will not be an easy ride, and throughout this never-ending process you will need to keep yourself busy. How would you fill the difficult time waiting to bring your gorgeous son home? You will have an overwhelming gut feeling that now is the time to get a real education. Kati, you will decide to put your head down and study hard for five long years, which will distract you from feeling the painful wait to bring your son home from South Korea. This will be a new experience for you, as you left school before doing your high school certificate, preferring to work so you could earn money. While you work to complete your degree, you will land a job as a counsellor at a drug and alcohol rehabilitation hospital in Sydney. Through this work at the rehabilitation hospital, you will hear many stories of families torn apart from addictions and mental health disorders. My dear Kati, you will watch many people put their lives back together, and most importantly, you will be able to help families heal and communicate with one another once again.

Through your work as a counsellor, your soul will finally sing a tune it connected with and is needed at this stage of your life. This is definitely your calling. What you don't realise is that through your work healing others, you will in fact simultaneously be healing yourself. As the years go on, you will be wondering how your current work could help you on your next journey of becoming an adoptive mother. How would you be able to help this little person relate to living in a different country with different smells, different faces, and a completely different language?' You decide to explore play therapy for children, and will go on to complete a postgraduate diploma in Art and Play Applications in Therapy. You will just know in your heart that this will be your go-to healing modality to use, not only with your own soon-to-arrive son, but eventually with the hundreds of other children and their families you come to work with over the years. You will find that play therapy provides a space of healing like no other for children suffering from emotional, psychological, mental, and behavioural issues. Your intuition will kick in again when working with children in this therapeutic space. Through using a child-centred modality, you will be able to connect on a deeper level with your clients, *and it will feel right!*

Six long years after filling out your initial paperwork to adopt internationally, you will find out that you are going to be a parent to a beautiful little boy from South Korea. He will be 6 months old and is a happy, healthy baby. After all the years of waiting, all the official paperwork, all the invasive interviews, psychological testing, fingerprinting ... finally, you will receive the phone call you and your husband have been waiting for. It is an understatement to say you will be both over the moon; you will be ecstatic. Once the initial phone call sinks in, you both celebrate. Your families will gather together, and you will all feel the electric energy of excitement in the air. You will receive photos of and updates on your son every couple of months; as much as it is delightful to see your gorgeous boy, it will be extremely hard to not have him in your arms. Months will turn into years, and dear Kati, you will feel that familiar anger and sadness sitting within you. Dear Kati, when you finally fly to South Korea to attend court and meet your son for the first time, he will be 2 years old. This first meeting will be wonderful, but extremely sad. You will see the bond that has formed between your son and his foster mother. The lack of communication between you all will be hard due to the language barrier and is not a comfortable feeling, to say the least.

The long wait will finally be over, and your son will be coming home to live with you in Australia. The next year that follows will not be easy, but it will be worth it. This little boy will need a lot of love, support, and stability. He will be scared, angry, confused, and very sad. Not being able to communicate effectively through language with this little soul proves difficult. Dear Kati, there will be times when you feel like withdrawing inside yourself, and that is okay. You will constantly feel tired and know that your body is not coping.

Well, look out, your third curveball is about to be thrown, and boy it's a beauty. Dear Kati, this again will challenge that oath you made to yourself. This time, you will need to be open to trusting others and accepting support and nurturance, especially from your family.

The tiredness and illness you will feel within your body are real. Your intuition tells you that there is something wrong with your health, and you start to suffer from chronic breathing problems. You will decide to seek professional help, and the initial scans and blood tests reveal you are suffering from a rare congenital lung condition called 'intra-pulmonary sequestration segment,' meaning you were born with an extra lung. The mucous covering your entire left lung is causing major breathing difficulties – and, dear Kati, you will need to pull up those big girl pants again to have major lung surgery. A few weeks later, you will be booked in to have your procedure. Waking up in the intensive care unit, you will be scared, confused, and worried about your future. Dear Kati, you must put your trust in everything and everyone around you. You will know in this moment that your recovery is out of your hands; have faith and hope that everything is going to be okay. Kati, those months in recovery allow your family to really get to know the real and vulnerable side of you. You will need them, and the rupture in your earlier years of life is about to be repaired. You will send that childhood oath flying out the window, enabling you to build strong, safe, and secure attachments in your future. You will allow the communication lines to open completely, giving your family the chance to nurture you through this time. Your relationship with your family will blossom. Every new year, you will feel stronger, healthier, and more full of energy.

This last curveball with your health will allow you to live a new life where you can breathe and feel supported, although everyone will call you the 'One Lung Mum,' which will make you laugh.

As I write this letter to you, dear Kati, you are 48 years of age and the healthiest version of yourself. You live in your own beautiful home on the Northern Beaches and run your own successful business, Britton Play Therapy & Counselling. Kati, your gorgeous son is now 8 years old, and he is smart, loving, and securely attached to both you, and your husband. Your son is thriving at school and has become quite a soccer star. You still struggle to let people nurture you at times; this is a work in progress. Nobody's perfect!

The biggest lesson you take from your journey as a parent now is the importance of keeping lines of communication open, offering a great influence on your son as he grows without the need to control him. The future holds more for you, Kati, and I can't wait to see what happens next.

Love,

me xx

CHAPTER 21

Dear Miss Wooler

Nyree Johnson

Dear Miss Wooler,

You are beautiful, kind, and intelligent. You are amazing and you are enough. Believe me!

You're going to come up against some challenging situations in your life, and the trick is to ensure you approach each challenge with grace and humility. It is important to remember that whatever comes your way, everything can be figured out. Remaining calm in the face of chaos is a talent and skill worth honing. You have an amazing gift to share with the world, and you will lead those around you when you decide to truly step into yourself. (Hot tip, this happens in your early thirties ... but do it sooner!)

You'll be taken advantage of over the years because of your empathetic nature and your care and compassion for those around you. People will see how kind you are and how big your heart is, and they'll use it to their advantage, before you realise what's going on. Don't let this get you down, though. You're strong, you're influential, and you're capable.

I know that what you went through at 7 was confusing and upsetting. Being groomed to be taken advantage of by a person who should know better, an adult ... You didn't realise at the time that there were awful people in this world, and Mum's warning of 'stranger danger' never really sunk in until this experience.

Don't go through life thinking, 'it'll never happen to me'; always be prepared to take care of yourself and to trust your gut. If you feel like something is wrong, believe yourself. Your instincts are always right, even if it takes you a moment for your brain to catch up and your decisiveness to kick in.

Unfortunately, all too often over the course of your life, you'll hear stories from people who went through something similar, and in most cases worse than yourself ... You were lucky. There are undesirable people in this world who see opportunities to target young and naïve children for their own sick indulgence, and as a young girl living in a housing commission home in a mixed-race household with a single parent doing her absolute best, you were an easy target.

Everything that has happened in your life, as painful as it may be, happens for a reason. This is always the case.

Your amazing parents enrolled you in Tae Kwon Do shortly after the incident and police involvement. Your dad, especially, NEVER wanted you to be in a situation where you couldn't look after yourself. Even though he doesn't live in the same house, Dad is very involved. As a unique individual who grew up in a large family among mostly brothers, having two daughters probably wasn't an easy transition, nor did it allow relatability. His upbringing, though, enhanced yours. You probably already know this at 10, but you are the luckiest kid in the world to have the parents that you do and a village that supports and raises you.

Strength, courage, discipline, and confidence are skills you craft between the ages of 7 and 21 during your practice in the art of Tae Kwon Do. Your love for the sport will see you competing and placing in these competitions. It fills you with such pride and happiness when you reflect on your achievements and life skills learnt, and it is with immense joy that your own daughter shows interest in the sport with absolutely no prompting from yourself.

To watch her train, grow, and develop through her own journey brings immense gratitude, especially as her journey doesn't start for the same reasons yours did.

Tae Kwon Do teaches skill, respect, confidence, and discipline, and it fills you with a sense of capability that I'm not sure you would have gained otherwise. The bonus here is the pride on Dad's face when he knows his eldest daughter can 'hold her own' and fight in self-defence if and when required. You won't fully understand this just yet; however, you will when you have children of your own.

Throughout your teen years, you're going to make some odd choices. Not necessarily bad choices, as they will craft you into the person you are today – and that person has an amazing soul. When you are in Year 10, you'll use your skill of Tae Kwon Do to defend your sister, Carly. You'll find her crying, walking with her friends and looking for you after being harassed and bullied at school. You instantly feel a rage that you've never felt before, and you seek out the person responsible and take action. Aggression and anger fuel your fire, and for the one and only time in your life, putting your discipline aside, you attack rather than defend (which is frowned upon). Your sister is your best friend for life, and even at the age of 35, you have no regrets at taking this action. However, be careful not to impact innocent bystanders; try to be a little calmer and more respectful when speaking with teachers and support staff to relay the incident.

You'll be suspended from school, banned from the semi-formal and the end of the Year 10 Great Keppel Island trip. With the help of your mum, you'll seek forgiveness from the headmaster and be granted permission to attend both end of year events; however, you will not be welcome back at school.

At the time, it will be a little hard to understand this, but please know that in life you can't always control what is happening to you or around you. You can, however, certainly control your reaction and response to it. Always be respectful, courteous, and considerate.

The lucky thing you have going for you is that you have an amazing family who are all doing their best and who also love you unconditionally. You can mess up as many times as you need to in order to truly figure out who you are, and they'll always be there for you. Don't get me wrong; they're not going to enable poor life choices, but they will be there to pick up the pieces when you fall in a heap and admit defeat. They'll keep you grounded and you'll never be short of feeling loved, even if some of them have weird ways of showing it.

Your grandmothers will have a significant impact on who you are and what you stand for. At the time, you won't realise the lessons that are on offer; however, it will be evident as you grow and develop into adulthood. You'll lose these two women far too early in your adult life, and you'll be broken for a long time. You'll feel lost and you won't know who to turn to for help. The good news here is that when you do find YOU again, you're even more amazing than you were before because of the lessons they taught you during your short time with them.

*Always give what you can. Time, money, food, clothing
etc. – Grandma Wooler (Sarah Wooler nee Brown).*

As a child, you look at Grandma Wooler and think that she is immortal. You look at her with a sense of awe as she represents so much history, so many memories, and so many life lessons. As an adult you start to see time show on her face, and you'll listen closely to tales unravel to reveal the woman she was, the heroine of her own autobiography.

Grandma loves deeply and fully. She is the kind of person who just has so much love in her heart that even when you bring new people into her life, she finds a spot for them, too. Everyone is always welcome at Gran's.

You'll love volunteering your time with Grandma Wooler, at a home for disabled adults where she is a nurse. She'll attempt to retire several times from this role, but even upon a successful retirement, she'll still be a volunteer. Treating people with respect and equality is paramount in life. People can't control the circumstances they were born into, and enabling a sense of community, understanding, and dignity is critical to maintaining a harmonious society. This is a big lesson you'll learn from this wonderful woman, and one which you'll carry for your entire life.

You can never keep Grandma Wooler still for too long, so don't try. The running joke in the family is that she has more of a 'life' than her children and grandchildren. Her volunteer work at a senior citizen's centre will see her cooking up a storm and co-ordinating activities for the 'oldies' on a weekly basis. The 'oldies' will in fact be younger than your Grandma Wooler.

One of the greatest gifts in life is to take care of those who once took care of you. Being able to return the favour and ensure absolute dignity and respect, always. Aged care homes and palliative care is what it is. The people who work in these fields are nothing short of amazing. You can't change it, but again, you can control how you handle it. When visiting Grandma Wooler, you'll be visiting not only your grandma but also her friends. Take the time to speak with them and listen to them; their stories are gold, and it's a privilege to have them shared with you.

*The way you hold yourself, present yourself and
keep yourself IS important. It may seem vain but
in all honestly, it's personal pride in appearance,
confidence and the way you present yourself to the
world. – Grandma Ross (Glenda Ross née Fritz)*

You'll often watch Grandma Ross getting ready for the day; this is where she'll teach you how to do makeup, take care of your skin, and do your hair nicely. You'll sit in the big bathroom or on her bed watching her as she teaches you what to wear and when, including how to dress for work and that if you are wearing a dress or a skirt in a professional environment, you must ALWAYS wear stockings. Yes, stockings. In Central QLD in the middle of summer ... stockings. You'll shake your head every summer but at the same time, you'll smile briefly and remember her and her lessons. It's a lesson that even your mum has instilled in her.

You'll carry those golden words of wisdom from Grandma Ross for your whole life. Listen carefully. You too will spend your mornings, 'getting ready for the day,' and when you spruik this quote in your home, your family knows exactly what it means. She has so much confidence and has earnt so much respect thanks to her passion and advocation for causes and groups she's involved with. She has a strong voice and a big presence, and is never afraid to speak up and share her insights.

Life is an ever-evolving learning opportunity to do better; be better, and always show up. In everything that you do, always do your best. No one can ask you to do more than that.

While primary school is a blast, high school isn't as much. You'll have a small group of friends but will struggle with fitting in and being different. You don't really know why you're different, but you are – and that's a good thing, trust me. The traditional school classroom and delivery method doesn't suit you – a large, hot classroom with a dictatorial style of delivery, minimal movement, and an ever-wandering mind. Your ability to concentrate for long periods of time without movement, interaction, or engagement is a significant contributor. You question why? when you must write word for word from the blackboard into a notepad that you know you're never going to refer to again. You may feel like you are dumb and like you just don't 'get it'; please know this is not the case and the exact opposite is the truth. It is simply a matter of the school system failing unique kids like you. The ones who need a different type of interactive and hands-on learning experience instead of the dictatorial style on offer. It's not their fault; they're catering to the majority, of which you are not.

Much later in life, you'll learn how to study in a way that suits you. Even though this is driven by a desire to prove yourself and your worth (which is not necessary, but you don't know that at the time), it works for you and leads to the successful completion of four 'bits of paper,' quantifying your experience and education, as well as opens an opportunity and invitation for you to complete a master's degree.

You are very clever – don't wait until your late twenties or early thirties to figure this out. Your mind is analytical and strategic; you think of solutions others don't dream of, and you know exactly how to make things happen. You're known for 'getting stuff done.' People will often ask you as an adult how you get so much more done than others, how there seem to be more hours for you in a day than for anyone else. You have a superpower. The way you work, your mind, the way you think, and the way in which you go about your life all complement each other – absorbing and implementing all the lessons on offer to create the very best version of you, every day.

Study for the lessons on offer, not the bits of paper. It's such a rewarding experience and opens you up to a world of possibilities, knowledge, and understanding which you can apply in life and in your work. Share your knowledge and skills with those around you who genuinely want to learn and listen, because the success and empowerment this brings is contagious. When you share what you know as well as your skills, people feel a sense of confidence when they too believe they can achieve. Help them on that journey because, after all, we're all in this together.

If there are any doubts in your mind about what you can do in life, STOP. Get out of your own way and get over yourself. Take action, because anything that you want to do, you can. Life is too short to worry about any negative thoughts your mind is playing tricks on you with. Most importantly, ignore anyone who dismisses you or puts you down, because their opinion of you is not your business. If you get worried, concerned, or upset about what people might say or think about you, please ignore it. It comes far more easily as you age, but can be very challenging as you grow into adulthood.

When you commit yourself to an employer, be loyal, respectful, and reliable, and do your absolute best work at all times. Don't play games at work, as tempting as it may be at times. You'll see this often during your adult years and you'll never really understand it, until you do.

Recognise those around you who are doing amazing work and surround yourself with a team of people who genuinely want the best outcome for all in the team. This can be tricky, especially as you may not have the decision-making power to hire and fire – but if your role, your company, or your team doesn't align with who you are and what you're about, leave. You're not a slave to the income, and you're so amazing that you'll find something else that will better suit you. Be happy in what you do and don't tie your self-value to your role. Never be afraid to start over or change careers if you need to. When you trust your instincts, things will work out for you. Take a chance.

You're going to make mistakes in life as an adult, just as you did as a teen. You'll even make mistakes that don't align with your values. Always trust your instincts and forgive yourself. Don't beat yourself up or dwell. Learn, grow, move on, and remember to always appreciate the lessons on offer while looking to the future.

When it comes to friendships, quality far outweighs quantity any day. Aunty Mars tells you this often through your teen years, and it's advice that really, truly sinks in. You remind yourself of this often as an adult, too, and you find yourself repeating it to your own children as well as to the youth you work with. Having a handful of friends you can truly count on and relax with enables you to be your authentic self. You don't have to be everything to everyone. Just be you.

Dream big, always. Enjoy daydreaming about your goals in life and write them down. Make a plan and take action. One of the most amazing practices that enables dreams coming true is gratitude. Start a gratitude journal at 10, not 34. Be thankful for the amazing life you live, your loving family (flaws and all), and, one day in the future, your own husband and children.

You'll be lucky enough to meet an amazing man who you'll want to spend your life with. His support and admiration for you is a gift and one that you'll be constantly thankful for. He keeps you grounded and well supported and enables your dreams while balancing his own. You're an amazing team, and you'll often talk about sitting together at ages 100 and 105, sipping rum together in the aged care home and reflecting on your lives together.

Being able to grow into adulthood together will see you learn life with your best friend. He'll teach you how to drive, you'll teach him how to manage money, and you'll both complement each other. You'll have big dreams together; you make a lot of them come true before the time you're 35, and there are so many more yet to happen. He's a dreamer and you're a realist, but don't let you hold either of you back. An equal balance is needed in order to grow and achieve, while also being smart with planning and investments.

From the very first time, you introduce him to your dad – on a day he'd just come in from Longreach, had been at the Fitzroy Hotel, and is strolling back to Gran's home in Depot Hill alongside a random backpacker he'd picked up on the way. He becomes a massive part of your family and he realises just how unique you all are ... and he still stays.

He picks you up more times than you him, and he never reminds you of the times you fall. Always willing and ready to be where you need him to be, with the running joke that he has a tough gig as the 'trophy husband.' He has seen you at your absolute worst but will still tell you that you are beautiful. He'll let you rant and rave, knowing that it's only his ears that'll hear it because of the dignified way in which you carry yourself. You'll respect each other, you'll love each other, and you'll forgive each other. Marriage is not easy, but it's worth it.

Reflecting on life and mistakes learnt ... if I could change the past and influence you at 10, I'd want you to stay healthy. Unfortunately, you're going to be very overweight for approximately ten years, and to turn this around and combat your chronic back pain (thanks to a hereditary condition ...), you'll submit yourself to gastric sleeve surgery. Weight loss alone won't help, but maintaining a healthy weight and a strong core will minimise some of the pain. Stay healthy; you're here for the long haul, and you want a physically fit body and mind. Even with chronic pain, you'll learn how to live an amazing life filled with fun and adventure while managing your condition. It can be done – trust me.

Your purpose in life is to be an inspirational influencer of positivity and change, utilising thought leadership skills, accepting diversity, and promoting equality, all while remaining humble. With an intense focus on empowering those around you, supporting your community, advocating for what you're passionate about, and inspiring resilience, confidence, and enabling success.

Be proud of the way you handle yourself, and be confident in your own ability to manage what is thrown your way. You've got this; you just need to believe it.

Always keep a check on your values and ensure you're aligning your life, your commitments, and your decisions to them. Be genuine, be authentic, be better than yesterday ... and always show up!

Always remember: You are amazing and you are enough!

Lots of love

Mrs Nyree Johnson

Written at the age of 35 xx

CHAPTER 22

Always Be
Uniquely You

Natasha Peake

Dear Tash,

Tash, I'm writing you this letter today to empower and inspire you in everything you do, with the goal of helping to guide and educated you for the choices you make today and in the future. And, perhaps, to remind you of how you can do things differently, to become the person you've always dreamed of being. That vision of you being superwoman ... that person is you – the unique person you are, Tash, and the person you will become in the future.

As you read through each paragraph, I hope you enjoy every word and experience. You will be happy, sad, angry, enlightened, and inspired – and you will feel the strength and loving heart and soul deep inside you. Your values and beliefs will come alive.

You always seem to be getting into trouble, no matter what you do. Remember riding home from school with your brother and his friends, racing down the river hill, sliding in the mud, and crashing the bikes? You fell into the river, but it's the bike that took most of the damage – you cracked the handlebars and broke the pedals. It was so much fun, but you're afraid to ride home, because you know Dad will be furious with all of you for ruining your bikes. In the moment, it was well worth it; none of you really cared about how much trouble you'd be in.

After the fact, though, you know how much trouble you'll be in. You and your brother hide the bikes in the shed before Dad gets home, hoping that he won't see the damage and you'll avoid a belting. This time, you get lucky; he won't notice it that night, and you'll be able to fix it tomorrow.

Sometimes it feels like no matter what you do, you always do something wrong and get in trouble with Dad. Between his job on the fire brigade and his time in the Army, you're always so anxious about doing something naughty or saying something wrong. I know you're scared of him, and I know he's always strict with you and your brother. But he really does care for you and want to protect both you and your brother. It may feel like it's too much right now, that he's just mean and you can't understand why, but trust me when I say it's worth listening to and learning from him. And I promise, in time you'll come to understand a little more about your dad and how he grew up.

It's okay, Tash. Things do get better, and you'll soon learn that this is part of growing up.

I love seeing you have fun. That time with the bikes and your brother and your friends, you laughed so much you ended up rolling on the ground with laughter.

But I don't like seeing you scared – and I know that that happens far more often than not.

At the age of 10, you're already a truly amazing girl. You get great school reports, complete your chores, listen to your parents (most of the time!), and respect and are cared for by so many people. But you're tired of being boring and well behaved. I know that right now you just want to let out steam and try to be different, to start exploring all the different ways to be naughty. You see your friends doing all kinds of silly things, like trying cigarettes, and want to join them.

Please, Tash, listen to me – don't rush to grow up. You have so much fun ahead of you yet.

Because you will grow up, and you will misbehave.

It starts with wagging school with your friends and stealing your mum's smokes, writing a note to your teacher and signing it as though it's from your parents. Some of the school days, you meet up with a group of new friends, thinking you're pretty cool because you have ciggies, even though you don't even know how to breathe in the smoke. You try puffing on the cigarette and just about cough up your lungs. *You think, I think my chest's just broken into little pieces – and honestly, I'm not even sure I did that right. Why do people think it's cool to do this?*

Oh, Tash, don't ever let people tell you that smoking is cool!

It's fun, though, isn't it? You know it's bad if you get caught, because you'll be in so much trouble, and you'll probably never see your new friends ever again. But it's just so much fun you can't resist.

And then you start drinking. And lying to your parents about where you are.

And the alcohol just makes you feel so good – no worries, no feelings … no control over your body at all, actually. It's awesome, and you wish life could be like this all the time. You don't even know what it is you're drinking; whatever it is, you don't really care, because you and your friends are all happy and laughing (and continuing to cough up your lungs, but never mind).

Then comes the moment when you realise you're going to be sick, and oh, gosh, you are not well at all. You know it's not good, but you don't stop there. It's on to marijuana – or, at least, what you *think* was marijuana. Or is it marijuana laced with another drug? It's hard to say. There's a lot you don't remember.

But there's that time you smoke bucket bongs in a sand and bush dug-out by the river. It could have caved in on you, but you're silly and so stoned you don't know where you and the danger doesn't occur to you.

This is a significant day because it's the time you need help to find your way home, and then blurt out that you're wasted to your parents. Dad sends you straight to bed – and you're so scared to wake up, because you always get in trouble and this time you're sure to get a hiding.

But for once, you're not in trouble. When you wake and go to face your parents, all Dad says is, 'I hope you've learnt your lesson.'

That's it. Such a shock!

When you grow up, you're going to look back on this time and face hard questions. How many friends did you lose? How many brain cells did you lose? How many of your organs suffered, so early in your life? How many addictions did you pick up?

I promise you, it isn't the end of the world. You have so much life ahead of you.

*

Football is a big thing in your family. You spend years watching your dad coach, going to training and games … You'll even umpire the boys' football. Dad always said that children should be involved in sports – but it seems that when he said that, he wasn't talking about you.

Because Dad won't let you join a club sport or recognise your talents.

In a few more years, you'll have a vision – you're going to be a great sports person. This time, you're determined to chase your dream, to be who you want to be, and no matter who gets in your way, you won't let anyone stop you.

Not even Dad.

It's your turn to make decisions, to do the things you want to do. You're 100 percent sure that people will respect you – that you'll earn their respect by showing others your true value.

This time, when you ask Dad if you can join Little Athletics, he says yes!

But he never attends any of your sports events or watches you in athletics, softball, or even soccer. Later, you'll come to learn why, but for now you're angry and upset and confused and hurt, and those feelings will affect you for many years to come. You'll feel hatred towards your dad, unloved, like you're an outsider in your own family. You just don't understand why your dad never seemed to care about you and your achievements – in school as well as in sport.

There's no choice but to carry on with life, regardless, but you'll carry that hurt with you for a very long time.

*

In a few years' time, you'll graduate from high school and await your university results. In the meantime, you'll work full-time at Coles, study at TAFE at night, play sports, party hard with your friends – and absolutely love volunteering, with one of your best friends, to work with less-abled children every weekend.

All that time at Coles bears fruit, as you'll be recognised and nominated for your volunteer work by Coles and the Retail Traders Association and will win the Western Australian Community Service Award. You'll be truly honoured, not least because the monies go to the not-for-profit organisation at which you volunteered for so many years.

Winning that award and handing the cheque over to the organisation spark all kinds of feeling in you. It's a magical and proud moment for you, the most rewarding and appreciative feeling in the world – and not even something you asked for. The realisation of the passion and love you have for what you do makes you start to rethink your life. It's at this moment that you decide it's time to make your own decisions of where you're headed – the vision of yourself you've always dreamt of, of who you want to help and where you want to work ... the award gives you the confidence in yourself that you ne to move forward, onto a different path. Coles was a stepping stone, but now it's time to learn what you can do for the community.

*

Your time at Coles is also made memorable because of the health concerns you experience while there: dizziness (similar to seizure-like symptoms), vision troubles, severe headaches ... You'll panic and try to work through the symptoms the first few times, but no matter what you do, these episodes leave you feeling off balance and unwell.

Those first few episodes, you just want to lie down, so you don't bother to get yourself to a doctor. But as the episodes continue and you start to collapse at work, you're worried, and so go in, hoping for help. But the doctors will just give you migraine tablets and tell you to rest.

Please follow up, Tash. It's extremely important and will become a major part of your life, and you *must* listen to your body. You know it better than anyone else, after all.

Tash, you were a sick kid from the moment you were born. You were in and out of hospital for many years during your childhood, suffering from whooping cough, what doctors thought was diabetes, nail in foot, rare symptoms, breathing issues ... the list goes on. A lot of the time, though, the doctors just couldn't work out was wrong.

I hate to tell you this, but unfortunately you won't learn about your condition until you're in your thirties, after what you think is your first stroke – which itself comes *after* a heart attack. And, I'm sorry to say, in the course of your life you will suffer from a number of strokes, major orthopaedic surgery, colon polyps, severe endometriosis, PTSD, anxiety, depression, suicidal ideation ... you're going to spend a lot of time in rehabilitation and therapy.

In the end, it turns out you have Sneddon's Syndrome – a rare, slow progressive disorder that affects the blood vessels in your brain. And you, lucky girl, also have a rare makeup and narrowing of those blood vessels in the brain, something that no one's ever seen before. Just think, your scans have gone to medical professionals as far away as San Francisco and Switzerland for further research.

And this brings me back around to Dad, and sports, and all those feelings of hurt that have haunted you since you were a child.

Dad made the decisions he did because he was extremely protective of you, and of every little thing you did from birth. You were so very ill as a baby, and the doctors just couldn't work out *why*. Dad was scared and didn't want to risk something happening to you – didn't want to risk you getting hurt. And he saw sport as something that could only endanger your health. It's his love for you that made him overprotective; when you can't explain why your child is getting sick, you go out of your way to try to keep them safe.

Your health will be with you the rest of your life, Tash, and will become one of the biggest stepping stones you encounter as you grow older. But please, don't let any of this scare you too much; you are incredibly strong, courageous, powerful – a survivor. You face life without ever trying to stop, and you overcome every hurdle in your path. There is nothing and no one that can stop you – you are truly an inspiration, to so very many people.

*

Your health has never stopped you from chasing your dreams, and it's on a trip with your best friend, Renee, that you first realise what you want to do with the rest of your life.

You're going to join the Army or the Police Force.

You research everything in the Army, first, in preparation for applying. It's not until you tell Dad about your aspirations and your decision to apply that you feel like you're unworthy, that he has no intention of 'granting' permission for you to become an officer. *It's a man's job*, he tells you, *not a job for girls – you need more real-life experience*.

You're hurt, but his words can't stop you. Of course, you don't quite realise how hard the whole process will be: the applications, the interviews, the exams, the preparation for training … the training itself! But it doesn't matter: you're determined. You watch the police officers train out on the dusty red fields, jumping logs, climbing ropes, bear crawls through tunnels, high knees through waterlogged trenches – it'll be difficult, but this is your dream job, and you're willing to fight for it.

And so you applied for the police. It's the next step in your vision of the future – becoming a service officer for the community.

I won't lie to you, Tash – this journey is going to be difficult. It requires strength, a high level of fitness, power, resilience, performance, skill, verbal communication, a sound mind, working as a team as well as individually, developing coping strategies, managing stressful situations ... and, most important of all, empathy and respect.

That's you to a T, Tash. Go for it!

*

So, Tash, what have you learnt?

First of all, let me tell you that you will experience so much more than you expected as a police officer, a career that, over the course of more than 13 years, absolutely changes your life, in ways you can never imagine.

Looking back, I realise that the discipline of your upbringing, and the rebelling, and the ability to make mistakes, all taught you much more than you thought. What's that old saying? 'You have to be cruel to be kind'? It's a phrase that will run through your head each and every day, and even now you sometimes wonder if it's still true.

You know Dad loves you. He always will. And he's extremely proud of you. Do you remember why you feel like he treats you unfairly? Might it have been your perception? Was it just you, or were other kids treated the same or worse than what you thought was bad? Or was it just normal for our generation, when canes were still used in schools and dads were overprotective of their daughters?

Thing is, Tash, none of that really matters now. What matters is how you manage the cards you're dealt (and whether you manage them wisely or not)! Everyone is different, everyone is unique, and everyone has faced struggles in their own way. By the time you're my age, you'll have experienced life for what it is. What's important is this: Did you grow? Did you learn from your mistakes and the decisions you made? Did you have the best possible experience at the time? Where are you now? Do you still have your dream of the future, or have you reached it and created a new vision? Are you respected in the community?

Do you love yourself for who you are today?

That's what should matter to you, Tash. If only you'd know it when you were 10.

*

Tash, you are most *definitely* a unique individual – tell yourself this daily, please! Step on each stone in your path and learn to crush it; your future will hold many more stones, some bigger and some smaller, and you have to learn to deal with them wherever they arise.

Keep on striving for uniqueness.

Keep on making mistakes and growing.

Live life and strive to be you – and *only* you.

And, Tash, always remember:

**STRENGTH AND COURAGE OF A WARRIOR, HEART AND
SOUL OF AN ANGEL,**

FOREVER BY MY SIDE, THE WIND BENEATH MY WINGS

Lots of love always,
Me

CHAPTER 23

Daydreams and Moon-gazing

Joanne Edge

Dear Joanne,

Happy Birthday!! You're 10 today – how does it feel to be in double digits? Looks like you've had a wonderful day, a birthday to remember, that's for sure! You're snug in your cabin on the ship, feeling warm and fuzzy after your busy day. You spent your birthday in Israel, absorbing all the sights, smells, and noises in the markets and shops of Jerusalem, watching as goats and chickens wander around and relishing the smells of the food – such delicious smells! Then a party on the ship with a mouth-watering buffet made by the crew – so many different types of curry, chutney and dips, poppadoms, delicious hot naan, desiccated coconut (lucky you didn't sneeze on it this time and send it flying!) ... It was a feast!

And, the pièce de resistance: a wonderful cake made by the chef, who also went to the trouble of putting ten candles on it for you!

... how is it that you love food so much, and eat so much, but are still so tiny, even skinny, for your age?

So, you're 10 years old now, and I'm writing to you in the hope that you read and take notice of what I have to say to you

187

– that you have a joy-filled life. I hope you continue to enjoy and appreciate your life, and the lives of others, and are able always to see the magic of the world around you. And, too, I hope that this letter offers some guidance, so that you don't waste precious time worrying about stuff that doesn't really matter anyway.

So! Please read on and take what you wish from my words below.

Daydreaming is a good thing, no matter what others may tell you – whether you're looking out to sea, gazing at the moon, staring into nothingness, or just spending time with your imagination. At least, as long as that's not all you do! Your imagination is the creator of your world and your dreams and your life. So dream your dreams big; live your dreams. Do a little bit of something every day towards them, and towards what you want to do and how you want to spend your life. Picture it, think about it, feel it as though it has happened – and feel how happy and grateful you are that whatever you are hoping for has happened. Believe in your dreams and in magic, and never give up on them.

It's a miracle to be alive, to breathe, to move, to see, to hear, to think, to feel, for your body to do all the things that it does to keep you alive without you even having to think about it. Those giddy feelings that fizz up inside you, just because you're excited ... for waking up to a snowy morning; for getting home from school to see your cat, Nat, and her kittens; for jumping into your cosy bed and getting under the covers to get warm and read your book with a torch because it's so cold in your bedroom that there's frost on the inside of the windows. Those fizzy feelings are special moments to treasure; savour them, bottle them, make more of them, and keep them ... not just for you, but for others that you can share those giddy moments with who might need a sprinkling of fizz in their life – and for you, if you need to top up on some magic! We are privileged to be on this planet, enjoying its beauty and the miracles that life and nature bring. See the magic in the everyday – in the beauty of flowers, tiny creatures, the changing of the seasons, mountains, the moon – and never grow up! (That is, never lose your playfulness, silliness, and giddiness!) And laugh – lots! Somebody wise once said that growing old is inevitable – growing up is optional!

Be yourself, no matter what. You can do and be whatever you wish to be with commitment and persistence; don't listen to others who may think differently, or try to tell you any different, and don't compare yourself to others. You are uniquely you. Nobody on this planet is like you, or can do what you can do, and do it just how you do it – so try not to listen to those who may try to make you into something that you're not.

You're eager to please, but don't feel you need to please others all the time – help others, but don't forget to help yourself, too. Your early years have had so many changes. You've lived in lots of different places and attended lots of different schools. It's just been easier to try and please people, and to have them like you. So for example, when Auntie Sue asks if you want to stay for tea – it's okay to say you want to, because you know you do; you're having so much fun teaching your cousin to fly by jumping down the steps in their lovely garden with balloons in your hands. It's okay to say yes without overthinking it or wondering if they'll think you're cheeky if you do, or if they'll be offended if you decline. Just say yes – it's okay! You're a reflector and analyser, which will be valuable skills in the future but are less so right now … not when you can smell the delicious aromas of Auntie Sue's cooking and you're dying to stay for tea.

The moves and unsettled times end here; no need to worry about more big changes, just embrace and enjoy. Care for your mind: Clear it, be aware of what you allow to seep into it, and what you close it to. Meditate daily. Your calmness is a gift, and others will be grateful for that in the future. You aren't genetically made to be a drama queen; you were made to be as you are, and your experiences will shape who you become. You're sensitive and subtle and don't want to cause offence; it's okay to be fluffy around the edges but stand up for what you believe in. You'll come across people who won't be kind to you, but that is up to them. Don't let them affect how you behave. How they feel is up to them, but how you feel is up to you; you can only control how you feel. But be kind, and whatever you do, do it with love and kindness, avoiding intentional hurt at all times.

Go the extra mile to keep in touch with people. You'll have some pretty special people in your life, throughout your journey, and it's too easy to lose touch with them. They won't be around forever, so make time for them. That said – some people are meant to join you for portions along your path in life, while others will be with you all the way. Those meant to be in your life will be in your life.

Protect your time – you will find that it's one of the most precious things you have, along with your health (and the special beings in your life, of course). Don't waste time doing things you really don't want to do; sure, there'll be things you'll need to do that you may not want to, as part of your learning. There'll be challenges and obstacles that you'll need to overcome, but these are challenges along the way that you'll learn from. Everything you will go through in your life is a lesson, preparing you for something along the way, leading you where you need to go. It's the stupid, pointless things that you don't need to do that you may feel you *need to do or should do*. Treat yourself and save yourself a whole heap of hassle-filled thoughts by taking *should* out of your vocabulary – there's no such thing. You either *did* or *didn't* do something and that's all there is; you either *did* or *didn't* do something because that was the right thing to do at the time, so take *should* have out of the equation. Follow your heart; whatever you do, do it from the heart or in response to the gut feelings you have; that way there can be no regrets or guilt or *shoulds*. While it may now feel that you will live forever, life is way too short for wasting on those negative emotions.

Be careful who you spend your time with. Feel the energies of those around you – if they make you feel good when you're with them, enjoy; if they don't, stay well away, as best you can, and where you possibly can. And beware of mood hoovers, those that seek to suck out your positive energy and endeavour to convince you that the cup is half empty, when you can clearly see, and know, that it is half full. Learn to manage your time and use it well, and work on your time keeping. You may live in your own world with your very own time zone, but others do not and may not appreciate this, so master it. It will save you hours of last-minute running around and others of having to wait. Otherwise it is likely to be 50+ years practising before you perfect it! And, too, don't waste time worrying what you want to be when you 'grow up.' Think about what you love, and what you love doing, and do it. It will lead you to where you are meant to be and what you are meant to be doing, and if you enjoy it, you will study and master it, whatever it is.

Care for your body and move it every day just because you can, in any way you wish. Walk, run, jump, dance – anything to get your heart beating and release the feel-good hormones. When you start doing yoga in your thirties, carry on with it – your body and mind will thank you, and it will save you struggling to touch your toes when you start again in your forties! Listen to yourself and your body: Your instincts, thoughts, and behaviours are real. If it doesn't feel good, don't do it. If you get a funny feeling in your belly, that's your intuition asking you to take notice, so take notice. It might be a good belly feeling or a not so good belly feeling; listen to it – it knows best! Listen to music and sing! It makes you feel good. Make songs up, make words up – it will make your children, and others, laugh in years to come. Try to remember where you are, though, like the time you were sleeping in your brother's room on a camp bed – just because you thought it would be fun to sleep on a camp bed – and starting singing 'Peace, Perfect Peace' because you couldn't sleep. He was not too impressed!

Be mindful about what you are eating. Remember when you first found out that lamb was really lamb? That's right, a baby sheep! The day you asked your nana why they called it lamb, as you were tucking into one of her lovely Sunday roasts, and you were told that it was lamb – and you realised that you were actually eating one of those cute, fluffy little animals. Stick with that horrifying thought that you felt at that time; it was a real, trusted emotion. And those times when you went to visit Nana Edie and were delighted to feed the beautiful goat and watch it in the garden, and again your horror when Mum and Arthur, auntie and uncle went there for dinner and you found out that they had eaten that very same goat!!!

You'll be brainwashed as to how much you need to eat meat for your health and growth – but you don't. Just take a look at some of the strongest animals on the planet! (When they tell you things are done in a humane way – don't believe them. How can killing be humane? Do some research and see what you think!) Plant-based food is the way forward, and while this may be quite unheard of now, more information will become available for you: You *can* live and survive on plants, and on the fruits and wealth of goodness that Mother Earth grows. Be a plant pioneer! You'll feel better for not eating something that has been killed, both within your body and in your mind – emotionally, physically, and spiritually, and also environmentally. As the years pass, more people will soon start to learn about this in terms of health, nutrition, and disease, and many more will join that cause as you go through adulthood, despite there always being lots of contrary information advising differently. Choose wisely; again, your body will be grateful in years to come. And, after all, you can never be too sure of what you're eating. Remember the chicken stew you ate and enjoyed? And you later found out it was rabbit stew. You were aghast, but what's the difference – a chicken, rabbit, cat, dog, fish, lamb, cow ... ? Why is it that more value is placed on some animals' lives than others? You can't say you love and care for animals and then eat them! Stick with those gut feelings.

We are guests on this beautiful planet, and need to respect all its inhabitants. Regardless of what else is happening in the world, the earth continues its life: The sun continues to rise, the oceans continue to flow, the winds continue to blow, and the moon continues to shine bright. Try not to stress about the stuff you can't control. Enjoy 'living' life, and enjoy and care for the beauty the earth shares with us during our stay. Every single day, the world and the beauty of nature create wonderful things for us to see and feel. Continue to appreciate and enjoy them; try never to lose that sense of wonder of the everyday things that are magical – the beauty of a night sky, the cuteness of a kitten ... Yes, you're going to continue your love of all things cute, especially cats, and babies, and goats!!

Read, and continue your love of books, as you never know where it will take you – that dream of you becoming a writer will come true if you want it to. Keep learning and keep reading – education doesn't stop. Nothing learned is ever wasted; it will come in handy for something someday, or it will have taught you a lesson that helps to take you forward to your future self.

Remember that recent conversation with Gran? You were both discussing how you would never get on a plane, because you were both so scared. You've no need to be, you soon will get on a plane. Enjoy the excitement and adventures this opens up for you. Go conquer more fears; travel the world. Experience different countries and cultures; you're lucky to have seen a lot of it already via your travels on the ship. Go and explore as much of it as you possibly can.

Become a mother – it's the most wonderful thing you'll ever do. Love your children with all your heart. You'll get information and advice from all sources, but listen to your heart; you'll know what's best. As long as you love them unconditionally, keep them safe, and give them your time, interest, and attention, you'll embark upon the most incredible journey with them, watching them develop and learn and grow into wonderful adults. Appreciate and love the people close to you – your family, and friends; you never know how long they'll be around. Appreciate people around you more, generally, not just the people close to you. Always be the best you can – caring for others, following your heart, and making decisions based upon your heart.

Take Computer Studies when it's introduced in school in a few years. Yes, I know that will fill you with dread, and I can see your eyes rolling reading this – and yes, the class will be full of boys ... but you'll need it. It will stand you in good stead for the high tech world that is about to unfold.

Technology is going to develop rapidly as you grow up, so much so that your phone will be a mini computer, camera, Walkman, TV, and purse, all in one. You'll be able to keep in contact with people easily, all around the world. But just as there is light and dark, night and day, there is good and bad, and there are a whole host of problems that can arise from the changes this technology will bring that, luckily, you can't even begin to imagine just now. Along with the impact of other elements of life and society, some children, even at your age, will no longer want to be on this earth, enjoying the delights it brings – so spread those caring, loving wings and share the joys of life with all that you can.

There's this phenomenon that will soon whisk its way around the world as technology evolves – social media. Use it wisely, and please try to encourage your friends to do the same. You know all the fun that you have now playing out – bikes, picnics and playing in the streams, tig, hares and hounds in the park? If humans aren't careful, social media may impact all of that. Just talking to your friends, for instance, on a handheld phone with no wires – a bit like a walkie talkie, but it will work from further than the next room! And it will have no crackles and interference – not half as much fun! If you were to have it and use it now, if you weren't careful you could become absorbed in this and miss real life. You'd be inside your house, your friends inside theirs. You'd go to school, come home, and talk to your friends on social media rather than actually seeing them and going out to play and having fun.

It's not all negative! Technology will also bring so many positives and benefits in years to come. Technology will enable all kinds of hope, communication, and entertainment, but most importantly will enable families and friends to maintain contact, even if they can't see each other in person. Sounds amazing, hey? It's actually incredible – at the click of a few buttons, you'll have a world of info at your fingertips. You wouldn't need to go to the library anymore to do your homework or to scour through Arthur's encyclopaedias; it'll all be there in an instant. But you love books, right? And the library ... imagine a world without books, libraries, and bookshops. No. Way! So, I emphasise strongly, use technology mindfully.

Anyway, back to your birthday. You're right to love birthdays; they're special, but then every day is special! Not just birthdays. So enjoy them all – every single one. It's a blessing to be alive, and to grow old is a privilege. You may not think so now, but it will be a pleasurable honour to have time to look back on, be thankful for, and reflect upon your life, to see your children grow, and to share memories. Not everybody makes it to their senior years; not everybody makes it through childhood. Think about how you would feel or do things if it were your last day, because you never know when it will be. Be thankful, be mindful, and be happy for each day.

But for now, you are snug in your bed, still feeling warm and fuzzy about the memorable 10th birthday you have just experienced. So, while there is a lot of information contained in this letter for you, don't be daunted by it. It is written in the hope of helping and inspiring you to go forward through life with confidence and belief in yourself, and to help you to focus upon filtering out all the garbage you don't need, while cherishing and embracing all the things you will.

All my love,
Your 51-year-old self Xx

CHAPTER 24

Life Lessons

Chelsey Jean

Hey Girl,

I see you.

The world is totally yours for the taking.

I know these words sound just like another fridge magnet, or one of those things stuck to the back of the toilet door, but geez – what if you actually believed it now, at the perfect age of 10? You'll hear these words over and over again, but it'll take another 30 years before they really sink in. Yes – when you're old! If you could only know how your life unfolds, know how proud I am of you.

This letter is to say you will never be on your own: I am, and always will be, here for you. The most profound lessons in life come from left field, but you've learnt to ride the unexpected twists like waves, taming them and surfing your way to the shore – learning a new move with each new twist. When things in your life get hard – and they will, from time to time – please stop and take a big breath and feel me there with you, like a protective guardian angel. If only you could know that you'll always come out on top.

Are you ready to take a peek into your future? I know, silly question – you've probably already skimmed through to the bottom and are reading this for the tenth time! But just think, your obsession with wanting to know the future is finally coming true.

You've always loved to delve into the imaginary world of infinite possibilities, a love that's made its way into your schoolbooks, decorated every day with infinity symbols. And, too, this love grows into an interest in card readings and telling the future, bestowed upon you by gifted people from all over the world. Now, as your grown-up self, I find excitement in the world of uncertainty – but I hold fast to a trust in us, to the strong foundation you built for me so I can grow and learn and move forward, secure in the knowledge that I can have all I dream of.

It's all here, yours and mine and ours, for the taking.

But for now, stick to the sayings Mumma has drilled into you even at such a sweet age and recite them regularly – you know the ones I mean.

Your best friend is your bank book.

Always have a cunning kick.

Stand toe to toe.

A thief can only steal from you but a liar can have you hung ...

These little one-liners help mould you into a strong, independent leader – the leader you are now and in the time that, for you, is yet to come.

When you grow up, you'll be asked: how did you get here? What were the steps? How do you do all of these things? The answer to each question is you – that 10-year-old still deep inside, determined and fun and loving. I've been becoming myself my whole life, guided by that little girl deep inside who never gave up on me. Who always said yes – to life, to opportunity, to love.

Never stop doing this, honey.

I love how you've interpreted the events in your life up to now.

At 10, your father had just left. (He really had nothing to do with you anyway, so that didn't change much.)

At 10, you moved from Cairns to Lota. (You already had six school moves under your belt, were already a pro at adjusting to a different uniform each year, so that didn't matter.)

At 10, you were playing representative hockey and softball. (You always hung out with older kids, anyway.)

At 10, you walked out on the babysitter. (Because you do a better job looking after your brother and yourself.)

At 10, you sewed your first bra out of elastic. (The same elastic you used to play elastics, the game that was making your little boobs bounce . . .)

So, here we go. You've got Mumma's list; now it's my turn to share some important life lessons. I know you're ready.

Over time, the universe will show you that it believes in you, in countless ways; I want you to keep on embracing the world like you have already, with a cheeky smile and an *I can do that* attitude. You've always been so open and transparent, taking ownership of your story and never being afraid to share your opinions and speak out.

Never stop doing this. Feeling no fear at your voice being heard is a superpower, one that allows you to own and change the future, without ever having to rely on anyone else. This ability is at least part of why people have always been in awe of how you fit so much into life and your ability to do all of the things ...

This is fantastic – but also a total pain in the butt! Wearing the crown of the Queen of Responsibility, as you label yourself, means taking on much more than you should ... but that, my girl, is who you are. You are a giver, a girl who stands up for your values and strives to be an example for others. I've always loved your ability to stay so strong to your values and lead by example.

Life isn't always rosy, but remember, your shoulders are only so strong. I know that keeping busy is your way to make yourself numb, to block out everything that's too much for you to deal with and lock it away where it can't hurt you. I promise, you're not alone – so many people do this, often without even realising.

Here's the thing: as you get older, all of those moments will start to poke their heads out from time to time. But when you're grown up, when you're me, you'll have the tools and the professional support to deal with them as they arise. And, even better? All those years in between mean you'll have learned so much that you can teach thousands of women how to do the same – how to deal with things that were too much when they were younger. I love this part of my life so very much, and I'm so grateful that you were so brave, so protective, so determined to deal with everything as best you could, even when it was hard.

You are so brave. Looking back, you carried so much on your shoulders, weighed down by too many responsibilities and life experiences even at the age of 10. I can just see you shaking your head – but it's the truth! Bravery takes many forms – being brave is showing up, telling the truth, standing up for your beliefs, shedding your armour and standing tall. Brave is saying *no*. *No* to the babysitter who wanted to use you, to make you look after the other kids. *No* to following the rules and instead making your own. *No* to asking permission to be and do you.

As you grow up, you'll gain the confidence to have your own back, to feel like you're all you need. But you aren't alone. You have so much support, even if you can't see it, even if you seem to be the only person who can feel that you're protected, that no matter what something will *always* show up for you. You are watched over by angels and guides, and they will be with you always. With each year of life on this planet, you'll find yourself trusting more and more in this universal power; no matter how many questions you ask, you'll never lose the feeling of being totally supported. Your confidence will extend to knowing that your invisible support will always, absolutely have your back.

I know Mum leans on you, relies on your support. It's a strong relationship, and sometimes it's more like you're sisters. She tries so hard to protect you from your father, from his selfishness and destructiveness, but she's only 29 herself. Your memories of – I won't call him Dad, because we both know he's never fulfilled that role – *that man* will never leave you, not least that awful day when he kidnapped Ty from the trash and treasure markets you used to go to with Mumma and Pop. In the end, Ty was safe and your uncle brought him back home, but you'll never forget. While t*hat man* will pop in and out of your life a handful of times, it's that day that shaped your future relationship. You will be at peace knowing that he is happy to live his own life on his own path, rather than walk with you on yours, And when Mum happily remarries, her new husband will fill the gaps that you need in your life. I won't lie to you: it'll be rocky at the start, as you both vie for mum's attention, but with time the three of you will come to support each other as an unbreakable unit.

I know it's hard when you're only 10, but try not to take other people's opinions to heart, especially when those opinions hurt. Try to remember that their problems are *their problems*, not yours; you can only do *you*. Remember that you hold the ability to manifest the things you desire: if you focus on something that you truly align with, on something that you love, you are unstoppable. When you focus on something, you will start seeing it appear everywhere – butterflies, red cars on the roads, Cabbage Patch dolls – until you finally achieve it. And, too, you'll find that the things your life is missing can suddenly appear and become part of your world; love what you wish for and be ready to receive it with open arms. Remember, your angels are always with you and always working for you.

Thinking back, you always instinctively took the steps that I've had to relearn as an adult, seeking help from the best life coaches across the world. Every day I remind myself that I already know how to do this, that I always have – it's just that now there's a name as well as specific help for it. But how did you know?? I suppose in the end, the *how* doesn't matter; I'm just so grateful that you did.

You will always see the good in people and want to help, with an unshakeable faith that things will always work out for the best.

I know that things are hard. You've never stayed at a school longer than a year, and I know it hurts that you never seem to have friends that survive each move. Every time it comes to pack again, it feels like your life is uprooted, taking away your friends, but I promise that one day you will develop beautiful, wonderful friendships that survive and thrive far beyond 12 months.

You know, looking back I realise that I rarely thought about how I look. Maybe not now, this year, but with time the boys will start noticing you – even if you remain oblivious! Try not to take things too seriously; you have so many years and so much more living to do before tackling something like true love. (Which absolutely exists, I promise!) Don't let go of being a tomboy; ride motorbikes; explore old boats down at the jetty; and slow dance with as many boys as you want to!

There is so much more waiting for you on your journey to become me. Everything that shapes me now comes from you, because you chose to thrive. Life progresses in waves, patterns, and flows, and because of you I can see these patterns, like how my sleep pattern coincides with the size of the moon. I encourage you to reach out and explore, to experience every day with an eye out for the important bits; the more you acknowledge them and hold them close, the fewer issues I have to deal with later! Your life – my life – has profound meaning and purpose. The real you is brave, fun, authentic, always learning and always making the most of each and every moment. And it's that realness, that authenticity, that will draw people to you as you grow up, and that will enable you to help people to live their best lives.

Of course, one of the difficulties of growing up is figuring out who to fight for – who you should strive just that much harder to keep in your life. I know you believe that the people you care about will leave you. I know that it keeps happening in your life, with new people coming and old people going each year, and I know that your default is to let people make their own decisions. If someone wants to stay, they will, right? But as you grow up, think about who you should fight for, and when you should fight for them. There aren't any easy answers, but try to keep it in mind as the years pass. Remember that every person is doing the very best they can; it's hard, especially when you find yourself disappointed, but it's something that you have to be able to understand and accept. It's easy to let people go, especially when your thoughts stray to negative assumptions and conclusions, but if you try to assume that everyone has good intent, it becomes easier to stay rather than jumping ship. By the time you're my age, you won't have to work as hard at giving people the benefit of the doubt, the chance to show you the important role they play in your life, because it's become second nature to let them in.

I suppose when it boils down to it, this letter is me checking in with you, to tell you that you are enough. That everything will always be okay.

No, you're not perfect, and yes, I absolutely love you anyway. But here's the thing – you can be manipulative at times. You need to always be right, to always have things done *your* way, to the point that you finish relationships and shut down, showing that you don't need anyone because you are fiercely independent and self-sufficient. Thing is, when you're on autopilot, you turn into a control freak, a workaholic, a woman so determined to get things done, even with no help. Even if it means you have to work all night to finish what you started ... because you gave your word, and giving your word is super important to you. Not everyone is like this, though, and it's easy to find yourself let down when someone else doesn't follow through. Try not to be too harsh on them – or on yourself.

Please know that the softer side of you is also worthy. You deserve to be cuddled and loved, to let people in to accept love. Don't let all the ways people have failed you stop from pursuing your dreams, or from accepting the love and joy life has to offer. Work to honour deeper connections you feel with people you are drawn to – and know that true relationships come from those who are also seeking connection. Stay in the game and follow your path of freedom. Pause to take in the beauty around you, be unafraid to attend parties you're invited to, and go to schoolies instead of working two jobs.

Because of you, my beautiful 10-year-old self, the life I live now is fulfilling. Take the words in this letter to heart; let the lessons

I've shared become a part of who you are. And remember: you will always have me as your number one cheerleader.

I freaking love you,
Chels xo

CHAPTER 25

The Girl Who Didn't Fit

Kelly Ledger

Dear Kelly,

Oh, my girl. Standing here, so many years from the day you turned 10, I can see the challenges and heartbreaks awaiting you, and wish you didn't have to go through all of it still. But I'm here to tell you that everything life throws at you – you'll survive, and you'll eventually find a life you love.

You will grow up knowing that you're different. You see life through a different lens, always thinking outside the box – and though you'll spend a good part of your life thinking this is a disability, later in life you'll realise that this has been your greatest gift.

As a kid, though, you'll constantly feel frustrated, like a square peg doing your best to push into a round hole. There's a photo of you at this age, standing in a line with the rest of your class – except you're facing in the opposite direction, posing. You always seem to have the urge to do the opposite of what everyone else is doing, not to be contrary, but because it's what feels right. Despite, or maybe because of that, everyone seems finds you weird, quirky … crazy. You'll try to get all the odd kids together, in an attempt to show that you're actually the popular group, and you'll learn the art of mimicking those people who everyone seems to like, wearing masks so that people won't see the real you – trying so hard to fit in when you don't, not really. I know you feel alone, in your own little world, with no one who understands you or wants to hear what you have to say. It will break your heart at times, and make you cry, but please remember: These are not your people. Hold strong, Kelly. Hold strong, because in time you will find where you belong.

Your bullies only care that you're different; they don't want to see who you really are, instead preferring to mock you with nasty nicknames like Can Opener (thanks to your brother Lee and your crooked teeth) and Dumbo (because your ears stick out of your hair). And because you're so lanky and thin, people are forever asking if you have an eating disorder, suggesting that instead of sponsoring hungry kids with the 40-hour famine, they ought to be feeding you instead. Everyone laughs, again, at your expense. It's a cruel world.

There are bright spots, though, despite the sadness and loneliness. Your Grade 3 teacher is the most wonderful human being you'll ever meet; she introduces you to the wonderful worlds of Roald Dahl and Dr Seuss, writes beautiful words on your report cards, makes you feel valued. She makes you feels safe, and it will mean more than you can imagine as you battle the rough seas of childhood and your teenage years. And your grandmother – from her you learn kindness, the beauty of treating others who are different or unique with compassion, not cruelty, and you will hold onto that ideal, even as life does its best to batter you into submission, when kids are unkind and bosses dismissive.

*

I wish I didn't have to tell you this, but the bullies at school aren't the last time you'll have bad luck with relationships. You'll meet a man when you're 17, and you'll believe him when he promises that he'll give you a wonderful life. Unfortunately, even though enough red flags pop up that you'd be able to see them from the moon, you don't take heed. Instead, you persuade yourself that it's better to be with him than to be alone – and you'll convince yourself all the way up to the altar, into a marriage that you know is wrong, because you just can't seem to work out that it would have been better to walk away. When you're older, you'll learn to trust your intuition – to believe that if something doesn't feel right, there's a reason for it. But it takes time to find that trust in what you feel in your gut, and at 19, being with him makes you feel special, worthy in some way – so different from how awful your life was at school. That's your ego, telling you that you're going to be someone … as long as you stay with him.

You realise eventually that you've put value into the wrong things, but by then it's too late to escape with any ease. Four weeks before your 21st birthday, you have your first baby – Michael. For a moment it seems perfect, a perfect family, with you and your beautiful baby boy and your husband. And then it goes wrong again. He doesn't want you to work and controls who you can see. You end up cut off from all of your friends and, to a degree, from your family and support networks. He starts to complain that you're getting frumpy, and opts to spend his time hanging out at the bar until all hours.

There is good news, eventually. When he refuses to go to counselling, you spend $60 to go and look at an empty chair … and have a moment of clarity. Your life is not the one you wanted, and you realise that the longer you stay, the worse things will get. So you gather up your courage, like the strong woman you are underneath the hurt, and start planning to leave. You finally tell him on your birthday, when yet again he's not been bothered to make an effort. And though you've imagined all the different ways he might respond once you tell him, in the end it's not 'I'll change' or 'I'll go to therapy' that you hear – it's 'but what are people going to say about me?' If you needed any more of a push to get out, that was it.

As much as it's a relief to finally move out and start your new life, you realise quickly that being a single parent is *hard*. Your mum suggests you move home, but it's important to you that you prove that you can be an adult, stand on your own two feet, be a good mum to Michael. For a while it's a mess – but somewhere in all of that chaos, you find yourself again, and it's a relief to realise that you're still there, deep inside, waiting to come back out.

It takes time, but then you meet Steve, and he's so different from your last relationship that it takes you a long time to realise that he's really, actually, a good bloke, one with no interest in hurting you or breaking your heart. But first and foremost you're a mum, and so you keep things quiet, not telling Michael, to protect him in case things don't work out. And then, oh, you'll learn yet again how much you love that beautiful boy of yours, when he learns about Steve for the first time and is delighted that you have a special friend – because it means you're happy, and Michael is glad to see you happy again.

The wedding is set for May, but leading up to the big day you realise you're pregnant, with Max. It comes as a shock to Steve

– and you! – but really it just means growing your little family a bit more quickly than you'd planned. A year later, on Max's first birthday, you realise that little Tommy's on his way, your family expanding just that much more. You're a long, long way from that bullied little girl – but you still have so much life and growth and knowledge to gain.

*

In your first marriage, before Michael is born, you spend time working at your (ex-)husband's family business, doing filthy jobs to try to work your way into running events and functions. Eventually you get interested in online shopping, and it doesn't take long for you to build a successful online jewellery business. But the more people start to take notice, the more your (ex-) husband dislikes it, until it becomes a huge point of contention in your marriage. You don't work again until you leave him, when you're lucky to get a job as a teacher and casting assistant at a talent agency. Later, you'll move from working as a travel agent to working with an airline, moving from marketing and sales to the VIP department and back to sales again.

Here's the most important thing you learn from your work, Kelly: Don't stay in a job where people can't see your value. You spend so much time over the years building castles on clouds when it comes to jobs, spinning gossamer dreams that collapse in on themselves when the work world you envisioned doesn't come to pass. Once, you put stock in inspirational quotes; after one disappointing job after another, you finally realise that they're just words, nothing more. No matter how hard you work, no matter how much you sacrifice, no matter which job you try, you always seem to come up short – never quite good enough, never quite fitting the mould, a great team player but somehow not the person that's wanted or needed. The instructor of a modelling course gave you one of the worst pieces of advice in your life: Fake it until you make it. And you do, thinking this will take you places ... but you just end up chasing empty dreams.

And oh, dear girl, you try so hard, for so long. You figure out each new role on your own, because no one ever seems to be around to explain it to you. When a 20-something co-worker constantly puts you down and makes you feel inadequate, you try to get over it, because she probably doesn't even realise she's doing it, and complaining won't get you anywhere. You try to go above and beyond, but no one ever seems to be around to notice. You snap the ligaments in your ankle and are taken away by ambulance – and the first thing you do is ask for your laptop, so that you can at least keep working. Surely, you think, they'll notice now? But no, they don't, and when redundancies are announced, you go into a really dark place. Sure that if you just work that little bit harder, it'll turn out alright for you, you dive into extra hours, putting in that much more effort, hoping beyond hope that it'll be enough … And then you hear about an incentive at work, to win a trip to fashion week. Losing isn't an option; you've lost too many things before. You throw everything you can at it – and you win! For the first time in a long time, you're sure that your future is secure, that this is your moment, that it's all uphill from here. You get on the plane – but then the event is cancelled, because (would you believe it), there's a global pandemic that's shutting down things all over the world. It's upsetting, but you'll survive, you think.

And then come the redundancies. You try, so hard. You go in early, clean up emails in the team inbox over the weekend, offer to be on call if needed. But in the end, you turn out to be the one on the chopping block – and all you can think of is how everything you sacrificed has been for nothing. All that time you didn't take off when you were injured. All those memories you missed with the kids as they grew up. All the days you turned up to work when you really shouldn't have. Sadly, the best person for the job doesn't always get the job, nepotism is alive and well and often favourites are played.

What was the point?

How can you begin to explain to the kids? What kind of message will this send them? You do your best – and sometimes it's just … not enough? In retrospect, of course, life is often unfair, and it doesn't hurt kids to know that no life is without disappointment. And, too, there's an important lesson for you here: If you aren't careful, you throw all of yourself into work. But you're so much more than just your job. It just takes time to realise it.

Anxious to move on, anxious to find a new source of income, you devise a crazy plan to sell personalised videos of yourself, dressed as the Easter bunny, on an online platform. And it works. Some days you end up making more money than you did when working for the airline. Even better, you find a sense of purpose in this role, and the messages you get from delighted customers helps to fill the void you've found yourself in. And, finally, you realise that you're not alone – no one else completely knows what they're doing, either.

In the end, you'll find yourself in a job in the entertainment industry, behind the scenes. Your ability to think on your feet, keep an eye on solutions, and adapt with ease makes you quite successful in this role. And this is what you learned, after every job you've worked: Hold out and remember your worth. So often you ended up working for companies who never saw you as a person, just a number on a spreadsheet and a potential redundancy to save money. Don't give up. Life is hard, but you'll find your worth in the end. And somewhere in all of the chaos, you'll find yourself again – and it will be such a relief to realise that you're still there, deep inside, waiting for the right to emerge and just be.

Kelly, every time life throws you a challenge, you'll learn something about yourself, even when it takes heartbreak and pain to find it. You struggle when you're young when it comes to being told what to do; you're much more likely to go rogue and do your own thing ... almost inevitably with disastrous results. You always want to be right, but you'll come to learn that it's important to acknowledge when you're wrong – to be able to take on other people's perspectives and evaluate the world from that point of view. It's so important to put yourself in the other person's shoes, see things as they see them, and only then make a decision to move forward. It's not something you'll learn overnight, but once you've conquered this lesson, you'll find yourself much more at peace. And here's a little peek at your future: You'll finally realise this playing scopa with an old Italian man. You spend a few games winning – and then realise that there's beauty in allowing him to win, just as there's beauty in allowing yourself to not always be right.

You have to keep your ego in check and your feet firmly planted on the ground, or you'll miss out on the beauty of your family. Trust your intuition. Don't give up easily. Be yourself, not what you think the world wants you to be.

Because, in truth? That self is pretty darn awesome.

Love you, dear girl.

xx Kelly

ACKNOWLEDGEMENTS

This book wouldn't have happened without a few people.

To my project manager, designer, and book formatter extraordinaire, Kathy Shanks, who kept me in line and stepped in to create a stunning cover at the last minute, when our initial cover designer was not available, and I rejected the first 10 concepts by other designers! Thank you so much for always being awesome.

To Makenzi Crouch, the incredible editor I have worked with since my own first book all those years ago. Your command of language, and warm personality make you a pleasure to work with. Only for you would I embrace all those red lines and corrections!

The lovely Nelika McDonald, who provided a perfect proofread at super fast speed when we were up against publishing deadlines and running behind with everything. We applaud you and I can't wait to do more work with you in our new programs over the coming years.

To Amanda Horswill, who wrote the beautiful back cover description of the book. Condensing an 85,000 word book down to a few hundred words is a skill that not many people possess. You're also an awesome person who I am proud to call a dear friend. Thank you for sharing your talent with us.

To Lauren, Annette, and Dee of The Audacious Agency, who provided stellar marketing and publicity services for the authors. Without you, the book would not be seen, and I'm so grateful to have met you and witnessed your incredible talents.

To my personal assistant, Shecainah Sagaya. Without you, my business would fall apart and my days would be darker. Thank you for always being there with your beautiful smile and generous, gentle nature.

To my family, Andres and Boston. Thank you for being patient with my early starts and late finishes, and all those times I was in angry bear mode and stressed about work, especially when they were on the same day. I love you.

Finally, to the authors who wrote these letters. Thank you for joining me on this journey. Thank you for opening your hearts and minds, and being open to the process of writing a letter you know could literally never be read by the recipient. I am so grateful that you chose to tell these stories, and the way you embraced it was amazing, and your letters are just perfect. You rock!

About the Authors

Amanda Horswill

As an impressionable 13-year-old, Amanda watched, mesmerised, as a 20-something Jana Wendt, clad in flack-jacket and khaki helmet, rode through a war-torn landscape, lipstick gleaming. From that moment, Amanda was hooked on news.

Fast forward three decades, and she has realised that dream, of sorts, covering myriad subjects, including hard news, property, lifestyle, data journalism, the arts, and careers. While she's (frankly) thankfully to never have had to wear a bullet-proof helmet, she served as Editor of *Brisbane News*, Deputy Features Editor and founding Deputy Editor of *U on Sunday Magazine* for the *Sunday Mail*, and a host of other senior positions at News Corp, prior to joining Australia's biggest financial comparison website, Canstar.

A passionate believer in the motto 'knowledge is power,' Amanda strives to translate the news into practical information that will help readers make informed decisions about their future.

When not analysing the news, Amanda can be found pouring over local property listings, searching for her next renovation project (she's up to eight so far), and running after two children (lipstick optional).

She holds a Bachelor of Arts in Journalism, Media Studies and Production, and Public Relations and a Graduate Certificate in Editing and Publishing from the University of Southern Queensland.

Amanda Horswill
Email   amanda.j.horswill@gmail.com
Facebook @mandyjaynee
Instagram @amanda-j-horswill

Anna Ball

I'm Anna, Founder and Director of Dot & Quill, a marketing communications consultancy focused on activating growth for small businesses. I'm a wordsmith extraordinaire, with a focus on developing actionable communications strategies to help my clients engage authentically with their audiences.

Since graduating in 2004, I've worked in London, New York, Sydney, and Brisbane and have developed communications strategies for many global brands as well as small businesses across the globe. In 2018, I found my courage to leave corporate life, bottled up my extensive knowledge across communications, and embarked on my entrepreneurial journey – setting up Dot & Quill. I'm honoured that my commitment was recently recognised by becoming a finalist in the recent 2020 AusMumpreneur Awards. It's this passion of helping small business owners find powerful words to activate growth in their own businesses which sees me jump out of bed in the morning.

My love for communication stems from being a languages scholar at the University of Exeter, England, and at the Universita di Urbino, Italy. The beauty of French and Italian captivated me, yet piqued my curiosity about how leaning on the nuances of language could change my message. I aim to use this ability to drive my clients to successful outcomes through human, authentic content.

Anna Ball I Dot & Quill
Phone   +61(0)477 329 223
Email   anna@dotandquill.com
Website www.dotandquill.com

Dr Catherine Jones

Doctor, mother, data scientist, wife, crafter, daughter, feminist, and sister. All words to describe Dr Catherine Jones, a 40-something based in Brisbane, Australia. This foray into creative writing is a new endeavour, taking her out of her comfort zone, far from the safety of academic writing.

Catherine is an avid learner and obligatory multitasker with many projects on the go at once. She loves to network and develop contacts in medical and other fields. She is never happier than when juggling far too many balls at once, which she finds it quite exhilarating.

Catherine's mantra is 'accept every opportunity and you'll never regret it.' She most recently founder herself in the fortunate position of being surrounded by interesting people and academically stimulating work.

Her husband and children balance out her innate tendency towards being a workaholic and remind her that life is nothing without the interpersonal connections. In her spare time, Catherine likes to travel, read, bake cakes, knit, dabble in photography, and practise riding her bike.

Dr Catherine Jones
Email   drcatherinejones@gmail.com
Instagram @blueyecath
LinkedIn   Catherine Jones

Charlie Giles

I am a descendant of the Wonnarua & Awabakal peoples on my father's side and Friesian (Holland) on my mother's. My father was born into an era when it was best not to talk about your heritage; however, despite this, it would be passed down anyway through intergenerational trauma once he started his own family. Uncovering the dark history and the truth-telling of these stories is what helped me to claim my identity; despite the fear of what others would say, the story of my parents gave me the courage to stand up and be my authentic self.

This has now empowered me to help others do the same. For 15 years, I have coached people to reclaim their authentic self and not be scared to live as the person they are meant to be.

I now work with traditional healers, learning energy healing and sacred ceremonies that reconnect and unblock the energies and patterns keeping them stuck in unhelpful behaviours. I initially studied a Bachelor of Arts in Social Science, then became a health coach and completed a Diploma in Astrology; I continue to study plant medicine and other Shamanic traditions.

Charlie Giles | Life Strategist & Energy Healer
Phone   +61(0)499 505 446
Email   Charliegee444@gmail.com
Facebook @charlieggiles

Chelsey Jean

I wake up each day excited to help others discover new, common-sense solutions for their healthiest and best life. I am a qualified sports therapist, naturopath, free thinker, awesome mum, and creator of the Advanced Natural Health Clinic and the Chelsey Jean label.

My passion for health and wellbeing began at 19 years of age, when I opened my first health and fitness studio, armed with a business diploma, knowledge of the health industry, and a passion for creating a niche in the health space. I soon began a movement towards detoxification and lymphatic health – conditions that are shockingly lacking but essential for immune health, fat transportation, metabolism, and energy. If it slows down, so do you . . . It took off!

My goal – to teach everyone how to 'pop the cork' and drain their lymphatic system – is now becoming true. I love making it fun and easy along the way, with my own special massage sequence that incorporates over 20 years of clinical experience and thousands of clients, as well drawing in all of the best bits of knowledge from my teachings all around the world.

As a self-described 'lymphoholic,' my innovative, naturopathically formulated LymFATic products and protocols can now be found in health clinics and retail stores all over Australia. I believe that amazing health should be accessible to everyone, and it's my family's and my mission to lead by example, supporting both women and men to uncover what is blocking them from becoming the best version of themselves – and have a ton of fun along the way.

Influenced by the great success of my in-clinic patients and winning the Innovation Awards at Natex 2020, I aspire to change as many lives as possible with my online community 'BooB CamP, LymFATics Alive and Body Wisdom' programs.

Both lymph and life need love and motion; I am so in love with this life.

Chelsey Jean I Naturopath, Lymphatic Queen
Phone   +61(0)412 333 209
Email   hello@chelseyjean.com
Instagram @chelsey_jean_lymfatics

Courtney Kynaston

I am a virtual assistant (VA) and Mindfulness Creativity and Anxiety Mentor. I work to help people within their businesses to gain back time to focus on their clients and family.

I also aim to help them approach both their personal and professional life with reduced stress and anxiety through creativity.

Over the last 20 years, I have explored all different ways to manage and cope with my anxiety. In that time, I have found tools and techniques that help me daily to stay in control of my anxiety. My goal is to share those tools and my story with as many people as I can.

My focus is to help people explore a variety of creative outlets and incorporate them with mindfulness techniques. Through understanding these methods, they can be applied and used to calm the mind and handle the situation they're in.

I have worked in music venues and music shops and art schools; I have also worked with clients as their VA, helping other people. Each role and environment has allowed for creativity to be encouraged and explored.

Through working primarily in customer service, I have grown a passion to share my story and help other people, and wish to explore these opportunities further.

I have a bachelor's degree in graphic design and marketing and a double diploma in marketing and administration. I am a member of the Mindfulness Meditation Teacher Training Program with Sean Fargo. I have mindfulness & life coaching certifications through New Skills Academy as well as various mindfulness and creativity courses through Udemy.

I would love to hear from you if you would like to learn more about what I have to offer, or to join my 'Mindful Creativity for Anxious Minds' Facebook group.

Courtney Kynaston
Virtual Assistant & Mindfulness Creativity & Anxiety Mentor
Phone   +61(0)466 663 925
Email   courtney@kismetva.com.au
Website   www.kismetva.com.au/mindfulness

Donna Gabriel

Drama Dance Educator, Health and Relationship Coach

A lifelong educator with a broad facilitation and event background, I love incorporating performance and communication skills to instil clarity of motivation with passion for life and healthy fun.

Dancing Donna. That's me. Since I can remember, I've pushed the furniture back to dance, rehearse, create that new move. How does it go? What if I spin here? I felt those moves, as a spirit, guiding me.

I've coached a Vic. Calisthenic Team to national victory, been awarded an Australian Sports Medal from Gymnastics Australia, choreographed hundreds of dancers for major events, and delivered assertiveness communication to people from all walks of life. On other days, I might teach creative writing to incarcerated women, introduce international students to Melbourne, or deliver sex education to adults with cognitive learning differences.

We connect and create as we talk, listen, share, learn, laugh, maybe even cry – and leave with more hope. I love it.

Donna Gabriel
Drama Dance Educator, Health and Relationship Coach
Phone   +61(0)414 250 932
Email   donna@donnagabriel.com

Ian Collins

For most of my life, I've been keeping other people safe while dancing on the edge of risk myself. I've travelled the world as an international Safety & Performance Coach, worked with many industry-leading organisations, and helped thousands of people from all walks of life to stay safe and realise their potential. I've lived on five different continents and explored a lot of this globe – walked on fire, jumped out of planes, ridden bobsleighs and motorbikes at breakneck speeds, swam with sharks, climbed mountains and active volcanoes, taken plant medicine in the jungle, come face-to-face with pirates in the Congo, barely avoided being thrown in jail in Libya, trained entrepreneurs in North Korea, and even sent flowers to Chairman Kim Jong-un in a gesture of peace. I have dedicated my life to curiosity and play, and it has been one heck of a ride to date!

My deep desire to understand what makes us tick has led me to specialising in Human and Organisational Performance – the science of systems-driven behaviour and understanding of how and why people make mistakes. I work with organisations on some of the riskiest frontiers to build more resilient and reliable systems that keep planes in skies, prevent oil rigs from blowing up and nuclear plants from melting down, and ultimately get people home safely to their families and keep the environment free from harm.

I also work on an individual level to help people recognise that behind fear is unlocked genius and joy. That the whole spectrum of life can be embraced and that we can meet ourselves at the edge of what's possible. Shall we dance?

Ian Collins is a Master Behavioural Coach.

Ian Collins | Human Performance Coach
Email   ian@safetycoach.com
Website   www.safetycoach.com
Website   www.ianpcollins.com
Facebook   @ipcollins
Instagram   @ianpcollins
LinkedIn   linkedin.com/in/safetycoach

Jess Weiss

I'm a mum of two beautiful children; my son is 2.5 years old and my daughter is 8.

Together with my partner, we live in Gympie, Queensland Australia, near the beautiful Sunshine Coast.

I am originally from Germany and immigrated to Australia seven years ago. Coming from a background of childhood trauma and abuse, I always struggled to find emotional stability in life. When I first became pregnant, married, and moved to the other end of the world, I believed I would find happiness.

But I didn't find it. Instead, I found myself in the darkest episode of my life ever.

My emotional well-being, self-worth and the sense of fulfilment went down in lighting speed.

When I hit my emotional rock bottom, I took a close look inside and realised that I've spent my life in toxic environments, toxic relationships, and toxic thought patterns.

I was overloaded with stress, anxiety, and negativity and was disconnected and emotional exhausted, slowly drinking myself away – divorced and a single mum with no social or financial support in Australia.

So I went on a journey to find myself and to find peace within.

Today I am extremely passionate and on a mission to inspire others to make positive changes and to tap into a happier and healthier version of themselves and to heal their wounds of the past.

Wildest Wings is about learning how to FLY – First Love Yourself.

Jess Weiss | Emotional Well-Being and Self Love Coach, Writer, Sobriety Mentor, and Mental Health Ambassador
Email   Jessica79.weiss@gmail.com
Email   wildestwings.change@gmail.com
Facebook Wildest Wings
Instagram jayjay_down_under

Joanne Edge

I have a special interest in psychology, particularly in human behaviour and relationships, and more specifically relationships within the early years and interactions between parents and their children. I have a passion for helping parents to enjoy their children and to recognise how their feelings, behaviour, words. and actions affect their children – even from conception and during pregnancy; and to help parents enable their children to grow up loved, safe, secure, and confident with love and compassion for others and the world around them.

I also have a keen interest in mindfulness, meditation, and yoga, reinforced by regular practice. I have more recently developed an interest in personal development and the power of the human mind. I also have a passion to share the importance of life-long learning and self-development.

My background is in working with children and their families, other than random jobs as a student! I am currently working as a team leader with nearly 19 years of service, leading a team of public health practitioners to support children, young people, and their families within the community. Through my work experiences, I have developed a great sense of warmth and emotional intelligence, as well as an ability to connect with and support people. We know from research that problems and difficulties in relationships and life stem from our early days, and that the early years of a child's life are critical for their growth, development, security, and trajectory through life. I am keen for people to be aware of this and to see how changing their perspective on things can have a positive impact.

I qualified as a nursery nurse after leaving school and went on to become an RN, midwife, and health visitor with a BSc Hons in Public Health Nursing.

My greatest experience of families has been in raising my own. My two wonderful sons are the reason for my desire to share my knowledge and experience, and to try and make steps towards the world becoming a more harmonious place for those who are to follow.

Joanne Edge
Email   joanneedgebooks@gmail.com
Instagram @Joanne Edge_edge_

Kati Britton

I am a registered play therapist with the Australasia Pacific Play Therapy Association and a clinically registered counsellor with the Psychotherapy and Counselling Federation of Australia. I am also an international member of the Association for Play Therapy in the United States.

Since 2009, while completing my bachelor's degree in social science, I worked as a counsellor in an addiction treatment centre on the Northern Beaches of Sydney, treating addictions and mental health issues. Seeing the trauma being presented by adults at the treatment centre, I decided to start working with children to break this cycle of harm before it begins in the adolescent phase and beyond. Becoming an adoptive mother was also a driving force behind my decision to become a professional play therapist. Since completing a postgraduate diploma in Art & Play Applications in Therapy, I now own my own private practice, Britton Play Therapy & Counselling, where I support children and their families who have experienced trauma and social, emotional, and behavioural difficulties. I am also an intercountry adoptive mother of an amazing boy from South Korea.

When I am not doing my therapy work, I am chief maker and founder of Evolve Candles. This is my creative outlet, as I love to make beautiful, natural, handmade products.

Kati Britton | Entrepreneur, Clinically Registered Counsellor & Play Therapist, Inter-country Adoptive Mother
Phone   +61(0)447 831 807
Email   info@brittontherapy.com.au
Website   www.brittontherapy.com.au

Kelly Ledger

A jill of all trades, Kelly is known for her adaptability and is not afraid to get her hands dirty when she needs to. She recently gave an impromptu keynote on leadership after a speaker pulled out at the eleventh hour. Kelly's leadership style is to never ask staff to do something that she wouldn't do herself. With an attitude of always saying yes and working out how to do it later, Kelly has found herself in some unique situations but has always managed through them like a duck takes on water.

After finally settling for a career in the travel industry, this all came to a crashing halt when Covid hit and she was made redundant. This lured Kelly back to her roots in the entertainment industry while finding a way to make an income selling personalised videos as the Easter bunny as something to pass time and find purpose again. This eventually led her to work for a company that provides services to the events, film, and TV industries. Kelly currently runs the QLD Business. Kelly is also an emerging comedian, and this has also led to her also being a keynote speaker and aspiring comedian.

Once I worked for an airline . . . Now I have fully grown my wings to fly . . .

Kelly Ledger I Mother, Wife, Comedian, Businesswoman
Email   mskellyledger@gmail.com
Facebook @iamthatkelly
Instagram @iamthatkelly

Lisa Boorer

I love education and find learning a greatest way of expanding our horizons and meeting wonderfully interesting people. I have an executive master's in business administration, a diploma in hospitality management, and a certificate IV in training and assessment, all for business purposes. For personal use, I have a master's NLP, a certificate I & II in craniosacral therapy, a certificate I in somato emotional release, and a master's in hypnosis.

I'm a senior consultant for Bill Lucas P/L. My role varies from hospitality training to written contributions for online course creation, social media marketing, and business consulting. There is never a dull moment or a day that doesn't make me think outside the square. (PS: I am terrible with punctuation; thankfully there are proof-readers).

I am the mother of three amazing people, who through their lives have taught me more about myself than has always been comfortable.

My greatest pleasure in life is contributing to the success of others, facilitating the change in a person's life or business that they are seeking and watching them get that lightbulb moment or to even learn about themselves and see those goals shift and change.

Lisa Boorer | Business and Personal Consultant
Email   lisaboorer@icloud.com
LinkedIn   linkedin.com/in/lisaboorer

Luke Amery

Luke Amery is a brain cancer survivor, best-selling author, speaker, sensei, and open-cut FIFO worker. He was awarded the 2017 Bright Future Award and 2017 Amazon Best-Seller Award for his first book, *Ganbaru Mindset*. A Japanese term that means 'to stand firm' in spite of circumstances, or to do even more than one's best, Luke developed *Ganbaru* into a strategy through which to tackle anything in life.

He was happily working as an "open-cut" miner in Australia when he began struggling with his physical balance and discovered he had been struck with brain cancer. As the father of two, working for long periods away from home, he already knew he had been missing out on so much. Coupled with the sudden, serious health issue, Luke knew a complete life change was in order.

Today, having conquered his golf ball-sized brain tumour, Luke lives with a sense of making up for lost time, and the importance of living in the now. He has found new joy in helping others achieve their dreams and rediscover their "mojo" along with their true purpose and passion in life.

A student of karate since 1998, Luke holds two blackbelts and is proud to have shared his passion for martial arts through teaching in his local community as well as his own practise.

He has appeared on *Hot & Healthy* with Nicole Vanhatten as well as on *Brandworking* with award-winning branding expert Lauren Clemett. He also spoke at Ronald McDonald House and Brainchild Foundation's 2018 Young Wild & Free Charity Gala.

Luke Amery
Email   info@ganbarumindset.com.au
Website   www.ganbarumindset.com.au

Makaela Moore

As an intuitive leadership coach, I help women in business shift their identity to become fearless leaders in life and work, so they can stop walking on eggshells and finally be the confident leader they aspire to be. Unlike other coaches, who focus on traditional goal-setting and leadership strategies, I use my signature framework, which combines brain science, subconscious reprogramming, and intuition with leadership principles to help women transform their lives from the inside out.

Leadership shouldn't only be a workplace trait. When we embrace the characteristics of our 'inner leader,' we are able to let go of our armour and step into a life that is fulfilling, courageous, and intentional.

My signature framework and coaching help women to achieve more out of their work and life from a space of confidence instead of criticism; to make decisions with clarity; and to gain back control by overcoming procrastination and perfectionism through self-mastery. When we become the fearless leaders of our own lives, our work becomes joyful and we become purposefully intentional and ultimately unstoppable!

With a degree in human resources/business management and a long career in human resources, I've taken all that I know about leadership and workplace relations and added in a good dose of intuition and brain science to create a methodology that is like a magical transformation. My biggest pleasure in life is passing all of this knowledge onto my most important coaching client, my 8-year old daughter, Sidney, to whom I dedicate my chapter in *Letter to my 10-year-old self*.

Makaela Moore | Intuitive Leadership Coach
Email   hello@makaelamoore.com
Facebook @makaela.moore.biz
Instagram @makaela.moore

Maria McDonald

I am an intuitive trauma healer, coach, and consulting professional. I work with people and purpose-led organisations to self-heal and reach their full potential so they can better impact the world.

I have always wanted to make a difference. I began my working career as a probation officer. But I played hard and worked hard and avoided my hidden intuitive talents for years. I was living a lie and not stepping into my power. Through a journey of self-discovery, I have now realised the amazing intuitive tools I have, and have always had, but have been fearful of displaying. I now use my full whole self, working in a way that I love to unleash the heart-led power in others. There is so much untapped potential holding back the positive impact that can be made on our world, and we need high-vibing leaders and influencers now more than ever!

My work includes ministerial recognition for the establishment of GPS monitoring of offenders in New Zealand, and recently I programme-managed the Christchurch Mosques attack sentencing. I continue my purpose-led work with Victim Support on their strategic capability and bringing heart and spirit to those who need to be lifted and healed.

I have a Bachelor of Social Science in Cross-Cultural Psychology and a Master of Arts in Criminology.

My greatest treasures are my two darling children and my husband, who is my best friend. They are my reason to make the world a better place, and they challenge me to be my best self. They're kind of like the grit in my oyster shell to create the pearl.

Maria McDonald | Intuitive Trauma Healer | coach | Consulting Professional
Email   mariamcdonald111@gmail.com
Facebook   @mariamcdonald111
LinkedIn   linkedin.com/in/maria-mcdonald-310a711b

Marta Madeira-Mulungo

The first 20 years of my life were a true revelation of who I am as a person and what my strengths are. When I look back, I see that I emerged from extreme poverty into what I now feel is great success. And I'm just getting started.

Inspired by my humble beginnings, I learned to believe in people, probably because I believed in myself. I knew that my mission would come to pass, as it did and it's still doing. I slowly developed a passion for inspiring people to develop confidence in themselves, and today this is my life passion. I help people whose doubts and fears keep them away from the life and success they desire. When they work with me, I help them dissolve the doubts and fears holding them back and create quantum leaps in their careers and businesses.

My life path and experience are true proof that if you know what you want, you can get it. I have a unique talent for boosting people's confidence and helping them step into their power. When I coach or mentor my clients around the world, I help them to see the true potential within themselves and to get to the root cause of their doubts and fears and lack of focus. My clients are typically professionals and business owners that aspire to more out of life.

I hold a master's degree in human resources management and development from the University of Manchester, an honours degree in organisational psychology, and a bachelor's degree in psychology. I am a certified results coach through the Proctor Gallagher Institute, USA, a humanistic coach through the MORE Institute, Germany, and an International Coach through International Coaching Community.

Marta Madeira-Mulungo
Entrepreneur I Life Coach I Results Coach I Human Resources Expert
Website   www.mmcoachingeng.com
Facebook   @mmcoachingeng

Mary Wong

Conversations underpin all successful relationships and can create enduring transformational impact.

That is why I work internationally with organisations, executives, and managers to create a culture of kindness, connection, and co-creation through powerful leadership conversations.

I am currently creating my podcast, Optimal Conversations, to maximise the effect of this work by taking it beyond the limits of the workplace.

With formal qualifications in coaching, counselling, leadership, and business, I draw upon my personal journey to becoming an excellent communicator, coupled with my many years of business experience when serving clients.

An international speaker and multiple Amazon #1 best-selling author, I have received several awards, including international awards for fiction, nonfiction, and poetry writing, and three Stevie International Women in Business Awards.

When I'm not coaching, speaking, or writing, I love to encourage my garden to grow (although it is often contrary) and to release my inhibitions through the organic creative process of doodling.

I live in Brisbane, Australia, with my three main men – husband, David, and sons, Daniel and Michael.

Mary Wong I Conversations Coach, Trainer and Mentor
Email   mary@optimalcoaching.com.au
Website   www.optimalcoaching.com.au
LinkedIn   linkedin.com/in/marywong-coaching/

Michelle Beauchamp

I have a life goal to teach others it is possible to grow beyond personal life pain and a misguided upbringing to be different than those responsible for raising you.

Working with Westpac Rescue Helicopter Service in Newcastle NSW, alongside the engineering team for heavy maintenance of four AW139 helicopters and 3 operational bases across Northern NSW.

My individual uniqueness comes in many shapes and forms. Managing life perspectives since the age of 13 in particular, I have an effervescent personality, with many of my friends describing me as inspirational, fun-loving, strong, empathetic, truthful, bubbling, benevolent, comforting, welcoming, brave, friendly, and a loving survivor and helper. I am well known for giving non-standard responses to regular questions. For example, when asked how I am, my response is often, 'Scrumptious,' which seems to delight people, and the smiles as a result enhance many a day.

I am a parent to two children of my own and have been a spare parent to an additional eight over the last 40 years. Meeting challenges along the way has strengthened my resolve in life and at times equally crushed it. Dealing with the devastation of losing our eldest son five and half years ago at the age of 27 to type 1 diabetes left our family reeling and remains difficult today. Having another seven adult children to stay connected with has helped me to move forward. Seeing them all as they continually strive to be great people is awesome.

My education post-school has been largely in the transport, procurement, and logistics field. I have Certificate IV in small business management and quality systems management, as well as internal auditor, fire warden, first aid, and various construction-based certifications.

Michelle Beauchamp
Phone   +61(0)437 953 052
Email   bickydippas@hotmail.com
LinkedIn   linkedin.com/in/michelle-beauchamp-4a97a436

Natasha Peake

I am the owner of Peake Performance Personal Training Perth.

Former retired Western Australian police officer with experience working and studying in the field of forensics.

Working in the Defence Force Industry taught me about resilience, persistence, discipline, self-defence, behaviour, reaction, action, fitness, consistency, and the fight or flight response. And not to forget the true-life expectations of a career in a dangerous, demanding profession – you swear an oath 'to serve and protect' the first day you put your uniform on.

I am passionate about health and fitness, rehabilitation, self-esteem, and lifestyle behaviours for all ages and abilities, and I thoroughly enjoy helping and watching others grow and strive to reach their own self values and desires. I love to share my own experience, knowledge, success, failures, mistakes, and laughter with others in a positive way that helps us all to shine and strive for longevity, through movement and lifestyle and most of all happiness.

My training philosophy is to maintain a healthy lifestyle through exercise, better lifestyle choices, healthy nutritional habits, reduced stress, enjoyment, relaxation, and developing a mindset made to deliver. I am extremely passionate about movement, whether mobility for the body and/or the brain or rehab for the body and/or the brain!

A healthier body = a healthier mind (vice versa)!

As a PT, I access the individual for who they are and use my skills, knowledge, and own life experience along with theirs to find out their why and how I can help them. For the ones that struggle, that's where I come to their aid and support, striving to guide and assist them in a positive outlook and outcome that's rewarding for the individual, both physically and mentally.

My motivation is simple and three words: VISION and LONGEVITY – Movement Matters - keep moving.

Natasha Peake I Fitness, Rehab and Lifestyle Coach
Phone +61(0)466 663 925
Email peaketraining@gmail.com.au
Facebook @tash.peake

Nyree Johnson

IAs an experienced corporate professional and owner/manager of multiple businesses, I love nothing more than to share my knowledge and experience with small businesses during their initial establishment and growth period. This allows me the opportunity to enable strategy and planning for success, while also bringing to the table tools and resources otherwise unknown. Watching a business boom from the side-lines and knowing I've had a direct impact in that accomplishment truly fills me with gratitude and modesty. Repeating this process with an individual who needs a hand up is even more rewarding, especially when informal.

I love speaking up and sharing positivity to empower those around me. Most recently in 2020, I've been given this opportunity many times on stage and via video. The engagement and connections I am able to make, coupled with sharing my message of truly knowing yourself and the magic that comes with that, as well as achieving an intentional imbalance, is an honour that I will be forever thankful for.

There are a multitude of balls I like to juggle, and I'm always keeping a check on which ones are glass and which ones are plastic and can bounce. What I can share for certain is that I only ever do what I love to do, and I am always exactly where I want to be.

Nyree Johnson | Corporate Professional
Email nyree@nyreejohnson.com.au
Website www.nyreejohnson.com.au
Facebook @Nyree-Johnson-111199940744527
Instagram @nyree.l.johnson
LinkedIn linkedin.com/in/nyree-johnson

Rebecca Lang

I am a naturopath and nutritionist and am passionate about helping people heal their body, mind, and spirit. At age 17, I knew I wanted to be a naturopath. I did initially work in tax and business, until my son was born. He had many food intolerances, which led me to follow my passion. My mission is to expand in abundance, success, love, and health every day, as I inspire those around me to do the same

I work intuitively and confirm my guidance with scientific testing. I love working with blood pathology and treating with natural medicine. I also use a unique Hair Testing for 600 Items. I work in all areas of health and wellness.

My other passions include creating and facilitating detox and wellness retreats for women. With my business background, I also enjoy mentoring naturopaths. I am the owner of Bargara Beach Holistic Health Centre. I also recently created Of the Earth Juice Bar & Health Shop, where I have designed a three-day juice cleanse.

My qualifications include Bachelor of Health Science in Naturopathy; Advance Diploma of Naturopathy; Advance Diploma Western Herbal Medicine; and Advance Diploma Nutritional Medicine.

Rebecca Lang | Naturopath | Nutritionist
Naturopath | Nutritionist | Retreat Facilitator | Entrepreneur
Phone   +61(0)7 4159 1834
Email   rebeccalang@healthandhealing.net.au
Website   www.healthandhealing.net.au

Simon Bryant

My identity and energy for life are founded on a strong and wonderful family life which is characterised by warmth, love, and acceptance. I am blessed to be a partner to my wife of 34 years, a father to three amazing children (two with partners), and an opa! I am strengthened by being deeply rooted in the semi-rural community of which I am a part, and I am particularly looking forward to starting a new chapter of my life as a scout leader in the local community and facilitating opportunities for youth to grow and develop through adventure experiences.

My work life across many different countries and continents has largely been divided into two major anthologies – working with information technology and working in youth and youth leadership development. The five years spent in training and facilitating volunteer leaders of youth to be empowering young people to fulfil their potential, are the years of my career I treasure most. They also, somewhat surprisingly, have proven to be of enormous value to the world of business and technology I now find myself in.

As a present-day technology and innovation leader, I am engaged in building the new digital world through leveraging the power of new technology and the huge potential of new sources of information and data made accessible as the result of new technology. The hope and intention is to help enterprises, governments, and communities uncover new insights and drive automation which will improve the human and community experience, enable businesses to be more effective and efficient, and hopefully help solve the big global challenges of our time.

Thinking ahead of the rest of my life, my dream is to create a place and space in the great outdoors for adventures to be explored, acceptance to be experienced, beauty to be realised, potential to be discovered, and wounds to be healed. To create a place and program for youth and young adults, where they can begin or continue a journey of fulfilling the wonderful potential of their lives.

Simon Bryant
Transformational Leader I Innovator I Ecosystem Orchestrator
Email   Bryant_simon@hotmail.com
Phone   +61(0)437 957 667
Facebook   simon.bryant.96
LinkedIn   linkedin.com/in/simon-bryant-8478a3

Tara Nelson

I am a naturopath with over 25 years of clinical experience, and I still absolutely love working with my clients to bring them into their peak state of health.

My health journey began after years of an eating disorder and low self-esteem and out of the love and desire to feel the best I can be. I aim to bring this to my clients.

My passion as a naturopath is about educating people about how to eat well and live well, for them to take control of their own health by making the changes of eating better and eliminating lifestyle practices that do not support this process.

My commitment to you as a patient is 100%, and when you commit 100% also, the results are phenomenal. I love to work with people who are ready to make the changes to their health to become a vibrant, healthy you.

My passion is working with clients suffering from a thyroid condition. I have Hashimotos thyroiditis myself, as does my 16-year-old daughter, and can relate to the symptoms of the thyroid client. Thyroid problems are increasing at an alarming rate, and most of my clientele come from a place of being under-diagnosed or diagnosed but still experiencing severe thyroid symptoms. I work holistically with thyroid patients to bring balance to their thyroid and reverse their disease process. I run an online Thyroid Recovery Program, as well as a six-week online practitioner thyroid training program, and I mentor practitioners specifically with their thyroid cases.

I have three amazing children, a loving partner, 5 acres in Yallingup WA, and absolutely love my life.

Tara Nelson | Thyroid Specialty
Phone   +61(0)417 945 333
Email   info@naturopathiccaresw.com
Website www.naturopathiccaresw.com

Taryn Claire Le Nu

I wake up each day excited to help others discover new, common-sense solutions for their healthiest and best life. I am a qualified sports therapist, naturopath, free thinker, awesome mum, and creator of the Advanced Natural Health Clinic and the Chelsey Jean label.

My passion for health and wellbeing began at 19 years of age, when I opened my first health and fitness studio, armed with a business diploma, knowledge of the health industry, and a passion for creating a niche in the health space. I soon began a movement towards detoxification and lymphatic health – conditions that are shockingly lacking but essential for immune health, fat transportation, metabolism, and energy. If it slows down, so do you … It took off!

My goal – to teach everyone how to 'pop the cork' and drain their lymphatic system – is now becoming true. I love making it fun and easy along the way, with my own special massage sequence that incorporates over 20 years of clinical experience and thousands of clients, as well drawing in all of the best bits of knowledge from my teachings all around the world.

As a self-described 'lymphoholic,' my innovative, naturopathically formulated LymFATic products and protocols can now be found in health clinics and retail stores all over Australia. I believe that amazing health should be accessible to everyone, and it's my family's and my mission to lead by example, supporting both women and men to uncover what is blocking them from becoming the best version of themselves – and have a ton of fun along the way.

Taryn Claire Le Nu I Spiritual Mentor I Practitioner of Hypnotherapy
Email   connect@tarynclairelenu.com
Website   www.tarynclairelenu.com
Website   www.diaryofadoctorswife.com
Facebook @lenuhealing
Instagram @tarynclairelenu